The cries for justice by
too often fell upon deaf ears and
God's prophetic messengers her____ ___ _____g Day when his covenant
people, indeed all peoples of the earth, would be judged with truth,
righteousness, and justice by the Messiah, Jesus Christ.

Dr. Amy Downey has crafted a contemporary interpretation and
application of their prophetic words through her book, *Missions in the Minor
Key*. Amy's own passionate love for and call to serve as a Christian missionary
to the Jewish people rings true in her explanation of these key Old Testament
prophecies. The reader may even hear echoes of the Minor Prophet's voices
whenever she seasons what she writes with a bit of her own characteristic
prophetic salt. She challenges the church today to return to the Lord and
fulfill Christ's global mission mandate!

Downey has done the scholarly work needed to accurately interpret
the biblical text and writes in a way that is accessible to both Christian church
leaders and lay members. The reminiscences of her own family history that
include brokenness and healing, combined with Israel's history of the same
in God's covenant family, invite us to receive God's forgiveness and healing
in our own lives and homes.

Missions in the Minor Key reminds each of us that God does not desert
but pursues us with an eternal love that is experienced through the gift of His
Son, Jesus Christ.

Larry C. Ashlock, D.Min., Ph.D.
President, Baptist Center for Global Concerns

Although often neglected by many pastors and Bible expositors, the
Minor Prophets have always been one of my favorite sections of Scripture.
From Habakkuk's solutions to the theodicy problem to the bizarre fishing
methodologies of Jonah, the Minor Prophets offer something for everyone.
However, Dr. Amy Downey approaches the Minor Prophets from a different
angle, that of missions. I had not considered the role that missions have in
the Minor Prophets until reading Dr. Downey's *Missions in the Minor Key*. Her
book will illuminate how major the role of missions is with the not-so-Minor
Prophets.

Brian G. Chilton, M.Div., Ph.D.
President, Bellator Christi Ministries

Missions in the Minor Key

Amy Karen Downey

IHP Academia
West Frankfort, Illinois

IHP Academia
An Imprint of Illative House Press
500 E. Elm St.
West Frankfort, IL 62896

IllativeHousePress.com

Hardcover ISBN: 979-8-9873886-9-3
Paperback ISBN: 979-8-9873886-8-6
E-book ISBN: 979-8-9915912-0-1

Cover Design: Illative House Press
Cover Images: Rijksmuseum, CC0, via Wikimedia Commons

Contents

This book could not have been written without my beloved mama, Barbara Ellen Downey, and my sweet friend Marilyn Greenblatt. Mama and Marilyn – who shared a similar childhood – were never able to meet in this life, but my dear mom often prayed for Marilyn over many years and was so excited to see the changes that God made and was making in her life before she died in 2020. Marilyn, I cannot wait until we are all reunited in Heaven and to see the giant mama hug that is given to you.

Foreword by Chris Price

It is with great pleasure that I write this foreword for Dr. Amy Karen Downey's insightful book, *Missions in the Minor Key*. As a long-term friend, I have witnessed Amy's dedication to Jewish missions and evangelism. Raised in a parsonage under her Baptist pastor father and devoted mother, Amy embraced Jewish ministries early in life. Her commitment to studying and teaching the scriptures is truly inspiring.

Amy's work is not merely academic but reflects a heartfelt ministry inspired by the scriptures and a genuine love for God's chosen people. Her unique perspective and experience bring a fresh voice to the discussion of missions, particularly in the context of the often-overlooked Minor Prophets. Like a minor key in music, this book provides depth and nuance that enrich our understanding of God's grand symphony.

Missions in the Minor Key fills a significant gap in pastoral and layperson libraries alike. While it delves into scholarly details, the book remains highly accessible, making it valuable for pastors, ministry leaders, and any believer eager to deepen their understanding of biblical missions. Amy's ability to communicate complex theological concepts in an engaging manner ensures that readers from all walks of life can benefit from its insights.

The Minor Prophets are frequently overshadowed by their more prominent counterparts, yet their messages are crucial for understanding God's redemptive plan. Similarly, the necessity and urgency of Jewish evangelism cannot be overstated, yet it remains an area often neglected in contemporary Christian missions. Amy addresses these overlooked aspects, bringing them to the forefront in a way that is both enlightening and convicting.

As the head of school at Spring Baptist Academy, I recognize the immense value *Missions in the Minor Key* holds for educational settings. Our high school students conduct extensive research often with a focus on the Old Testament. I am eager to place this book in our library, confident that it will enrich our students' spiritual and intellectual growth. Amy's work not only informs but also inspires action, encouraging readers to engage in missions with renewed vigor and commitment. This book is written in a way that is easy for high school students to understand, making it a tremendous addition to our library.

Just as a minor key in music can evoke profound emotion and reflection, Amy's writing stirs the heart and mind toward a deeper commitment to God's mission. In *Missions in the Minor Key*, Amy reminds us that missions is not an optional aspect of our faith but a central component of our calling as believers. The Minor Prophets, with their powerful messages of repentance, restoration, and redemption, provide a rich foundation for understanding our role in God's mission.

In addition to placing this book in the library of the school I lead, I will also be purchasing it for the Lanier Theological Library in Houston, TX. I am excited to share this with the researchers at the theological library and to see the impact *Missions in the Minor Key* will have. It will benefit scholars, theologians, small group leaders, schoolteachers, students, and local community leaders. Dr. Amy Karen Downey has provided the church with a much-needed resource, and it is my hope and prayer that *Missions in the Minor Key* will be widely read and embraced, to the glory of God and the advancement of His kingdom.

In Christ's service,

Dr. Christopher D. Price
Head of School, Spring Baptist Academy

Foreword by James Drawbond

It has been my pleasure to know Amy Downey for the past sixteen years since having her as my professor at a small Baptist college in Texas. She not only taught each course (and there were several!) with passion for the particular subject she was teaching at the time, but more importantly with a passion for Jesus, and sharing Him with the world. And, as the readers of this work will soon learn, Amy's love for Messiah Jesus was also shared by her father, Jack, and her mother, Barbara, who we, as the "college kids," affectionately called "Nana." If you ever had the opportunity to know "Nana Downey," you were truly blessed!

Over the years, I have had the chance to see Tzedakah Ministries move and grow from Dallas to Waxahachie to New York. I have also had the opportunity to get "down & dirty," from installing insulation in the ministry office to standing with Tzedakah in support of the Dallas Holocaust and Human Rights Museum. Despite all the hardships and struggles that a small ministry can endure, the one thing that remains steadfast is Tzedakah's commitment to "Jesus, Jesus, Jesus" (as Nana Downey used to say.)

In her work, *Missions in the Minor Key*, Amy presents a unique perspective on the Minor Prophets, offering an honest summary of their teachings while sharing the calling and challenges of Missionary work. Her approach is both truthful and transparent, with a touch of humor. She fearlessly tackles difficult issues such as social justice, war, human trafficking, grief, theodicy, and slavery, handling them with grace and writing as if she is having a genuine conversation with the reader. Her work skillfully blends the explanation of Hebrew grammar with down-to-earth illustrations, and it serves as a reminder that we are allowed to be "real" with God!

We avoid the Minor Prophets because their words make us feel uncomfortable, but their words are much needed today. *Missions in the Minor Key* offers a challenge to heed the words of these Prophets in a world that is used to "only" feeling comfortable and provides a call to repentance. Amy's work reminds us of the hope of redemption and restoration found in Messiah Jesus. She also issues the challenge of "Who will follow? Who will take up the mantle and be the next generation of missionaries and pastors?"

It is my hope that as you read *Missions in the Minor Key*, you will find it as insightful, challenging, informative, convicting, and entertaining as I have. To use a quote by the author, "The world needs our whole hearts and the whole message of Messiah Jesus. Nothing less will do."

James Drawbond

Publisher's Preface

Reading Amy Downey's writing on the Minor Prophets is like taking a guided tour through the ancient lands of the Old Testament. As any good tour guide should, Amy enriches the journey with interesting and relevant details, great stories and personal anecdotes, and a cleverness and wit that make the trip truly enjoyable. However, Amy is more than just a tour guide. She is a first-rate scholar and passionate disciple of Jesus the Messiah. What Amy offers by way of careful and convincing scholarship is matched by a zeal for the mission of God to bring all people to Himself, especially the Jewish people. Buckle up and hold on, as this journey with Amy into the world and words of the Minor Prophets is sure to inform, inspire, and challenge.

T. J. Gentry, D.Min., Ph.D.
President, Illative House Press

Author's Preface

I recognize that very few people read a book's preface unless they know that they are mentioned in it. However, I hope that people will at least glance at this preface because I am going to mention some people who changed my world and made it possible for me to write this book. Yes, everyone writes this sentence, but some of these people will surprise you ... I think, or at least I hope.

I always have to express my deepest appreciation to three teachers from elementary years and undergrad who changed this nerdy and awkward student profoundly – Virginia Dailey, Ketta Casey, and C. Barnwell Anderson. Mrs. Dailey and Mrs. Casey allowed this elementary student to push forward beyond what was perhaps comfortable for them and pursue interests that were outside the curriculum. Thank you from the bottom of my heart is not enough to say but it is all I can write at this moment. I will never forget Professor Anderson from Jacksonville College and will always miss him until I see him again.

Upon further reflection, I must include a fourth teacher, and that is my late music teacher from Leedey High School, Melba Britton. Mrs. Britton was a rock to me during some difficult high school years. She was a steadying force to many students in the late 1980s who experienced another teacher who was less than kind. What would any of us have done without you, Melba Britton? I can only hope that I was a teacher/professor like Mrs. Britton, Professor Anderson, Mrs. Casey, and Mrs. Dailey to at least one or more of my students at one time or another.

When I was at Southwestern Baptist Theological Seminary, I was profoundly impacted by the great Old Testament professor Harry Hunt, who is not as well-known as he should be. Still, I hope people will consider his influence because they read this book. I was able to work for Dr. Hunt and the legendary Systematic Theological professor James Leo Garrett, Jr., and knowing them is an honor that I am still amazed that I was able to have. Both of these men forgot more about their respective subjects than most of us will ever know, and I am humbled that I was able to call them my friends.

As you will discover as you dig further into this book, my parents were and still are the most influential people in my life. I was in a church service from the time I was three days old, and my daddy was with me when I prayed to receive Jesus as my Messiah on 18 September 1977 as an eight-year-old. Mama was my mission's teacher for so many years when I was a child, and after my dad died, she became my unofficial chief of staff in the work of Tzedakah Ministries. They loved the Jewish people and longed for the salvation of the Jewish people. I am who I am because Jack and Barbara Downey were my parents.

Josef, Agnes, William, Rosalie, Suzanne, Jack, and Vera. These names, in isolation, might not mean much to anyone. However, to me, they mean the world as they are seven people who survived the Holocaust and who I was able to call my friends. They have all died now, but I am the bearer of their history both before, during, and after the war. I know who they lost and what they went through during the Shoah. I love them all, and I know who I believe I will see again in Heaven and those who never came to faith in Jesus and to quote one of them – "would rather go to hell with their family who died in the camps than go to Heaven without them." They all had heard the Gospel of Jesus, yet my heart and soul still hurts at the thought of…

This is why I wrote *Missions in the Minor Key* so that Christians and churches will have a sense of not only the "minor prophets" but also so that they will have a greater understanding of missions and the urgent need to share the Gospel to all the world – including and never forgetting to the Jewish people. And lest I forget, thank you to all the supporters, volunteers, and board members of Tzedakah Ministries, it is only because of you that this book could even have been written.

Amy Karen Downey, Ph.D.
President, Tzedakah Ministries

Introduction to *Missions in the Minor Key*

Many years and moons ago while in college, I became curious about the books in what I continually to this day call the unwrinkled vellum between Isaiah and Matthew. You know those books in the Bible that never get read except for Daniel for prophecy conferences and Micah for Christmas sermons. Oh, I realize that people intend to read the "minor prophets" in their efforts to read through the Bible in a year but then get bogged down in Leviticus or Numbers and never make it to Nahum and Obadiah. Even a few people claim to have read Hezekiah when one mentions the minor prophets – never knowing I promise you that Hezekiah is not a book in the Bible, but Habakkuk is.

I became fascinated, even though I have to admit that as a college student, I did not truly understand what I was reading. With those prophetic books, we still insist on calling it "minor." Hosea was always a favorite of mine as I could not imagine that a woman truly was named Gomer and a man whose obedience to God would willingly extend to such lengths as to marry a woman who now, let us whisper in hushed tones – is "a prostitute."

Today, as a middle-aged missionary to the Jewish people of approaching thirty years and more than a few seminary degrees behind me, that sounds impressive, but just mean that I have student loans that I truly have every intention of paying back. I am still fascinated by these prophets who served God so faithfully (except for Jonah) and who do not deserve the label "minor." For while the moniker "minor" has been designated because of the size of their contributions to the canon, there is nothing small regarding what they had to offer to the Jewish people back then or what they have to say to us today.

And while I might be going back and forth between my "wrinkled vellum" of the actual written word and my iPad today, I can promise the missionary insights they still share with me, and I hope with you as well – whether pastor, layperson, Sunday School teacher, or even college or seminary student – will still change the world if only they were read and not merely safeguarded for mysterious ideas in prophecy conferences or the occasional advent sermons during Christmas season.

For in this volume of all twelve "minor" prophets, I have divided these prophets into six sections: (1) The Bad, Good, but Not Ugly Prophets; (2) The Long and Short of Sinful Living; (3) Truly Understanding the Day of the Lord; (4) If God Hates Divorce Why Does It Seem He Is?; (5) Why Don't People Learn – Lessons from Before the Fall of Jerusalem; and (6) People Are Just Stupid – Lessons from After Babylon. Each of these six sections will examine two prophets from a perspective perhaps not considered before – a missional perspective for the twenty-first century.

Chapter One covers the story of Jonah. However, the question I have often asked myself is simple—was he really that great of a prophet? In fact, Jonah was simply a whiner the whole time he was "on mission." From the time he was given the task until the last verses of Jonah, Jonah was nothing but a complainer. And actually, if we are honest about it, he did not finish the job given to him by God. He left the mission task half-done. Yet, God wanted the whole story of Jonah in the Hebrew Scriptures not only for the sign in the Gospels (Mt. 12:39-41; 16:4; Lk. 11:29-32) but also for a teachable lesson for us today. The question is then—will we learn the lesson that we are given even if Jonah refused to do so? And just exactly what is the teachable lesson for us today?

Chapter Two relates to the unsung story of Nahum. Nahum was tasked with cleaning up the mess/disaster/calamity/catastrophe that Jonah left behind. Ninevah reverted back to their sinful state because Jonah had not finished the task he had been given. Sadly, this is what happens so often when missionaries become discouraged or complacent or believe the task is beneath them. Then, it is up to a modern-day Nahum of the mission world to complete the task, and often, the work is left undone. A work that is unpleasant and filled with pronouncements that no one likes to consider but which must be given and heard. There are Nahum's today who must clean up after modern-day Jonah's and are never given the recognition or honor that is their due, and honestly, they do not expect it. However, we need more Nahum(s) in the world, but where can they be found?

Chapter Three recognizes the greatness of the faithful layperson such as the great Amos. It is often overlooked that Amos and Isaiah shared the role of prophets during a similar era and had unique paths and tasks. They courageously delivered God's messages to a stubborn audience, a testament to their unwavering faith and bravery. Their roles and backgrounds set them apart, but their shared courage inspires us all.

Isaiah served in the Temple, and Amos was a sheepherder. Amos was a man of the soil, and Isaiah was more than likely a man of refinement. Isaiah was a professional, and Amos was a layman. However, I am certain that Isaiah would have and perhaps even did tell the people to listen to this layman's words, for Amos was speaking forth the words of God. A well-deserved chapter is needed for the missionary service of the laity today who serves behind the scenes but nothing would or could be accomplished without them.

Chapter Four is about the unknown Obadiah. When was the last time a sermon series was delivered from the book of Obadiah? Is there often even a sermon given from Obadiah? If you asked the average church member if Obadiah was in the Bible ... what would they say? Yet, Obadiah delivers one of the most stinging indictments against a nation ever delivered in Scripture. In twenty-one verses, Obadiah promises Edom's destruction due to their treatment of Israel. Their wealth, their power, and their supposed indestructibility will not be able to save them when God chooses to allow them to be destroyed by their own supposed allies. Obadiah was a lesson for the past and has a lesson for us today if only it will ever be read or even found by many Christians. It is a perfect bookend for Amos as well.

Chapter Five is the story of Zephaniah. This is another book of Scripture that is often overlooked, sadly to our detriment. For one, they can often be stopped in their tracks of smug self-satisfaction by a simple verse. Zephaniah 3:2 is such a verse – "She has not obeyed *His* voice. She has not received correction; She has not trusted in the LORD, She has not drawn near to her God." (NKJV). While this verse is speaking exegetically of Judah before the Babylonian Captivity, it could be speaking on an applicational level to an individual, a nation, or even a local church.

If we are honest, we should not go past this verse without feeling the stinging pangs of condemnation. Yet we so often want to point out the sins of the other without humbling ourselves for a good dose of self-examination. This was Zephaniah's urgent message, a call to self-examination that is as relevant today as it was in his time.

Chapter Six considers the book of Joel. The average person only knows about maybe five verses in Joel, and that is 2:28-32, in which we see the promise that old men will see visions, young men will dream dreams, sons and daughters will prophesy. However, if you ask them what these verses mean in the "Day of the Lord," the interpretations one will hear will run the theological and denominational gamut from Baptist to Pentecostal and everything in between. Ultimately, no one understands the missional purpose of these verses, much less the message Joel was seeking to share. It is beyond time, that churches regardless of denominational preference consider the entirety of Joel's message and why Joel was so urgent in his message of 2:28-32 and beyond.

Chapter Seven takes us to one of my favorites of the "minor prophets, and that is the story of Hosea. Before we begin to consider the biblical issues of Hosea, we need to ask ourselves two questions: (1) Why would he marry a woman named Gomer who "shared her affection everywhere?" (2) Did Gomer come from a town called Mayberry? Honestly, and with tongue in cheek, the second question is often easier to answer than the first. The emotional and spiritual issues of Hosea's quandary are more complex than a Francine Rivers' novel (no offense implied) could fathom. The great metaphor that God asked Hosea to live out before the people is one that perhaps even Job himself could not imagine. We must ask and attempt to answer—did God divorce and then reconcile with the Jewish people by the end of Hosea's message? And, if so, what does this mean to the great covenantal promise?

When I was a professor at a small Baptist college, I often called some of my students into my office for what came to be known as a Downey "come to Jesus" meeting. My students knew that those meetings would not be pleasant, but they also knew that I conducted those meetings because I loved them and wanted them to be more than they were at the moment. **In many ways, chapter eight and the words of Malachi could be called a "come to God" moment for the people, but most especially for** the leaders of the people. Yet, and for too long, Malachi is reserved for "Stewardship Month" sermons and the passage from chapter three. There is so much more to Malachi's warning to the people – before the 400 hundred years of silence. A person can find the last prophecy of the Hebrew Scriptures or a "come to God" moment that can even outdo the one that caused a burned-out basketball player who was ready to drop out of college and try his hand at the European Leagues to become an outstanding high school history teacher that he is today.

In my view, chapter Nine is often shortchanged. Micah is not simply about one prophecy in chapter five – even though that is a significant Messianic prophecy. Micah tells the story of a prophet divided internally because of what he sees coming for his people in the immediate sense and what he sees for them in the future. Micah knows the people of God deserve the punishment awaiting them, but he is also one of them. Yet, the prophecy we see in 5:2ff gives him, and we all hope that is joyous beyond measure. Micah is a "minor" book with judgment, mercy, justice, grace, sin, and hope. So … ultimately, Micah is a text that applies to all of us in this day and time.

Habakkuk can often be mistaken for Hezekiah. There is no book of Hezekiah in Scripture, but there is the small but powerful book of Habakkuk. In **Chapter Ten**, we find the prophet struggling with why God would allow heathen countries to triumph over God's chosen people. We also see the prophet struggling with why he is the one who is being forced to share the vision with the people. We find a man who struggles a great deal with what God is asking him to do, and that struggle is one with which many people can identify daily.

God often asks us to do things we do not want. God often asks us to share a message with people they do not want to hear and that we do not wish to pronounce because it will make us unpopular. Habakkuk struggled, and we struggled as well. Yet, we must do as Habakkuk did, share the message anyway, and find a way to "rejoice in Jehovah and the joy of God's salvation" (3:18).

Ultimately, **Chapter Eleven** reveals people's selfishness and that Haggai was the prophet who called them out on it. Therefore, is it no wonder that Haggai is so rarely spoken about from the pulpits and Sunday School lecterns? Haggai is not made for comfy and cozy moments.

Haggai called out the people who had returned from the Babylonian Captivity for their selfishness in building their own homes but allowing the Temple to continue to lay in ruins even though it had been years upon returning. Additionally, the people suffered from a lack of want but could not figure out why God was seemingly punishing them. Pardon for me for being less than academic for the moment, but … "Duh!"

Any people, much less God's people, cannot be blessed if they choose their comfort over God's purposes. Yet, even today, we continue to operate in this mentality and wonder why God's blessings are denied us. Please know this is not a "health and wealth" argument but an obedience argument, and again, I write out the word, "Duh!"

It seems so appropriate to end this book with Zechariah. **Chapter Twelve** of this book could quickly turn into a book on prophecy, and there is a great deal of prophetic hope in this book but the crux of Zechariah's message begins in 1:3 – "Return to me, says the Jehovah Elohim, and I will return to you, says Jehovah Elohim." Zechariah's message is encircled by the prophetic messages in the "minor" book that provides so much hope to all of us. Returning to God, following God, doing the will of God, sharing the message of God, and living out the hope of God will bring out the purposes of God for not only the people of God but also the whole world. Indeed, Zechariah and all the "minor prophets" are not minor at all.

With this brief glance at these not-so-minor prophets, I hope that these twelve men lived, died, and served the Living God of the Universe on a dusty wilderness called Judea thousands of years ago. Yet, they have a message for us today as well. They have a missional message for us as we live in the spiritual wilderness that is sometimes of our own making. We must learn this message as the twenty-first-century church must impact the world for Messiah Jesus as they live in modern-day Babylon, Assyria, Edom, etc., and do not even realize it. They need the hope that is only possible through the God of the Hebrew Scriptures – the Scriptures of Messiah Jesus.

Special Notes

1. The book will seek to avoid excessive notations of Hebrew grammar and grammatical/exegetical terms. However, if it proves necessary to pull out

the full richness of the text, I will do my utmost to keep it short. Grand and detailed explanations are never needed, from my experience, and only serve to make someone appear as if they are trying to be smarter than they really are.

2. If the Bible text says Lord, I will be taking writer's privilege and using the term Jehovah as this is the best English translation of the Hebrew. However, do not worry. Despite the fact that I live among the Jehovah's Witnesses … I am not one!

3. Many of the prophets choose to focus on a specific title (such as Malachi and Zechariah choosing to utilize Jehovah Sabaoth – Lord of Hosts) in reference to God. If a prophet chooses to do so, I will spend a few words explaining why this term is important to the book and to the prophet's message to the people.

4. I am choosing to utilize both BC and BCE as it relates to questions of dating. The reason for this choice is from more of an academic and traditional perspective than for any other reason. It is recognized that Jesus was more than likely born c. 6-4 BC/BCE and not 1 AD/CE. The "Common Era" attribution has been assumed to be an effort to erase the significance of Jesus' birth, but that is not the case and actually began several hundred years ago. I have included an article that explains the academic rationale for your edification: https://www.worldhistory.org/article/1041/the-origin--history-of-the-bcece-dating-system/.

Section One:
The Bad, Good, but not Ugly Prophet
Jonah and Nahum

Of the two prophets we will be examining in this first section, Jonah is the more well-known one of the two prophets. However, Nahum, the prophet, truly fulfills the task he was called to deliver. Indeed, it is interesting to me, at least, how the story of a big fish story catches the limelight. Still, the work of delivering an uncomfortable message, as Nahum did, is often ignored or overlooked. Yet, both messages are found in the Scriptures and have an essential point to convey, so we must tell it.

From one sign used by Jesus in the Gospels (Mt. 12:39-41; 16:4; Lk. 11:29-32), the prophet Jonah has received a lot of press. However, I have often asked myself—was he that great of a prophet? He whined the whole time from when he was given the task until the last verses of Jonah.

Additionally, if one carefully reads the job God gave to Jonah, one can see that he did not finish the job given to him. He left the mission task half-done. Yet, God wanted the story of Jonah in the Hebrew Scriptures not only for the sign in the Gospels but also for a teachable lesson for us today. The question is, then—will we learn our lesson? Will we finish the task set before us, or will we be as guilty as Jonah and leave the work only partially complete and hope someone will finish the job? Someone like a Nahum who serves as a custodian to clean up the mess we often leave behind.

Indeed, Nahum was tasked with cleaning up the disaster/calamity/catastrophe that Jonah left behind. Ninevah, not long after the "revival" that was begun during the preaching days of Jonah, reverted back to their sinful state because Jonah did not finish the task he had been given. Sadly, this is what happens so often when missionaries become discouraged or complacent or believe the task is beneath them. Sometimes, it even occurs when missionaries or pastors focus on numbers instead of discipleship, but I might be stepping on toes with that sentence so that I will move on. Then, it is up to an underappreciated Nahum to complete the task, and often, the work is unpleasant and filled with pronouncements that no one likes to consider but must be heard.

So … let us move on and begin to examine these first two not-so-minor prophets, who have some significant lessons for us today.

1. Jonah: Perhaps He Should Have Stayed in the Big Fish

Introduction

It would be a remarkable story of faith and obedience if I could write that I immediately responded to the mission call on my life. It would be a remarkable story, but it would be a lie. I first knew I was called to be a missionary when I was sixteen years old and my dad was preaching a sermon from 2 Cor. 12 about Paul dealing with his thorn in the flesh, but he could depend upon the sufficient grace of God to see him through the darkest moments of life.

From the moment daddy began to break apart the phrase "my grace is sufficient for you," I was being called to what Baptists like to call "full-time Christian service." However, even more than that, I knew as I squirmed during daddy's sermon that I was being called to **mission service**. Those two words terrified me as a Baptist young woman because of two other words … Lottie Moon.

Lottie Moon (1840-1912) is perhaps one of the greatest missionaries of Southern Baptist life. And without a doubt, she has raised more money in her death for international missions than anyone else has ever done.[1] Her work as a single missionary to China in the late 19th and early 20th century (especially during the height of the Boxer Rebellion) should never be forgotten by Christians. There is not enough room in this introduction to write of it here. Ultimately, she died of starvation on Christmas Day 1912 in Kobe, Japan, because she was using her own salary to feed the children of her orphanage. One can visit her simple grave, as I have in Crewe, Virginia, and see the words "Faithful Unto Death" on the tombstone and realize that Lottie Moon gave it all until she had no more to give.

I squirmed during this 2 Cor. 12 sermon of my father's. I fidgeted at the thought of surrendering to the call of missions. I resisted. Yes, I even resented the idea of missions. I had been a Preacher's Kid since I was the age of 4. I had moved across the country – New Mexico, Kentucky, Texas, and now the middle of nowhere Oklahoma. I was attending my ELEVENTH school as a senior in high school. Had I not done my duty for God already? Was I now being asked to do more? And did God not know what was expected of women missionaries – singleness, loneliness, and if the story of Lottie Moon had not taught us Baptists anything, starvation and an offering named after we died out of Baptist guilt for allowing us to die? I did not want to become the "Amy Downey Flag Day Offering!"

---

[1] "Lottie Moon," International Mission Board (of the Southern Baptist Convention), https://www.imb.org/about/lottie-moon/, accessed 21 March 2024.

And so, I metaphorically ran from the calling. I ran and received my undergraduate education with plans to become the best schoolteacher that God had ever seen. And I tried my best even though I was spiritually miserable. I ran to Southwestern Baptist Theological Seminary (an odd choice ... I know) because I thought I could serve God my way and maybe pick up a husband and children along the way. I earned my MAComm degree even while avoiding any whiff of people telling me that they just knew I was called to mission work.

I became the equivalent of a BSM director at a small Baptist college in East Texas, and there was a revival on the campus. Students' lives were changed for the sake of Messiah Jesus, and students surrendered to missions. A mini-revival broke out on campus, but their spiritual life leader was spiritually miserable. Until one day late in 1998, I finally broke down and told God that I surrendered to HIS CALLING on my life, even if that meant singleness, loneliness, and that infernal Amy Downey offering named for me after I died.

The reality of who my people group were—the Jewish people—is a story for another chapter. However, I finally stopped running from God's mission calling on my life and grabbed hold of the plow of Luke 9:62. I have never looked back since that day. And, indeed, God's grace is sufficient for my life, just as daddy said way back in 1986...

So ... why am I so hard on Jonah? He ran but eventually went to Ninevah and preached the Gospel. But did he really? Yes, he preached to the people, but he did so begrudgingly. He did so half-heartedly and only halfway, as we shall soon discover. His words changed the people of Ninevah for a time but Jonah's own words did not change Jonah. It is for these reasons and others, as we shall uncover in this chapter that I consider Jonah the good, the bad, and the ugly prophet.

Who Jonah Was and the Biblical Background to This Awkward and Often Nauseating Message

As you saw in the book title, my name is Amy Karen, but it has a backstory that is both amusing and telling—even in a time when the name Karen can be seen as derogatory. Shame on whoever began using the name Karen as an offensive term! I am just glad my mama is not alive, or she would be offended because she took such care in naming me.

Mama and daddy were arguing about my name before I arrived on 3 September 1969. Mama had chosen Amy Karen because she had discovered that Amy meant "beloved" and Karen had the meaning of "graceful" or "pure." Daddy wanted something a little less elaborate, like Susan or Jane, which were very popular in 1969.

Well ... I was almost three weeks late in arriving, and I took nearly 36 hours of labor to "pop into the world" once I decided to come. Hey! It was the summer of Manson, Woodstock, and the moon landing, and I think I was a little hesitant to arrive in such a crazy world as 1969. But I arrived, and after I did, my dad decided to run an errand, clear his head, and get some air.

After he left, the nurse arrived with the birth certificate for Baby Girl Downey, and mama filled it out with the name of Amy Karen Downey. Daddy was a little upset when he returned to the hospital, but as the nurse told him – "Your wife just spent 36 hours in labor after the little girl decided to come three weeks late. Who should have the naming rights?" So … my dad took the high road and the smart road, and I have been Amy Karen Downey since 1969.

Jonah's name is just as unique and special. His father, Amittai, whose name means "trust or worthiness," chose to call his son after a unique bird in Jewish and biblical history – the dove. The dove was the bird who discovered the dry land after the flood in Gen. 8:6-12. The dove was the offering that Joseph and Mary took to the Temple for her purification sacrifice of two doves (since they were poor), as required in Lev. 12:2-8. The dove descended from heaven to signify God's approval of his son as Jesus' baptism (Luke 3:21-22; John 1:32-34). Even today, the dove is the symbol of peace/shalom.[2] Yet, Jonah's mission to Ninevah and his reaction to his calling was anything but peaceful. So … what are to make of Jonah's name in light of his purpose? All I can write is to keep reading…

One can roughly date the writing of Jonah, if you hold as I do to a literal interpretation of Scripture, to 786-747 BC/BCE. One does not need the assistance of commentaries to have that information – even though commentaries are beautiful resources. One only needs to go to 2 Kgs. 14:23-29, esp. v. 25b, and one will discover this phrase, "which He had spoken through His servant Jonah the son of Amittai, the prophet who was from Gath Hepher ("*winepress of digging*"). The 2 Kings passage relates to the reader an account of the evil King Jeroboam II of Israel, who reigned by all accounts for 41 years (c.785-744 BC/BCE) and was then followed by his son Zechariah.[3] What is interesting about this 2 Kings passage is that evil Jeroboam II was powerful and had been able to reclaim much of what had been lost to the Assyrian Empire by previous weak kings (both Israel and Judah). Yet, the prophecy of Israel's future demise (Isaiah 8:1-10 for example) and Jonah did not want to go and give "those people" a chance to repent. He believed it was better to have them die at God's hands than to repent and, at a future time, have them destroy the Northern Kingdom – or at least that was Jonah's view and why he ran from God.

---

[2] While I did not focus on the historical nature of the dove from biblical times, there is an interesting article about the bird in *Biblical Archaeology* that might prove helpful to you as a reader. Dorothy Willette, "The Enduring Symbolism of Doves: From Ancient Icons to Biblical Mainstay," *Biblical Archaeology* (Online), 27 July 2023, available at https://www.biblicalarchaeology.org/daily/ancient-cultures/daily-life-and-practice/the-enduring-symbolism-of-doves/; accessed 28 March 2024.

[3] Steven Barabas, "Jeroboam II," *Zondervan's Pictorial Bible Dictionary*, Merrill C. Tenney, gen. ed. (Grand Rapids, MI: Zondervan Publishing House, 1967), 416-17.

Theme of Jonah – Anger and Pity Are in the Hands of Jehovah Alone (Jonah 4:4, 9 & 11)

In August 2017, the world appeared that it could be on the brink of nuclear war. Do you remember those days? It was revealed that North Korea was able to launch an intercontinental ballistic missile that could reach the United States and had enough nuclear material to create warheads to attack South Korea and perhaps even reach American territories in the region.[4] Of course, those horrific mushroom clouds never appeared in the sky, and the world pulled back from whatever destruction could have happened, but I was surprised to discover that the hearts of many were darker than I presumed.

I engaged in many Facebook debates (yes, the bastion of social media civility) on whether nuclear war was a good idea with people who called themselves pastors and even missionaries. And when I noted that the vast majority of North Koreans (approximately 25 million) have no control over the actions of their government and with a GDP (Gross Domestic Product) average of around $650 per year, survival would likely be the average North Korean's main preoccupation. Those same individuals did not seem to care. When I pointed out that such organizations listed North Korea as Open Doors and Voice of the Martyrs as the greatest persecutor of Christians and that our primary concern should be to reach out to North Korea with the Gospel and not with a nuclear weapon. My debaters did not care and wanted to nuke those 25 million souls into oblivion with the attitude of better them than us.

And as I reflect today back on this debate, I wonder if they would have agreed with Jonah's attitude both when he was called to Ninevah and after the response of the city in 4:1-3:

> But it displeased Jonah exceedingly, and he became angry. So he prayed to the Lord, and said, "Ah, Lord, was not this what I said when I was still in my country? Therefore I fled previously to Tarshish; <u>for I know that You are a gracious and merciful God, slow to anger and abundant in lovingkindness,</u> **One who relents from doing harm.** Therefore now, O Lord, please take my life from me, for it is better for me to die than to live!"

Jonah was upset that God saved the Ninevites. I think he was even upset that he was not around for the destruction in some sort of Sodom and Gomorrah light show sort of way. He wanted vengeance, and he was observing forgiveness. And Jonah was angry about it!

---

[4] Peter Baker and Choe Sang-Hun, "Trump Threatens 'Fire and Fury' Against North Korea if It Endangers U.S.," *New York Times,* 8 August 2017, available online at https://www.nytimes.com/2017/08/08/world/asia/north-korea-un-sanctions-nuclear-missile-united-nations.html; accessed 29 August 2024.

But … anger (i.e., what we falsely like to call righteous indignation) is not our prerogative. And sometimes, I admit, that does not seem fair – does it? We want revenge and twist those words that say, "Vengeance is mine, says Jehovah," to "Vengeance is mine alone." I have been there myself more than once – especially when I was younger and saw the crushed look on my parent's faces as they had to tell my mother it was time to move again because the church no longer wanted him as their pastor because he would not back down for racial integration when he discovered that church members were also members of the KKK or some sort of similar nonsense. And, yes, that actually happened.

For vengeance is not ours to seek. Ours is only to share the message of the Gospel and to follow what God told Jonah in 4:11 – *"And should I not pity Nineveh, that great city, in which are more than one hundred and twenty thousand persons who cannot discern between their right hand and their left—and much livestock?"* The word "pity" in this passage can also be translated as "spare" or "look upon with compassion…"

Looking upon with compassion is not a sign of weakness in this day and age. It is a sign of strength. Compassion has been shown to us and should be shown to those presently living without a personal relationship with Messiah Jesus. However, pity is not something we often find in today's world or even in today's church, and it is something that we must find again both within ourselves and especially within our church.

The Command and Jonah's Futile Effort to Hide
from the "Presence of Jehovah" (Jonah 1:2-3)

As I stated in the introduction, this book will not be an exercise in showing any Hebrew knowledge. However, I am beginning chapter one by looking at the Hebrew verbs in verse two. There is a reason for doing so, and it is because God gave Jonah three distinct commands in this one verse – "arise," "go," and "cry." These three words are all in the Qal Imperative sense. What does this mean for us today? ARISE! GO! CRY! In other words … God is telling Jonah to do it and to do it now.

What could be of interest is that the first time a reader finds such words as "arise" and "go" is when God instructed Abram to do the same. Abram went, but Jonah did not. The other word, "cry," should and perhaps could be translated as "proclaim" against the city of Ninevah due to their wickedness.

We then find the conjunction "But" in response to God's command – "But Jonah rose to flee to Tarshish from the presence of Jehovah." I do not know about you, but I find this a surreal or bizarre sentence, especially since it is repeated twice in verse three. How in the world could Jonah believe he could rise up to Tarshish and then go down to the bottom of a ship with the thought that he could hide from the presence of God?

Yet … is that not what we often do when we seek not to do what God wants us to do? I tried it for years when I sought to bargain with God. I sought to make deals with God by telling him how I would serve Him – maintaining a veneer of Christian service to those who did not know better but internally running from God with all my might.

Yes, I never missed a church service. Yes, I always tithed off the gross and not the net. Yes, I graduated from seminary and "served God," but only in my way and not his plan. That is … until I found myself facing a spiritual storm and a fish's belly in the guise of a long line at a bank and some train tracks, and I could not run from God anymore. And do not worry; I will explain this last sentence in just a few sentences.

What Does True Obedience Look Like In Jonah? (1:4-17)

I hope you have heard sermons and/or lessons about the faithfulness and obedience of the sailors on Jonah's boat. If not, I am going to discuss it here. For what was displayed by the sailors in 1:4-17 is what Jonah should have displayed in his attitude towards the Ninevites.

First, they experienced true fear when they saw the power of God (v. 5), and they called out to their gods. Yes, it was not the true God, but they knew what they were seeing and experiencing was beyond human control. They also sought answers for who was causing the problem (v. 7), and when they realized it was Jonah and his God – they experienced not only fear (v. 10) but also sought answers from Jonah and his God for what to do (v. 11).

This seeking answers from Jonah's God is key to this section as they realized that their gods were inferior to the God of Jonah – who is "Jehovah Elohim who made the sea and the dry land" (v. 9). Sailors of this time worshipped gods that were very specific – the god of the sea but Jonah was telling them that the God of the Hebrews was the **God of it all**. Jonah was, thankfully, a missionary, but in the wrong direction! And the sailors believed, listened, and obeyed even if the directions scared them senseless.

For Jonah told them to throw him overboard (v. 12). And while they tried to reach dry land (v. 13), they ultimately threw Jonah overboard even while calling on Jehovah in the process (v. 14-15) and then performed sacrifices to Jehovah (v. 16). This is the actual obedience that Jonah should have exhibited when he was called to obey but did not. And because of the lack of obedience, this great fish was awaiting Jonah in the sea (v. 17).

As promised in the previous section, I wrote of my personal storm, a long line, and some train tracks. Here is the time I will share what I mean by that strange sentence. When I finally surrendered to missions in 1998, I knew that I might also have to consider a life of singleness, an issue many women missionaries must consider.[5] I did not want this for my life, even though I had known as far back as 1986 that God had planned it for me.

I had been in love in my mid-twenties when we were both at seminary – desperately, profoundly in love with a godly man who I thought had also been interested in me. Things had not worked out, but I had not gotten over him, and even to this day (I am 54 when I am writing this paragraph), he is the one. A part of my heart will always belong to him even though I was not his one. So, knowing deep in my heart that being a missionary also meant being single for the rest of my life was a commitment that I wanted to run away from desperately, but God had me run instead to a bank where the line was just ridiculous.

This was in the days before ATMs, and I needed cash as I was having lunch with a prayer partner to talk with her about what God was asking me to do. I was waiting in this line, and I was running late. As I was waiting to get cash, a train rolled by with a line of cattle cars. I watched the cattle cars roll by, and I began to think of the cattle cars that took the Jewish people to the concentration camps in World War II. I then began to think of those who died in the camps without Messiah Jesus because they had never heard the Gospel from anyone. By the time I reached the Tea Room and had lunch with my prayer partner Lisa, I knew I could run no longer, for if I did … I would be forever out of God's will and in my own "great fish" from which I could not escape. And even if that meant singleness and loneliness … so be it. It would be better than running from God any longer than I had been.

Jonah's First Prayer … Humble or Kvetching? (2:1-10)

"Then Jonah prayed…" These three words are perhaps the three most restrained words in Scripture. He is in the belly (most likely the intestines based on the Hebrew word *mimmeh*) of an enormous fish, and the writer pens the words, "Then Jonah prayed… (2:1)" If it were me in the middle of the intestines of a huge fish floating around in what can only imagine, my words would have involved screaming and the single word, "HELP!"

---

[5] This might be a generalization more than a reality; however, the reality of single women missionaries is an issue for every generation. This is just one article that I chose from a plethora that could have been selected -- More Women in Missions: Four Reasons Why - Pioneers | Pioneers.

Thankfully, in Jonah's prayer, we can see from this prayer a mixture of repentance and self-pitying on the part of Jonah that often reflects our own prayers to God. Prayers that blame God for our circumstances, circumstances that are caused by sins of our own making, and then ask him to rescue us from it. Prayers that involve repentance, but sadly too often, repentance mingled with a sense of "at least I am not as bad as other people" notions. Prayers that promise God a great deal but often do not deliver when God does. And I will admit that this is often the prayer of too many missionaries– or at least this missionary.

Yet God hears and answers our prayers (2:2, 10) even when we do not deserve his ear. God listens to us. Whether it is from our recliner or from the intestines of a big fish. And while Jonah recognized that God had **cause**[6] to cast him into the sea (Jonah goes into great detail about the experience of being tossed overboard, but does he not? (v. 3, 5-6a), Jonah also feels as if he has been driven out/expelled from God's sight (v.).

And I want to say … "Wait a minute, Jonah, what are you saying here? You ran from God. How can you say that you were expelled from God's sight?" But then I realized that all of us, even those who are recognized as prophets such as Jonah, can speak bad theology at times. This is definitely bad theology, for as David tells us in Ps. 139:7- 12, there is nowhere we can run or hide from the presence of God.

So . . . can we give Jonah a break because he is in the disgusting guts of a humongous fish? No, we should not because this lack of faith, this **kvetching** (Yiddish for complain, be ineffectual, show reluctance for life itself) illustrates to God, to ourselves, to others that while we do not want to do what God wants, we will do it anyway. This is not faithful obedience but an effort to alleviate God in order to "get him off of our back" and out of fish guts.

Perhaps you believe I am being too hard on Jonah? Let us look at the rest of Jonah's prayer in chapter two. In verses 7b-9, Jonah does and says all the right things. Jonah remembers God and prays (v. 7b). He recognizes the futility of following false idols because in the darkest of dark times, those idols are worthless (v. 8). Jonah promises to sacrifice and fulfill his responsibility as a prophet (v. 9).

---

[6] The Hebrew grammar for the word "cast" is a Hiphil Imperfect 2nd Masculine Singular. And while the Hiphil is an important case in the Hebrew that the book will go into a later chapter, please note at this time that when a verb is in the Hiphil it shows that something is in the causative form. *"For you had cause to cast me…"*

These are wonderful things to do, but why did Jonah do them? and the answer is in verse 7a – "While I was fainting away, I remembered Jehovah…" The bottom line is that as Jonah reached his end (or what he believed to be his end), he remembered God, prayed and made all those promises. I hesitate to judge the truthfulness of those promises … BUT I want to judge because we have either all been there or seen people make promises that were based on the fear of death more than on their fear of God.

In fact, there is a funny movie from the 1970s starring the king of 1970s movies – Burt Reynolds – called *The End* that perfectly describes such a scenario. Reynolds was a man who was afraid of dying and who promised God all sorts of things only if he could live, but as he realized that his death was not as imminent as he once believed, he began to "crawfish," as is said in the South on those promises. One can only wonder that as Jonah headed back to Jerusalem after the Ninevah was spared, did he make the sacrifice he had once promised God?

Regardless, all we know is that at the end of chapter two, God caused that mysterious fish (another Hiphil verb) to vomit Jonah up on dry land. And while we can only imagine the stench and the appearance of Jonah after being in that fish for three days. It was God who rescued Jonah, and it was God who still had plans and a mission for Jonah to complete. Indeed, God never forgets what he wants us to do. Never.

Jonah's Half-Hearted Mission Outreach? (3:1-10)

I admit as we begin this section that I have a different perspective on one group of verses in chapter three (v. 3-4) that some books do not; however, I believe that Jonah's response in chapter four and the resulting response that we will see in the chapter on Nahum will bear my interpretation out. So … if you are surprised by what you are about to read, give me a chance and consider my opinion. However, and as always, be a Berean as Paul encourages us to be in Acts 17:10-15 and evaluate my view against Scripture itself.

As we begin chapter three, and as I am sure as Jonah is still cleaning off seaweed and other things that can be found in fish intestines, God speaks once again (or for the second time) to Jonah and gives him what appears to be the same message as he did in 1:2. One can find again the three words – ARISE, GO, and PROCLAIM. And once again, these three words are in the Hebrew imperative (command) case. Nothing has changed from God's message in chapter one, for Ninevah is still wicked, and Jonah is still responsible for delivering this message to the city.

Finally, Jonah went to Ninevah, where the questions about interpretation began. Theological academics have debated for a long time whether Ninevah was "really" so large that it would require a three-day walk for Jonah to cover it with God's message.[7] I would argue that the relative size of the city is not the actual issue that should be discussed, but Jonah's motivation is to share the message God has bestowed upon him.

In my view, Jonah's message, if given appropriately, would take three days to deliver to the people of Ninevah (v. 3). Yet, we see in verse 4 that Jonah delivered the message – "Yet, forty days and Ninevah days shall be overthrown" in one day. How could Jonah **adequately** deliver such an important message **to the whole of Ninevah** and see such a massive revival in only one day? A message that Jonah did not want to deliver in chapter one and a message that Jonah was upset to see was received in chapter four.

My view is that Jonah did not and that he only went to the portion of the city that would impact the ruling class and, thereby, the whole of the city. For we must understand in today's 21st-century world that if the rulers of that time (i.e., the king) declare something that everyone in the whole of the city must abide by the edict of the king[8] – whether they believed it in their heart or not. Yes, Jonah's words changed the heart of the king … which was an amazing thing. However, kings came and went during this time, but if the people of the city had not been changed, how long would the revival have lasted? As we will see in the next chapter, it is not long. The argument could be made, and this is my position, but at least I am not alone in this one. It is as if Jonah did the least amount of work he could do to finish his job so he could get away from those amoral Ninevites that he seemingly hopes (based on his Ch. 4 reaction) will not repent.[9]

---

[7] Craig G. Bartholomew and Heath A. Thomas, *The Minor Prophets: A Theological Introduction* (Downers Grove, IL: IVP Press, 2023): 152-53 and C. Hassell Bullock, *An Introduction to the Old Testament Prophetic Books* (Chicago: Moody Press, 1986): 46-47. Bullock allows for what can only be a cosmopolitan or metroplex understanding of Ninevah, similar to what today would be found in Texas. Dallas and Fort Worth are often called DFW in that all the cities/towns between them are separate, but one cannot leave one city without going into another town. The whole of Dallas/Fort Worth is an enormous metroplex that is beyond the cities of Dallas or Fort Worth itself.

[8] Bartholomew and Thomas, *The Minor Prophets: A Theological Introduction*, 153.

[9] Ibid. See also, Jack M. Sasson, *Jonah*, Anchor Bible Commentary (New Haven, CT: 2007), 224, 236-37.

Sadly, actions of half-hearted missions outreach are too often the norm and not the exception in the history of missions. The efforts to reach the Hawaiians in the 19th century are just one example of when good ambitions turned tragically wrong. The lure of easy money among the sugar cane turned those missionaries into slave owners, and today, Hawaii is a state that is not reached with the Gospel. I cried throughout the beautiful and woefully underappreciated Martin Scorsese movie **Silence** when the 17th century Jesuit missionaries sought to evangelize Japan but were inadequately prepared for the conditions of the country and ended up doing more harm than good in the "Land of the Rising Sun."

We cannot be examples of a half-hearted Jonah today when the work of missions and evangelism is being prosecuted and persecuted but is still required in a world that is unaware of its need for the Gospel. The world needs our whole hearts and the whole message of Messiah Jesus. Nothing less will do.

Jonah's Second Prayer … Straight Kvetching! (4:1-11)

I have had two encounters with the Phelps family of Topeka, Kansas. The first encounter was when I was in seminary in the mid-to early-1990s. I was part of a Baptist chatroom (do you remember those?), and Fred Phelps' young grandson Benjamin would occasionally pop into the chat room and spew his vile and hateful nonsense all over the group. Interestingly enough, Benjamin was a personable and bright young man in a one-on-one conversation, and one could sense that in another world, he might even be redeemable if he could get away from his family sometime in the future. Sadly, I do not believe he ever has.

The second time I encountered the Phelps family was around 2010 when they decided to come to Dallas and to protest at the Dallas Holocaust Museum and at the Dallas Jewish Community Center along with a few other pre-selected sites that hot summer weekend. I was there along with my mama and a few of my college students at the counter-protest to show solidarity with the Dallas Jewish community against the hostile and angry hatred expressed by the Phelps family, who were blaming the Jewish people for everything wrong with the world. The hatred of the Phelps' was so distasteful and so unbiblical, yet they were there supposedly in the name of God. I was hurt that day because, as a missionary to the Jewish people, I knew that the *charah* lies of the Phelps' would do more to hurt the cause of Jewish evangelism than any words of love that I could say that day.

Charah is the word used by the writer in 4:1 to describe Jonah's emotions when he saw Ninevah turn towards God. It is often translated as angry, which is entirely accurate, but it could just as well be translated as "jealous" or "incensed." As I was considering how to begin this final section for this chapter, my two encounters with the Phelps and their *charah*, their anger/jealousy, came to mind. Just as Jonah was displeased by God's turning away from wrath, the Phelps' are maliciously vengeful towards those of us who do not hold to their same anger or *charah*.

Interestingly enough, the first time that the word *charah* is used in Scripture is when Cain is angry at God (Gen. 4:5-6) for accepting Abel's sacrifice but not accepting his. This is the level of anger that Jonah felt towards God, towards the Ninevites, and most likely towards himself. This was a murderous anger, a dangerous anger, and why Jonah had the chutzpah (gall, brazen nerve), as they say in Yiddish, to, in essence, tell God, "See, I told you so," in verse 2 and why Jonah asked God to kill him in verse 3.

Again, Jonah's responses throughout chapter 4 can define the essence of chutzpah, from asking God for death to weeping over a gourd. Yet, God is merciful and exceptionally patient throughout the chapter. Instead, God repeats twice a question that I believe he must often ask us: "**Do you have good cause to be angry?**"

Oh yes, the righteous indignation question mentioned in the section regarding the book's theme. Did Jonah have reasonable cause to be angry when there were so many people we can only assume were young because they did not know their right from their left hand? Can we have reasonable cause to be angry at the world's distasteful and sinful condition when so many do not know Jesus because we have not told them of Jesus? We can only assume Jonah was disgusted when he first entered Ninevah and saw what he encountered. We complain bitterly on our social media accounts about what we encounter on TV and social media, but what do we do to change things today? We become *charah,* but do we do anything but perhaps a one-day walk-through instead of the three-day encounter that the world needs? Perhaps we need to become angrier with ourselves and less with the world. Perhaps?

Addendum Issue:
Why Is Jonah Read Today for Yom Kippur?

Occasionally, there will be an opportunity to cover a topic related to the theme of this book but one that is not necessarily connected to the biblical focus of the prophet. One such topic comes in chapter one, and it is the question as to why Jonah is the focus reading for Yom Kippur in Rabbinic Judaism today? Why is Jonah, who skipped town when given an order by God is, the focus on the most holy day on the Jewish calendar? Does that make sense to you? Well ... let us examine the Rabbinic Jewish response/rationale for reading Jonah today and see what sort of response we could make to them missionally and evangelistically. Indeed, the Jewish people need Jesus just as the Ninevites did so long ago.[10]

As I researched the religious spectrum of Rabbinic Judaism today (from Kabbalah to Reform and everything in between), I found a large mixture of answers. Indeed, the one constant answer I did find across the board was two words, "contradictions" and repentance (teshuvah), as it related to the Book of Jonah. In the Hasidic sect (ultra-Orthodox) known as the Lubavitch, Rabbi Mendel Dubov desperately seeks not to blame Jonah for his angry reaction. Still, he does note that according to the Talmud that, any prophet who directly disobeys God's command is worthy of death.[11]

Others focus on how Jonah is the symbol of repentance that Jonah needed to follow for himself even while preaching it to the people of Ninevah, and it is also the symbol for the Jewish people today.[12] And if this is the message that is being taught today, this is a message we could share with the people as well. Repentance is needed. A repentance was achieved as Jesus was in the grave as Jonah was in the fish for three days – Mt. 12:39-41; 16:4; Lk. 11:29-32.

---

[10] I could provide you with anecdotal evidence as a missionary to the Jewish people; however, I will instead give you information from the Joshua Project— https://joshuaproject.net/clusters/197. According to the Joshua Project, only 1.5% of the Jewish people in the world (more than 16 million) could be considered Christian. However, less than 1% of the 16 million would label themselves as Evangelical.

[11] Mendel Dubov, "The Story of Jonah and the 'Whale,'" see article online at https://www.chabad.org/library/article_cdo/aid/4510730/jewish/The-Story-of-Jonah-and-the-Whale.htm, accessed 30 March 2024. The actual Talmudic statement (*BT Sanhedrin 98a*) is found to say: But with regard to one who suppresses his prophecy because he does not want to share it with the public, and one who contemptuously forgoes the statement of a prophet and refuses to heed it, and a prophet who violated his own statement and failed to perform that which he was commanded to do, his death is at the hand of Heaven...

[12] Maya Bernstein, "Jonah and Yom Kippur: 4 Reasons We Read This Text on the Day of Atonement," My Jewish Learning, see article online at https://www.myjewishlearning.com/article/jonah-yom-kippur/, accessed 30 March 2024.

The final idea prevalent today is amazingly given from a perspective called Kabbalah. In a nutshell, Kabbalah is Jewish mysticism, and we should avoid it if possible because of its dangerous mystical issues. However, it is a finding a growing attraction in Judaism because the Jewish people are longing for something beyond the dryness of Rabbinic Judaism. Michael Laitman, a teacher of Kabbalah, notes correctly that Israel is to be a light to the nations but ignores the Scriptural passages of Dt. 4:4-8 that speaks of Israel's responsibility to draw the nations to God. Instead, he quotes other Talmudic passages and rabbis, which is the practice of Modern Judaism. He also ignores the Suffering Servant Songs of Is. 42: 6 and 49:6 (i.e., Messiah Jesus), which fulfills the truth of the light of the nations image.[13] The reasons for avoiding the Suffering Servant passages are apparent. Still, we can use these verses for evangelism today – especially since Yom Kippur is the holiest day of the year and is all about ultimate forgiveness, atonement, and repentance.

---

[13] Michael Laitman, "The Meaning of the Jonah Story Read on Yom Kippur (Blog)," *The Times of Israel*, 1 October 2017, available online at https://blogs.timesofisrael.com/the-meaning-of-the-jonah-story-read-on-yom-kippur/, accessed 30 March 2024. I need to note here that Laitman is a Kabbalist teacher and one should be careful before taking his words or teachings seriously.

2. Nahum: Cleaning up Jonah's Mess(Age)

Introduction

I am a missionary. I love being a missionary. The story of my missionary calling is available on Tzedakah Ministries' website for all to see—the good, the bad, and the ugly. However, my first love was not missions. My first love was studying history in all its forms, periods, and ages. In fact, my PhD from Liberty University, which is in Theology and Apologetics, has a concentration in church history.

From the earliest church fathers to the American leaders of the Christian church – George Whitfield and Jonathan Edwards and modern Christian history – I relished the opportunity to study the history of those times and their impact on the world. My fellow PhD students used to say that I had a habit of disabusing them of the view that many of our old Church Fathers (i.e., Augustine, Justin Martyr, Tertullian) were paragons of virtues. For some of these men – especially the three I mentioned above and others as well – were guilty of anti-Jewish views. So sadly, the spiritual impact of these movements and individuals was sometimes good, bad, and ugly. However, it was never dull, or at least not to me.

Let me explain what I mean as an introduction to this chapter for Nahum. Perhaps you have heard of The First Great Awakening of the 18th Century, which revolved around the revivalist preaching of George Whitfield and the pastoral focus of Jonathan Edwards.[14] The oratorical preaching power of Whitfield and Edwards' most famous sermon, "Sinners in the Hands of an Angry God" (first preached in 1741), changed the eternal destiny of untold numbers of people, and the colonial period was never the same. Indeed, Whitfield and Edwards were flawed men who shared the Gospel in America as few ever have, even with their human flaws and foibles.

---

[14] It has been brought to light recently that both men owned slaves, which has diminished their status in today's world. I am not defending their behavior, which is indefensible, nor excusing them by stating that this was a different time and a different world. Owning humans at any time is never allowable. Therefore, if you would like a good explanation of Edwards' conflicted view on the subject, George M. Marsden, *Jonathan Edwards: A Life* (New Haven, CT: Yale University Press, 2003): 55-58.

However, by the early days of the 19th century, the harvest of the First Great Awakening was but only a memory. In fact, Jonathan Edwards had been summarily dismissed (READ ... fired) from the church that had first heard the "Sinners in the Hands of an Angry God" (1741) less than a decade later in 1750.[15] Revival fires were less than simmering ... they were ice cold across the Northeastern areas of the country, but there was hope in the far distant horizons of the country. The frontier areas of Kentucky and Tennessee held the promise of revivals with upstart denominations called Methodist, Churches of Christ, and those crazy fellows called Baptists.[16]

Men like Francis Asbury (Methodist), Barton Stone and Alexander Campbell (Churches of Christ), Richard Furman and Francis Wayland (Baptist), and even women like Julia Foote and Harriet Livermore, revival meetings which focused on the conversion of the lost and what we would today call social justice influenced what was then the western edges of the United States.[17] However, the so-called "Second Great Awakening" would not be famous today if not for Charles Grandison Finney.[18]

Charles Finney was initially trained to be a lawyer before coming to faith in Messiah Jesus in 1821. There is nothing to doubt that Finney's encounter with the Messiah, but as Mark Noll observed, he did not see the need for theological training before beginning his ministerial career as an itinerant preacher in upstate New York and then revivalist across the land – an observation that should be a cause concern for us all.[19] Finney soon found himself at Oberlin College (Ohio), home to a place that allowed education for all people – men, women, and former slaves. Finney's focus in his revival sermon, as those of the men and women mentioned earlier, was both a salvation and a "social justice" message – a message that was not always welcome, especially as the United States was rushing towards the Civil War.[20]

---

[15] Ibid., 357-365.

[16] Mark A. Noll, *The Old Religion in a New World: The History of North American Christianity* (Grand Rapids: Eerdmans, 2002): 62-67.

[17] Ibid., 59-67.

[18] A portion of my bias against Finney and the "Second Great Awakening" comes because of my esteemed American History professor C. Barnwell Anderson at Jacksonville College when I was a freshman in college who described this period as neither "great" nor an "awakening" one day in class. However, nothing from my studies after Professor Anderson has caused me to deviate from his position. In anything, my studies only affirm his position.

[19] Noll, *The Old Religion in a New World*, 96-97.

[20] Ibid.

Finney was a dramatic speaker in the mold of Billy Sunday of the 1920s or even Jimmy Swaggart of the 1970s and 1980s in that he could sway the masses to a decision, but his theological depth was not deep at all.[21] While his revival meetings could last for months, the results of those dramatic events are noted not for mass conversions and increase of church attendance in the community so much as the results of creating emotions that often resulted in large numbers of child births nine months later (see fn. 5 for who and how I received this tidbit of information). Or, as my folksy grandparents used to say, Finney was a mile long but only an inch deep when it came to theological insight.

So ... what does the story of Charles Grandison Finney all have to do with Nahum? I am glad you asked. Often, someone called the local church pastor in the community had to come in after Charles Finney left town to repair the emotional and spiritual damage he left behind (i.e., clean-up). Nahum was the clean-up man years after Jonah – the famous or infamous guy from the "Big Fish Story" and chapter one – left a spiritual landfill called Ninevah, and this is Nahum's message that we are about to explore.

Who Nahum Was and the Biblical Background to This Clean-up Prophetic Message

The prophet, whose name means "comforting" and/or "full of comfort," definitely sent out a tough message to the people of Ninevah. One can reasonably wonder if this was the message that Nahum wanted to send. Still, it was the one that needed to be delivered to the people who had only partially heard the message (remember from chapter one that Jonah did not preach to all of the people Ninevah) as it was time for judgment as their repentance was temporary at best, and indeed, did not last long at all.

Nahum's autobiographical background is a mystery. All that we know is that he is an Elkoshite. Where is Elkosh, you might ask? There are questions as to where this ancient city was. However, the only certainty we have is uncertainty. Some speculate the Galilee region around Capernaum, while others surmise Southern Judah. The bottom line is that no one knows for certain today, but everyone knew where Elkosh was during Nahum's day.[22]

The timing of Nahum's message is less unpredictable for those who hold to Nahum being a prophetic book (i.e., those of us who believe in the inspiration of the Biblical text). Therefore, a reasonable guesstimate of 650 BC/BCE honors the prophetic message and respects the historical message.[23]

---

[21] Ibid., 130, 196, 264.

[22] Bullock, *An Introduction to the Old Testament Books*, 217.

[23] Bartholomew and Thomas, *The Minor Prophets: A Theological Introduction*, 202-203. These authors are open to a later date for Nahum; however, they offer a good analysis of the views, which is why I included them as the source here.

However, what I found most interesting in the introduction to the book (1:1) was the word choice that Nahum provides for the reader – ***massa***. It can be translated as either "vision," "burden," or even "oracle," and the various translations that one chooses to read will offer the either/or and "or" options. However, it might be wise to determine the best selection before going forward, for it is a vision because Nahum provided a prophecy. It is also an oracle for the same reason.

I do like Martin Luther's (yes, the Protestant Reformation guy) option for choosing "burden," but he picked up the idea from St. Jerome – the cave dweller guy from the early centuries of church history. Jerome and Luther chose "burden" because Ninevah, the city, was now under the weight of their own sins, as well as the fact that there was no hope for the people of God. The "burden" that Ninevah had been placing upon Israel/Judah was now being switched to the people to whom it belonged.[24] Now ... is this the perfect word choice? I am not certain because any of the three words are acceptable; however, "burden" does provide a nice visual, so let us go with that option for now.

Theme of Nahum – Never a Good Idea to Repent and Then Renege

As a pastor's kid (PK), I had to learn many tough lessons. Here are a few of the tough ones: (1) Always be polite to even the most uncivil of deacon's wives; (2) Never let anyone catch you sleeping during your dad's sermons ... even if it was a sermon you had heard a time or two; (3) Always eat everything placed in front of you when you are visiting a church member's home – even turnip greens and beets – which are disgusting(!) to almost any ten-year-old; and (4) NEVER, EVER renege on a promise given to anyone even if something more fun comes along.

I realize that "renege" is not used often anymore, but it is an excellent word in this setting. It simply means to go back on or to break your word. As a PK, I was often invited to attend exceptionally boring preacher meetings and sing for them (because I was a cute and fairly decent child singer). And I can assure you that for a young teenage girl, sitting through sermon after sermon after sermon from pastors on a Saturday is cruel and unusual, but if you promised to do it for your dad and those pastors ... you were committed to doing it. Regardless of whether it was a Saturday during the summer and there was a possible trip to Six Flags waiting or not. Your reputation was at stake; however, most of all, your dad's reputation was at stake. No reneging on promises was allowed...

---

[24] Martin Luther, *Luther's Works: Lectures on the Minor Prophets* (vol. 18), ed. Hilton C. Oswald, trans. Richard J. Dinda (St. Louis, MO: Concordia Publishing House, 1975): 283.

Yet, Nahum was responsible for writing a vision/burden to God's people and to Ninevah that dealt with the fact that the Ninevites had done precisely what I was not allowed to do. They had reneged not to their dad or the king but to God himself.

They had put on the sackcloth and ashes. They had mourned. But they had not done the most important thing of all … they apparently had not passed on the message to their children. And their children had abandoned Jonah's warning (albeit a message half given, half-heartedly) and gone back to a hedonistic, idol-worshipping lifestyle. A lifestyle that was vicious at best and barbarous would be a better description given all that we know of the Assyrians.

And now, the people of Ninevah (the Assyrians) would be judged by what we read in the oracle/burden. Judged harshly. Judged severely. Judged fairly. And all because they chose to renege on a promise. Warning given. Warning not received. It is a lesson for us all, but the question is … will we learn it?

Avoiding the Tendency to Isolate a Verse for Personal Use (i.e., Twisted Scripture – Nahum 1:7)

For every Scripture that can stand alone because of its clarity and beauty and comfort – such as Gen. 1:1 and John 3:16, there are other verses that just cannot. **However** … we too often have a tendency to want to grab an isolated verse here and there and claim them "as our own." Claim them as our comfort verse, our life verse, or whatever verse.

Now, is there anything wrong with having a life verse? I hope not, for I have one, and it is the statement I use instead of "Respectfully Yours" in letters or emails. My life verse is Acts 20:24, in which Paul proclaims to the church elders at Ephesus before he returns to Jerusalem and the prison chains that will follow him the rest of his life … *"But none of these things move me; nor do I count my life dear to myself, so that I may finish my race with joy, and the ministry which I received from the Lord Jesus, to testify to the gospel of the grace of God" (NKJV).*

Acts 20:24 truly define my mission calling. I have no reservations, no regrets, and no concept of retreating from the call to seek to share the Gospel with the Jewish people.[25] Thankfully, the context of the passage fits the verse as well. Unfortunately, many "favorite" verses do not fit what many people believe they mean, such as Jer. 29:11 or 2 Chron. 7:14 or even Phil. 4:13. Yikes, I know, I just stepped on some toes just now, and what will some famous stores do with all that wall art? However, truth is truth, and Biblical context is important because taking Scripture from its biblical background is how bad theology begins. Yikes … again!

In the book of Nahum, we do not find many verses that fit that situation, but there is one verse and that is found in the first chapter:

Jehovah (is) good – a stronghold in the day of trouble. And he knows those who put trust/seek refuge/seek protection in Him. (author translation)

In isolation, this verse can/could offer great comfort. It is a verse that perhaps even sounds like it could come from one of the authors of the Psalms – another place rife with verses taken out of context. However, if one reads verse seven in the context of the chapter itself and the whole of Nahum, God is not in a good mood at all.

God is angry at the Ninevites and the situation his people are in at the moment. While there is the promise of hope for those who take refuge and comfort for those who seek protection in God, I do not believe any of us today would want to be where God's people are finding themselves. At least American Christians would not wish to find themselves in this situation…

Yet, many Christians around the world do find themselves where perhaps they can claim this verse as a promise of victory and future hope. Christians in North Korea, underground churches in the Middle East, and in countries that we dare not mention lest our brothers and sisters be at risk for their lives. Places, where to even whisper the name of Jesus, is to invite a *fatwa* upon their head or ten years in a re-education camp (i.e., working waist-deep in a rice paddy for ten or twelve hours a day).

---

[25] The phrase "No Regrets, No Retreat, No Reservations" is written beside this verse in my Bible, but it is not original to me. The heir to the Borden dairy fortune in the 19th century is proposed to have the honor of first writing a version of these lines – William Whiting Borden. His story of leaving fortune behind for the sake of the Gospel calling should never be forgotten. Jayson Casper, "The Forgotten Final Resting Place of William Borden," *Christianity Today*, 24 February 2017 (https://www.christianitytoday.com/history/2017/february/forgotten-final-resting-place-of-william-borden.html), accessed 16 March 2024.

For Nah 1:7 is a verse not for those who are living in a comfortable setting but for those who are living in a place of hardship yet know that God is on their side and will not allow evil to claim ultimate victory. This verse is for our fellow believers who have or are bearing the shackles of verse 13 but know that the celebration promised in verse 15 is soon around the corner. This is a verse for missionaries and missions. This is a verse for the 10/40 Window. This verse is for our brothers and sisters who know what it is to suffer for Messiah Jesus.

Is Nahum a Justification of Jonah's Complaint or an Indictment of Jonah's Failure to Truly Evangelize the City? (1:3)

In chapter one, I admittedly was harsh towards and to Jonah – his narrow-minded character, his approach to preaching to the people of Ninevah, his unbearable attitude afterward as it relates to the people turning to God, and the results of his evangelistic efforts. And we now see in Nahum why I feel justified in my harshness. Ninevah returned to their pagan ways in no small part, in my opinion, because of Jonah, and the destruction of the city and the destruction of a people are the result.

Now, one could say fairly that the Assyrians, the people of Ninevah, were enemies of the Jewish people. And this was Jonah's argument after all … "they deserve to die!" However, God used Jonah to give the people a chance. While the people of Ninevah are ultimately responsible for their own spiritual demise, Jonah's, dare I say, lazy and half-hearted approach to evangelism also holds a portion of responsibility. And Nahum's burden/vision/oracle gives us the message, the result. Yes, it is a difficult read, but it is an important message to understand.

John Goldingay, in his work *The Lost Letters to the Twelve Prophets,* states this overall concept well when he writes the following:

> So Yahweh lives with the tension between being the God of love and the God who cannot simply turn a blind eye to evil, and he has to decide from time to time when and how to give expression to the first or to the second. And for Nineveh, this is a moment when it is time to treat a guilty city as guilty. Judah will not be doing the destroying, but Yahweh's action will also mean relief for Judah.[26]

---

[26] John Goldingay, *The Lost Letters to the Twelve Prophets: Imagining the Minor Prophets' World* (Grand Rapids, MI: Zondervan Academic, 2022): 138. Although I would not utilize the word Yahweh and choose to use the word Jehovah due to Jewish sensitivity over the word, I decided to quote Dr. Goldingay directly.

In 1:3, one can read the following (author's translation): *"Jehovah (is) slow to anger and great in power and Jehovah will never leave (the guilty) unpunished (for) his way (is in) the whirlwind and the storm and clouds of dust beneath his feet."* God gave the people of Ninevah a great opportunity – despite Jonah – and it was ultimately lost in the debauchery of their own making. It was lost because of their own pride and presumptions that they were invincible.

But and despite what some might think, the answer to the question given in the title to this section is not a both/and. There is no justification for Jonah's complaint or perceived justification that the Assyrians (the people of Ninevah) did not deserve to hear the truth of God. We must remember that the people of Israel had been given the charge to show the other peoples who and what God could do (Dt. 4:6-8). Throughout the Hebrew Scriptures, we see that it was the responsibility of the Israelites (aka the Jewish people) to welcome the strangers and those who wanted to come into the household of God, but only if they abandoned their foreign gods. Indeed, what would the lineage of David and even Jesus be without Tamar, Rahab, Ruth, and Bathsheba, who were all foreign-born? But … it was this overall failure of the Jewish people to be the "light to the Gentiles" that led to the coming of the Suffering Servant that we know to be Messiah Jesus (Isaiah 42:6; 49:6).[27]

The lesson we can then learn today is to finish the job we are given, whether we be missionaries and/or churches. We have been given a Great Commission task. Still, far too often, we do not finish the task because we decide to be God and determine that "those people" do not deserve the Gospel because of some perceived flaw in their character, their ethnicity, their personal sin, or perhaps in how they vote in an election. We play Jonah and do not finish the task, and then someone else is left to write the obituary as Nahum did after us. Meanwhile, we also forget that the Apostle Paul, who once was a murderer (perhaps one could even call him a serial killer), once wrote these words:

> *Do you not know that the unrighteous will not inherit the kingdom of God? Do not be deceived. Neither fornicators, nor idolaters, nor adulterers, nor homosexuals, nor sodomites, nor thieves, nor covetous, nor drunkards, nor revilers, nor extortioners will inherit the kingdom of God. And such were some of you. But you were washed, but you were sanctified, but you were justified in the name of the Lord Jesus and by the Spirit of our God. (1 Cor. 6:9-11 – NKJV)*

---

[27] The Suffering Servant Songs of Isaiah before Isaiah 53 are sometimes read as both/and. However, I (the author) choose to read them as solely in the domain of belonging to Messiah Jesus. This avoids the confusion of identity and the anti-missionary argument that Isaiah belongs to Israel, which is a pronoun impossibility.

The Great Commission and American Arrogance (2:1-4:19)

During my seminary days, I went to Wedgwood Baptist Church in Fort Worth, Texas. Wedgwood Baptist is remembered tragically for what was perhaps the second mass church shooting on 15 September 1999 that resulted in seven lives being cut short and eight others being wounded before the shooter committed suicide.[28] What is not often known about my seminary church is that it was a great missionary outreach church during that time as well and that my seminary pastor, Dr. Al Meredith (aka "The Singing Preacher" as many of his sermons were interrupted by hymns as illustrations), loved to help missionaries on the field and enjoyed training national pastors on the mission field when he could.

One time, Brother Al spent several weeks in Russia training national pastors, and upon his return, he spent one Wednesday night sharing about his experience. The worship center was crowded, and people were asking questions about the work in Russia. One man asked a question that stopped everyone in their tracks by its audacity and, dare I write, hubris – "Brother Al, should we send our worship team over to Moscow to teach those people how to worship God?"

Thankfully, I was not the one who answered the question because I was much younger than him and would not have been as kind as Brother Al was. He patiently explained to the man that Russians tend to have a different style of worship than we do, which is perfectly fine. Meanwhile, I was thinking to myself – "Idiot, this is why other nations think of us as 'Ugly Americans!'" I told you that it was good that my seminary pastor answered this man and not me … as I have discovered my edit button since my seminary days.

---

[28] There are many references about the shooting that can be found online. A friend of mine was shot, and a church friend was one of those killed. I was not at church that evening due to a God-ordained happenstance that still haunts me to this day.

Yet, we, as American Christianity, do tend to want to import our brand of faith and practice to the world. While I do understand that missionaries have to be very careful not to allow syncretism (combining of Christian views and the opinions of the world so that the exclusive truth of the Gospel is ultimately lost)[29] seep into our world as we share the Gospel with our people groups,[30] We must also never allow the sin of pride and false arrogance of American exceptionalism to seep in either. This has happened in the past, and sadly, it is rearing its head again in today's churches. It is a false wall to the sharing of the Gospel.

Pride and hubris (one of my favorite great vocabulary words) have brought down many empires and people. The Assyrian Empire (Ninevah) was no different when standing in the way of the King of the Universe. Nah. 2:1-2 reminds us of this truth very clearly. For while Nahum almost mockingly challenges them to prepare for battle against the God of the universe, it will be useless for Jehovah *"will restore the splendor of Jacob like the splendor of Israel even though devastators devastate them and destroyed their vine branches"* (v. 2).

The remainder of Nahum is almost one continuous litany of devastation after destruction after desolation for Ninevah. The disgrace is made manifest in 3:5 when Jehovah Sabaoth (Lord of the Armies)[31] states that He will cause the other nations (in an allegorical fashion) to see the utter nakedness of Ninevah – and if we want to be allegorically blunt about it – their female private parts. Yes, God was taking Ninevah down to the very dregs of society for not only what they had done to Israel but also for not truly accepting God's gracious opportunity for forgiveness.

So, all of these graphic gores might have you asking … what does this have to do with the American hubris of today and the earlier example from my seminar days? Again, and as always, I am glad you asked. While it is very dangerous to allegorize Scripture, I am going to take a little bit of artistic license with this example while still seeking to hold true to Nahum's message.

---

[29] Gailyn Van Rheenen provides a fuller definition that needs to be provided: "blending of Christian beliefs and practices with those of the dominant culture so that Christianity loses its distinctiveness and speaks with a voice reflective of its culture." See Gailyn Van Rheenen, "Contextualization and Syncretism," Missiology Blog, 7 January 2011, http://missiology.com/blog/GVR-MR-38-Contextualization-and-Syncretism, accessed 19 March 2024.

[30] It should be noted that sharing the Gospel to the Jewish people today is very difficult, and the issue of syncretism is a very difficult topic. Syncretistic terms and concepts like "Torah-Observance" and "Two-Branch" exist within Messianic Judaism, and they must be avoided as they are, dare I say, heretical.

[31] A full amplification of this description of God will be uncovered in chapter 11 (Haggai).

Ninevah presumed that they were invincible, but they found that they were not in a devastating way. I am fearful that today, we (American Christianity) have a prideful view of our evangelistic methods. We believe that we know best in all methods, and we seek to import our evangelistic tools to every corner of the world—even though there are times when our efforts "to teach those Russians how to worship" might be the worst thing we could ever do for those Russian churches/Christians.

Imposing American-style Christianity on other people groups – especially when we need to examine ourselves spiritually at the present time – is to rob those people groups of their identity, their peoplehood, and their humanity. And ultimately, it often turns those same people groups away from the Gospel and not towards it. By seeking to turn tribes in Africa or Indigenous people in Asia into Americans but yet losing the opportunity to have them truly become fellow believers in the Messiah, Jesus must cause us to ask the question – what has been gained? For as I read the final pages in Revelation, I see many tongues, many peoples, many nations around the throne and no one cares if any of us carries an American flag.

Section Two:
The Long and Short of Sinful Living
Amos and Obadiah

Amos and Obadiah are almost bookends in many ways. Amos is one of the longer books of the "minor prophets," and Obadiah is the shortest of the prophetic books. In fact, it is the shortest book of the Hebrew Scriptures. However, both of these men, whose words are almost never considered in churches today, give us words from God that we ignore at our own peril. Both of these prophets provide a clarion warning of what happens when the hubris of the powerful meets the powerful wrath of an almighty God.

Hubris, which is the idea of being excessively arrogant and/or overconfident, is the perfect description for the world in which both Obadiah and Amos were asked to prophesy words of "doom and gloom." A world in which the people of God presumed they were from judgment. A world in which the Chosen People assumed they were protected from punishment because they were somehow untouchable from anything wrong happening to them. A world in which the words arrogant and overconfident fit the Jewish people perfectly.

And Amos and Obadiah are commanded to "burst the bubble" on that hubristic balloon. These men of God definitely did not follow the suggestions of the original life coach, Zig Ziglar, on how "to win friends and influence people." Yet, they had to warn the people of the cost of not following God. They had to inform the Jewish people of what it would mean to live a sinful life. And I admit that I am excited that I finally get to use one of my favorite words, hubris, so many times in one setting!

Obadiah is overlooked today. Amos is overlooked today. Overlooked to our spiritual detriment. However, both of these men of God shared the truth that He will judge those who do not follow his commands. Perhaps this is something we should remember as well today because God does not overlook it when we forget the message that these two prophets sought to share.

3. Amos: Do Not Discount the Words of the Laity

Introduction

Every church should have Roy and Val Blair as members. They were, in many ways, "the perfect church members." Now, I am not saying they were perfect, but they were wonderful, godly people. The world is much less colorful and kind because they both passed away a few years ago.

My dad was a pastor for most of his ministry life. However, he went to Bible College and majored in children's ministry. This enabled him to serve in three churches as their Children's Pastor in the mid-1970s and early-1980s, which was also the zenith of the "Church Bus Ministry" days. Luckily for one of those churches, daddy was an excellent "shade tree" mechanic, and luckily for daddy, at that same church, Roy and Val Blair were members.

This particular church in Dallas, Texas, had eleven buses and three vans that went out every Sunday morning. There were also 4 or 5 age-graded children's churches going concurrently during the main worship service. My dad was responsible for all the children's churches – and he led the worship in the 4th to 6th-grade children's church – and supervised the bus captains, bus drivers, and volunteers on the 14 vehicles that went out every Sunday morning. Indeed, it was a 60-70 (if not more!) hour-a-week job. In addition, daddy was also in charge of church benevolence since many of those who came on the buses would reach out to the church for financial and food help, but that is another discussion for another time.

I was a bus captain at the age of 14 since my dad had trouble finding adults who would volunteer to head up a bus route in a tough neighborhood (Mr. Litton was the bus driver, and he could handle any "situation" that might arise). So, I was at the church's ministry banquet for the members in 1983 or 1984 when the Volunteer of the Year award was given. Daddy gave the award to Roy (and Val) Blair, and no one deserved it more…

There was not a week when one of those buses (or vans) did not break down, and since my dad was a mechanic and could save the church some money… daddy was under the hood of some bus/van trying to apply duct tape and bubble gum for one more week. And who was there beside him – Roy Blair. My dad met every bus/van on Sunday morning to find out how many were on the bus and if there were any problems that needed to be taken care of immediately (mechanical or problem child) – and Roy Blair was usually right beside my dad to help him out and greet every child with a smile and a howdy.

Val Blair was also there in her children's church to teach the children about Jesus. I believe it was the 1st and 2nd-grade children's church, and it was the one children's church that my dad never was concerned would have discipline problems or have an issue about anything taught from Scripture that might be incorrect. Daddy knew he could trust Val Blair with the children's emotional and spiritual needs. And Val Blair was not only concerned about those children on Sunday but also prayed for them daily and followed up with them on a Thursday if necessary. Indeed, Roy and Val Blair were the perfect church members. They were the perfect laymen/laity in today's language.

So why am I mentioning these wonderful people that I still miss, but I can imagine they are having coffee with my parents in Heaven at this moment? To me, they represent the modern-day Amos. Amos was a layman, and this is something we will discuss further in the next section. He was there and available to be used by God whenever and however he was asked. And we truly need more Amos' in the world today. So where are they, or are we just missing them when they are so willing to be used?

Who Amos Was and a Little Biblical Background

Amos was a burden-bearer for Jehovah, which is reflected in his name's meaning. It had to be a burden to be a prophet for God during this time when the responsibility of sharing difficult news would not make you a popular individual. Yet this layman and sheepherder/sheep breeder from Tekoa took on the burden given to him by God and delivered the visions to those who did not want to hear what they needed to learn.

As readers of Amos, we are given a very specific timeframe (c.760-750 BC/BCE) for when the prophet took time away from his sheep to share God's message. First, we know that it was during the days of Uzziah, the king of Judah, and King Jeroboam of Israel. However, verse one provides more information that allows us to narrow down the time period of Amos' ministry— "two years before the earthquake."

We find mention of this earthquake again in Zech. 14:5 in a prophetic sense – *"Then you shall flee through My mountain valley, For the mountain valley shall reach to Azal. Yes, you shall flee. As you fled from the earthquake in the days of Uzziah, king of Judah. Thus the Lord my God will come, and all the saints with You."* And while earthquakes are not uncommon in this part of the world, is there evidence that an earth-shattering event occurred that would have deserved mention in the text? Evidence beyond that which is mentioned in both Amos and Zechariah. Actually, yes. This is much to the consternation of modern-day archaeologists who often believe that their research will disprove the Biblical record but, when digging through the dirt, discover that what they find proves that that the Scripture was right all along.[32]

Theme of Amos – Seeking the Justice of God

Tragically, when many consider Amos, the only verse that comes to mind is 8:11, which is a wonderful verse – *"'Behold, the days are coming,' says the Lord God, 'That I will send a famine on the land, not a famine of bread, nor a thirst for water, but of hearing the words of the Lord.'"* Indeed, this is a wonderful verse and one that will be considered in great and more detail in a later section of this chapter. However, very few people examine the next verse (v. 12), which is heartbreaking, and I believe the core theme of Amos: *They shall wander from sea to sea, and from north to east; they shall run to and fro, seeking the word of the LORD, but shall not find it.*

---

[32] Amanda Borschel-Dan, "Archaeologists Unearth 1st Jerusalem Evidence of Quake from Bible's Book of Amos," *The Times of Israel*, 4 August 2021, available online at https://www.timesofisrael.com/archaeologists-unearth-1st-jerusalem-evidence-of-quake-from-bibles-book-of-amos/; Livia Gershon, "Researchers Find Physical Evidence of Old Testament Described in Old Testament," *Smithsonian Magazine*, 6 August 2021, available online at https://www.smithsonianmag.com/smart-news/scientists-find-evidence-8th-century-bc-earthquake-described-old-testament-180978385/; Nathan Steinmeyer, "Evidence of Biblical Earthquake Discovered in Jerusalem: Sites Across Israel Damaged by Eighth-Century B.C.E. Quake, *Biblical Archaeology Society*, 10 August 2021, available online at https://www.biblicalarchaeology.org/daily/ancient-cultures/ancient-israel/evidence-of-biblical-earthquake-discovered-in-jerusalem/; and Steven A. Austin, "The Scientific and Scriptural Impact of Amos' Earthquake," *Acts and Facts*, Institute of Creation Research, 1 February 2010, available online at https://www.icr.org/article/scientific-scriptural-impact-amos-earthquake/, all accessed 12 April 2024. Perhaps sharing all four articles might be considered a little bit of "overkill," but I chose to do so because all four articles come from different academic and religious perspectives – from conservative to liberal. Therefore, the evidence is irrefutable that Scripture and academia agree.

Perhaps I should also wait and examine this verse in a later section, but since it is what I believe represents the theme of Amos, I am going to do it here. The people of Israel, as they were Amos' mission people group, will be found wandering around in every direction and literally from port to port (i.e., "sea to sea"). The wandering in Hebrew represents people who were drunk, begging, and/or even harlots. This was the level of degradation they had been reduced to in their sinfulness. And while they go everywhere desperately seeking a God they abandoned as described in the Hebrews, they will never find it. Why? I believe Martin Luther says it better than I can when he wrote:

> You see, they believe that they have no need for God. **They go on in their blindness to act wickedly until they are caught by the judgment of God and perish.** The Word is declared to them in vain, as we see in this prophet. Amos, therefore, prophesied at a very ill-starred yet very opportune time. From all this let us learn well that in adverse times we must have good hopes for the goodness and mercy of God, but that in good time we must live in fear.[33]

I added the emphasis in the Luther quote above because this could also be said about us today. Many believers/followers of Jesus are walking around blind when it comes to their walk with God. They are spiritually ignorant if one can be so blunt as it relates to their biblical knowledge and the reality of what Paul wrote to his primary disciple Timothy about the church in the latter days being swept about by every wind of doctrine (Eph. 4:14; cf. 1 Tim. 4:1-5). It is not enough to read a book, even one as brilliant as the one you are reading now. One must delve into the Scriptures lest there be famine.

A famine that resulted in a lack of justice, which Amos condemned. A famine resulted in a lack of awareness of God's message, which God prophesied but which he himself was condemned for preaching about in the later chapters of the book. A famine for the actual land that Israel will lose because of their sinfulness and which should serve as a warning for us today.

---

[33] Luther, Luther's Works: Lectures on the Minor Prophets, 128. On a personal note and since I am a missionary to the Jewish people, I personally struggle in acknowledging any contribution by Martin Luther due to his later antisemitic works. However, I do recognize his contribution to the Reformation Period and what he offers as a theologian in any period.

Does God Care About Social Justice? (1:3-2:3)

On 7 January 2023, Tyre Nichols was killed by five African-American police officers in Memphis, Tennessee. The video of what happened to this young black man with his whole life ahead of him was difficult to watch, but it should be watched by anyone who cares about the words "justice" and "peace." His mother and stepfather were and should be applauded for their calls for calmness and compassion in the midst of their grief and loss. There is no doubt in the minds of many that their calls for peace and civility reduced the strife that erupted from riots that harkened back to the riots of 2020. Yet, we all should ask ourselves why this keeps *happening in 21st-century America.*

In reflection on this question, one can also consider the tragic ministry story of Walter Rauschenbusch. You can search the internet for his whole story because I can only summarize it here. He was a German Baptist pastor in the early days of the 20th century who was idealistic in his missionary desire to reach the lost and dying of New York City. He went to the Hell's Kitchen area of Manhattan, which deserved the moniker in those days. The area was filled with prostitutes and saloons. Children lived in squalor that would boggle the mind. For while my beloved city has regressed from the progress it made in the latter days of the twentieth century, the squalor of Rauschenbusch's days would make the dankness of this decade for NYC seem like the Garden of Eden.

Yet, Rauschenbusch did all he could to share the Gospel of Messiah Jesus with the saloon owners, the prostitutes, and the children who survived on what they could steal or beg for on the streets. However, and for lack of a better explanation, Rauschenbusch soon began to believe that the only means to change the world of Hell's Kitchen was to focus on their physical needs **over or even instead of** their spiritual needs. Out of this change from a mission's focus, Rauschenbusch was one of the first developers of a movement that would grow into the Social Gospel Movement.

So … what was the Social Gospel Movement, and why does it have a lingering impact on American society? I can answer the last part of the question first because it is easy … YES. Especially if any of you reading this book ever took swim lessons at the YMCA or the YWCA, as both organizations are wonderful examples of the genesis of the Social Gospel Movement.[34]

Both the YWCA and the YMCA were founded to provide housing and religious Bible studies for men and women who were single and seeking employment. Indeed, George Williams, along with ten other men who founded the YMCA, wrote the following as a basic charter statement for the YMCA's founding in 1844 -- *"Our object is the improvement of the spiritual condition of the young men engaged in houses of business, by the formation of Bible classes, family and social prayer meetings, mutual improvement societies, or any other spiritual agency"* (see fn.). However, declining numbers and finances changed the focus of the organization from a mission-sending organization to focusing on physical fitness[35] and song of the "Village People" in the 1970s to signal homosexual men that this was a good place to … "connect."

Defining the Social Gospel Movement is a lot more difficult and a lot more loaded because it has a lot of connection to what we call Social Justice or Biblical Social Justice today. However, it is relatively easy to define the Social Gospel movement because it can be examined from a 20/20 hindsight perspective. Social Justice or Biblical Social Justice is a lot more difficult because EVERYONE has an opinion. However, we need to try to have a better understanding of the term because Amos and many of the minor prophets devoted a lot of time to the idea, and that indicates it was/is important to God as well.

---

[34] As I was reading through my research, there was a great temptation to go into great detail about the "backsliding" history of the YMCA and the YWCA. However, this would take away from the focus of the book. Therefore, I can only briefly highlight how they fall into what they are today – a good place for swimming but definitely not a Christian organization. However, and if you are interested, I am noting here two places to go for additional information. Dorothea Browder, "A 'Christian Solution of the Labor Solution': How Workingwomen Reshaped the YWCA's Religious Mission and Politics," *Journal of Women's History*, vol. 19, no. 2 (2007): 85-110, accessed 15 April 2024 and "Sir George Williams – Founder of the YMCA," World YMCA, available online at https://www.ymca.int/who-we-are/the-worldwide-ymca-movement/the-ymca-history/sir-george-williams-founder-of-the-ymca/, accessed 15 April 2024. It should be noted that the YWCA website does not give a history of the religious founding of the organization and so I had to go outside of their website to find this information; but, the YMCA did at least give the religious history of its founding.

[35] Peter Greer and Chris Horst, *Mission Drift: The Unspoken Crisis Facing Leaders, Charities, and Churches* (Bloomington, MN: Bethany House Publishers, 2014): 67-69.

Tim Pietz for Christianity.com does a reasonably good job of examining the history, goals, and problematic theology of the early Social Gospel movement in his article; however, he even struggles to provide a clear definition.[36] Therefore, I have attempted to write my own definition of the term Biblical Social Justice. *Biblical Social Justice* is defined by the following verses: Isaiah 1:17; James 1:26-27; 1 John 3:17-18. Scripture puts no preconditions on how or who should receive help; Scripture only calls on believers to help people who are in need, and Scripture does not expect input or output. So, our only question, from my perspective as churches and believers in Jesus, is whether we are doing enough to help those in need.

For there is nothing wrong with focusing on the physical needs of the people; we are seeking to reach the Gospel of Messiah Jesus. In fact, I would argue that if someone is hungry, it might be impossible for them to hear the message of Jesus over a growling and grumbling stomach. However, Rauschenbusch and the others of the Social Gospel Movement of that time chose to abandon the message of the need to receive Jesus as Messiah to answer the temporary physical problems a person might have. Ultimately, I would argue that true Biblical Social Justice is not an either/or concern but a both/and resolution. This is something that Walter Rauschenbusch unfortunately missed entirely.

Thankfully, the prophet Amos understood the balance needed between biblical social justice and biblical truth. Unfortunately, very few people read the book of Amos today, or we would realize this balance today. So ... let us look at the prophet's words for ourselves...

Amos the Sheepherder begins his work as a prophet by condemning enemies of Israel/Judah, but I believe we can and should make modern comparisons today without doing exegetical harm to the text.

---

[36] Tim Pietz, "What Is the Social Gospel and Its Movement?," Christianity.com, 4 January 2023, available at https://www.christianity.com/wiki/christian-terms/what-social-gospel-movement.html, accessed 15 April 2024.

Brutal Military Tactics (1:3-5)

Damascus was condemned for utilizing brutal military tactics to subdue their enemies (specifically against the people in Gilead). Basically, God accused and found them guilty of "war crimes" and "crimes against humanity" in modern vernacular. I believe that by reading the text, we as believers and churches would affirm God's verdict – as if we had the nerve to question the Almighty. However, I would ask you, where were we when President Obama used military drones on terrorists that also hit innocent civilians or when President Trump threatened to use nuclear weapons on North Korea back in the early days of his administration? Notice how I mentioned both a Democrat and Republican president so no one could accuse me of being partisan. During World War II, many "good Christians" justified their actions against the Jewish people with the adage that they were just following orders. Does that give them a pass on the Holocaust? I hope you would say no.

I recognize that protesting against the government and its military strategy is a touchy subject in this day and age. The question of "just war" and valid military defensive actions is a dilemma for any government. However, we, as Christians and churches, do have the responsibility to investigate and know what our leaders are doing in the name of our country. And when they overstep, we have the responsibility to stand up and defend the defenseless.

Human Trafficking (1:6-10)

Both Gaza and Tyre were condemned for what we would today describe as human trafficking. Therefore, I decided to examine and provide you with some statistics on the reality of human trafficking in the world today (https://www.ilo.org/global/topics/forced-labour/lang--en/index.htm).

(1) 50 million people on any given day are considered as victims of "modern slavery." This means that 1 out of every 150 people are slaves in the world.
(2) What is "modern slavery" according to the September 2022 International Labour Organization?
    a. 27.6 million people are in forced labor in the world today
    b. 6.5 million people are considered to be sexually exploited with 3.3 million of this number considered to be children.
    c. 22 million people are in what is considered forced marriages around the world
(3) 199,000 people are human trafficked every year in the United States. The top state per 100,000 is Mississippi with 6.32 per 100,000. Out of the top ten states per 100,000, five are in the South — Mississippi, Missouri, Florida, Arkansas, and Texas.

Fratricide/Sibling Rivalry (1:11-12; 2:1-3)

Moab and Edom, who were descendants of the daughters of Lot, sought to destroy each other – and there are all sorts of ways I could take this exegetical interpretation. I could show this geopolitically, and it would apply. However, I decided to take this in-house and consider how Christians are destroying each other with denominational and theological wars. Go to social media (especially Twitter or what we know called X, thanks to Elon Musk) and discover how Southern Baptists, for example, are destroying the Convention over whether someone is "conservative enough" anymore. The battle on social media is not about the Gospel but whether one is a 4-Point or 5-Point Calvinist, for example. The battle is not about the truth of Scripture but whether one can or cannot be simply friends with someone who is a homosexual. We are destroying ourselves before the lost world so loudly that the world can no longer hear the Gospel message we profess that we want to share with them. We are becoming guilty of fratricide and do not even realize it.

Genocide (1:13-15)

Ammon was guilty of nothing less than attempted genocide. We have seen multiple examples of attempted genocide in the 20th and 21st centuries. Rwanda, the Killing Fields of Cambodia, today with the starving children in Yemen (look it up if you have not heard of it), and, of course, the Holocaust of World War II. However, most Christians and churches stood by and still stand silently and apathetically while these genocides occurred because they did not want to get involved. Bystanders instead of upstanders were our motto, and the ethical high ground was lost – and when the ethical high ground is lost, then the opportunity to share the Gospel message of Messiah Jesus is also lost.

Walter Rauschenbusch got lost in Hell's Kitchen's morass and hellish conditions. The German Baptist pastor who intended to show the love of Jesus in the skid-row circumstances lost his focus on the Gospel in the early days of the 20th century. However, today, we are lost in the morass of our own making and have lost any heart for Biblical Social Justice AND Biblical TRUTH. Therefore, we must ask ourselves, who will God judge more harshly? Dare we ask God himself a question?

Does God Care About Social Justice? – Part II (2:4-4:15)

Amos began his prophetic ministry by pointing out the sins of Israel and Judah's neighbors. I can almost imagine the people of God hearing the condemnation of Moab, Edom, Gaza, Tyre, and Damascus and almost salivating over the punishment that was heading their way. As I was studying those passages for myself, I could also envision the Jewish people as if they were at an old-fashioned Baptist pastor's meeting, shouting out the "Amens, Hallelujahs, and Preach it, Brothers" every time Amos began a new attack on one of their neighbors. They must have loved it because God was going to punish those evil Edomites once and for all.

But I wondered as I was reading, "Did they really think they were going to escape God's condemnation?" HINT: We will get to that question/answer in a later section of this chapter. Anyway ... Amos is not turned towards the kingdoms of Israel and Judah, and I can almost hear him say, "Now, it is your turn to hear what God thinks of you."

Were they terrified? Were they bemused because they had regressed so far into their sinful lifestyles? Were they certain that God would not carry through on his warnings? Just what was their reaction to Amos' warnings? Perhaps I am the only one to ask these questions when reading Scripture, and while I dare not read into the text to provide an answer, I did ask myself these questions.

Judah's Turn (2:4-5)

As we look at Judah's three "transgressions/crimes," it could be easy to assume that we are exempt today from being guilty of these same transgressions – but we are not. Amos tells Judah that they have <u>first</u> "rejected," "abhorred," or "despised" (as any of these English words are acceptable choices for the Hebrew word) the "Torah of God." I know that most English translations say, "law of God," but that would be incorrect as the word in Hebrew is Torah, and we miss out when we do not recognize this word.

As we know, the Torah is the whole encompassing message of God from Moses of Genesis to Deuteronomy. Therefore, when we read the "law of God," we can focus on what we perceive to be the finer points or details in the Torah, such as not mixing milk and meat together and believing that that was for then and not for now. While there exists among some Christian groups who love to debate those issues that I am not going to touch with a 10-foot pole argument because I happen to believe it is a useless and ridiculous argument, the Torah of Genesis through Deuteronomy today is as much Scripture as Jude and Philemon and 1 Peter. All sixty-six books have messages for all of us that we need to take seriously.

Anyway, and before I continue down that rabbit trail(!), the message of Amos to Judah was that they were guilty of rejecting God's Torah. They were also, and this is the <u>second transgression</u>; they had not guarded God's statutes/boundaries. Today, and in reading this verse, we should recognize that this statute/boundary was a protective measure that had been established for the people. Some might believe this refers to the Oral Law, but I am not one of them. I believe (and this is only my opinion) that this refers back to the idea that is found throughout Leviticus in this simple but exceptionally difficult phrase to live out – "Be ye Holy, as I am Holy."

God established the Torah/Law so that the people of God would be set apart as a "light to the nations," and they had not guarded those boundaries, and their light to the nations was now barely a nightlight in their own house. The people of Judah had lost their distinctiveness, which made them different from anyone else in their geographical area. No, it is not easy being different. It is much easier to blend into the crowd than to stand out, and that was their third transgression – they had been led astray from the original paths that their fathers had walked.

Time and space do not permit a return to the warnings of Joshua and Judges to see where the people were forced to remember the lessons of what happened when they forgot the original paths. Moses and Solomon both warned them not to remove the ancient landmarks which their fathers had set before them (Deut. 27:17; Pro. 22:28). Therefore, God was going to send them fire and destruction upon both Judah and Jerusalem – destruction that would not occur for nearly two more centuries (586 BC/BCE) but an inferno that certainly did happen.

Israel's Turn (2:6-16)

Now it is Israel's turn, and their sins are just as heinous as those of their neighbors – Gaza, Tyre, Moab, and Edom. In verses 6-7a, the righteous and needy are sold (human trafficking) for a pair of sandals as they are found guilty of diminishing the needs of the humble, the powerless, and the insignificant. In verses 7b-8, Israel is found guilty of the same sins as the people of Moab and Edom – the sin of incest and prostitution. Finally, and the greatest sin of all to God (v. 9-12), Israel is discovered to be negligent in recognizing that it was God who protected them all along and guilty of forcing the Nazarites and the prophets to disregard their calling.

Each sin is repugnant in and of itself. Yet, Israel was guilty of all three, and their guilt would not go unnoticed by the God who had protected them in Egypt and chosen them among all the peoples of the world (3:1-2). Their punishment was fair. Their punishment was just. Regardless of whether they realized it or not, the words of Amos were coming far more swiftly than they realized, for the Assyrians would soon arrive – less than a century later in 712 BC/BCE. And there would be no refuge for the strong, the swift, or the brave (v. 13-16).

The remainder of chapter 3 provides an explanation as to why God is wholly justified in his actions. This is done through a series of rhetorical questions that Amos answers for God in verses 7, 13-15. The actions of the Northern Kingdom had become so evil that God had no choice but to bring this judgment upon his people. Sin brings judgment. Sin brings pain. Sin brings death. Indeed, the great houses of Samaria (Northern Kingdom) ended, as we see in the concluding verse of chapter 3. For when God's people fail to live up to the expectations of justice, love, and mercy towards others and begin to live just as their neighbors – judgment will come to our great houses as well.

65

Do Not Challenge the Message(Enger) of God – (7:1-17)

One could spill a great deal of ink dissecting chapters 4-6 – especially analyzing how women are compared to the cows of Bashan. And, yes, I have written a sermon or two on how women are like those Bashan cows! Additionally, the words of woe are ones that we should consider, but they will have to be done in another setting, for we must move on to chapter seven. These seventeen verses in chapter seven reveal an Amos who intercedes much like Moses did for the people of God (v. 1-9) and an Amos who reprimands a false priest much like all the other prophets did during this time (v. 10-17). Yet, Amos still, and for some reason, refuses to call himself a prophet (v. 14).

Changing the Mind of God? (7:1-9)

The Jewish people consider Moses the greatest leader for many reasons, including but not limited to the following: (1) leading them out of Egypt, (2) leading them to the Promised Land, and (3) defending them before God when the Almighty One wanted to rightfully punish and/or destroy them for their sinfulness (Ex. 32:9-35). In many ways, Amos stepped in and performed the same action for the people of God. No, God was not planning to destroy the people, and he began again with Amos (7:1-10), as he indicated with Moses in the passages mentioned above. However, on two separate occasions in this passage, God was planning a punishment – a swarm of locusts and a massive fire – that would create a famine great enough to bring the people to their knees in starvation.

Amos stepped in with almost the same plea in verses 2 and 5 (author's translation) – *"PLEASE pardon (v.2)/stop (v.5)! – How can Jacob stand? For he is small?"* The force of Amos' plea in both verses obviously is at the beginning of Amos' statement to God. Some translations have the phrase "I pray!" but in Hebrew, the word is simply transliterated as *Na* as the interjection of PLEASE! Perhaps it is because some translators were uncomfortable with the idea of a prophet, or anyone for that matter, shouting out to God – "Na se-lah!" or "Na ha-dal!" – but that is precisely what happened when Amos begged God to cease the punishment he was dishing out to the land of Israel.

While I would not suggest that we all shout those phrases out to God in our prayer times (because we are not prophets, after all), we should understand that God understands our heart pain more than our "proper prayers." We can also see that Amos' words actually impacted God. We find these remarkable words in verses 3 and 6: *"Jehovah changed His mind."* But what exactly does that mean?

Is it possible for people to change God's mind? Well … the answer is actually no. We find definitive statements about this concept in Mal. 3:6 and Num. 23:19. C. S. Lewis once said in connection to why he prays the following amazing quote: "I pray because I can't help myself. I pray because I'm helpless. I pray because the need flows out of me all the time, waking and sleeping. It doesn't change God. It changes me."

God knows everything, both past, present, and future. What has and will and is happening has already happened in the timeframe of God. So … what did it actually mean in these Amos verses as well as Ex. 32:14 that God "changed his mind" or "relented?" The word in all three verses is *nacham*, and it can (and I believe should) also be translated as "Jehovah was moved to pity…" or "Jehovah had compassion…" The idea of *nacham* in the context of both Moses and Amos would then be like a parent who established a severe grounding punishment on a wayward teen but then decided to ease up after a certain period had passed. It is not that God changed his mind then. It was a test for Amos (as well as for Moses in the wilderness period) to see if Amos was willing to step up for the people.

However, the final punishment of the plumb line (v. 7-9) was one that Amos could not ask God to have *nacham* on the people. For, and to again use the wayward teen analogy, it was time for tough love and for the people to learn a lesson that they will definitely not forget. The best way I can explain this in more detail is to tell you the story of the final spanking I ever received from my dad.

I do not want you to think that I received many spankings from my parents because I did not. There was an occasional pop on my bottom for this or that, but I do remember distinctly three spankings in my life, and it was not because those spankings were violent or vicious but because they left a spiritual impression on me. The first was for running in church when I was four – for not showing reverence to the house of God. The second was also when I was four for lying to daddy about something so silly in hindsight. The final one was when I was about fourteen, and that was for speaking disrespectfully to my mom.

Being fourteen is a tough age, but I have to be honest with you my awkward period began at about the age of twelve and ran until I was sixteen. I started puberty late, which is somewhat normal, but it was compounded by the fact that I had skipped the second grade, so I was already much younger than everyone else in my class. I had a horrible vision, which necessitated thick glasses and then contacts. I needed braces, which I had put on my JUNIOR year in high school, but not before going through two different appliances to fix my TMJ and narrow upper jaw issues. My only hope for those years is that no one finds my junior high or high school annuals and discovers my school pictures.

My parents were incredibly patient with me. They tolerated my emotions. They put up with my tears. They hugged me when I came home and pouted because of bullies and the fact that I was, as I used to say, "Always going to be a hideously ugly creature." Oh … and did I tell you that I was also really smart and nerdy and had a small quantity of a sassy mouth on her?

Well … I did, and my parents tolerated it as long as they could, with my mom stopping my dad from giving me the spanking that I truly deserved many times before. Until that one final time, I sassed (backtalked if you are not from the South) my mom that one last time and daddy could not tolerate it anymore. He grabbed his belt and my arm and gave me what I deserved. After it was over, He sat me down and told me how much he loved me and that we all deserved better than what happened. He cried. I cried. Mama had never stopped crying since it all began, and the lesson was never forgotten. This was also the lesson that God intended for Israel to learn in Amos 7:7-9 even if it was (and it was) incredibly painful.

Amos and Amaziah – Don't Mess with the Message (7:10-17)

This lesson of 7:1-9 leads us into the story of Amos and Amaziah (v. 10-17), and it should teach us another lesson or two that I think is invaluable for us today. A lesson that involves recognizing the word of God when it is delivered by a man of God and a lesson that involves recognizing the gifts that God reveals to someone (even oneself) for others. The encounter between Amaziah and Amos involves a story of status, pride, and elitism – three things that can all change in a moment.

Amaziah, whose name means "Jehovah is mighty," is a priest at Bethel, according to verse 10. The fact that Amaziah is serving in the role of a priest at Bethel indicates to us one obvious detail – Amaziah is not where he belongs. Priests were to serve in Jerusalem and at Bethel, where idol worship abounded – one of the sites where King Jeroboam I had set up in the Northern Kingdom to keep his subjects from returning to Jerusalem – was to deny the proper place of worship for the Jewish people.[37]

Amaziah was serving at the will of Jeroboam II by this time (c.750 BC/BCE). And while he delivered a truthful message to the king, the intent of the delivered message definitely was not edifying towards Amos. Amaziah used the word that is translated as "conspired" and blamed Amos, the messenger, and not God, for giving him the message (v. 10-11). The priest also told Amos to return to Judah to eat bread and prophecy (v. 12) because Bethel is the home of the king of Israel (v. 13). We, on a human and rational level, can understand why Amaziah told Amos to return to Judah but what did he mean by the phrase "eat bread and prophecy?" The answer is an attempted slur towards the "school of the prophets" concept, which Amos answers in verses 14-15.

---

[37] Howard Z. Cleveland, "Bethel," *Zondervan's Pictorial Bible Dictionary*, 109.

So … you might be asking just what is the "school of the prophets?" I must admit there is no official term called "school of the prophets." Still, the idea of it is found in the Hebrew Scriptures, beginning with Samuel and continuing on to the days of Amos with Elijah, Elisha, and even Obadiah.[38] Ira Price further notes that these schools and their students depended upon others for their room and board.[39] Therefore, we can better understand Amaziah's slanderous statement about returning to Judah to "eat bread."

This is why Amos responded that he was not a prophet nor a son of a prophet but a sheepherder, and we also, in verse 14, a grower of sycamore figs. The reason as to why Amos felt the need to respond as he did is something that we should not analyze – no matter how great the temptation. Amos' calling as a layperson is not something that should be defended nor something that should be struck down. The work of sharing God's message could not be achieved without the work of the laity today, and anyone who thinks otherwise is naïve.

I am the president of Tzedakah Ministries, and we are not a large ministry by any measure. We do what we are called to do, but we could not do what we do without our volunteers and our board, who volunteer their time willingly and without any form of payment except my eternal gratitude and prayers. Kathy, Diane, and Patti are amazing people who I appreciate more than they can ever know, and the administration could not function without them. Our current board members – Chris, Bruce, Laverne, Alex, Diane (she double dips), and Mark – put up with me more than they need to do so. These volunteers to Tzedakah Ministries are modern-day Amos' to the work of Jewish evangelism in my eyes.

And so … when Amos told Amaziah what would happen to Israel and his wife/family in verses 16-17, I wonder why this Bethel priest did not hear him. Perhaps pride, status, and elitism got in his way. Regardless of what it was, we should never forget those who assisted missions, evangelism, and churches in achieving the work of the Gospel today. For my dad, it was Roy and Val Blair. Who is it for you?

---

[38] Ira M. Price, "The Schools of the Sons of the Prophets," *The Old Testament Student*, vol. 8, no. 7 (March 1889): 244-249, available at https://www.jstor.org/stable/3156528?seq=6, accessed 17 April 2024.

[39] Ibid., 248-49.

Behold! The Days Are Coming (8:1-14)

This chapter can be summarized by one word … dark. God again lists the sins of the Northern Kingdom (Israel). God determines that the end has come for Israel. He states by the "pride of Jacob" that he will not forget any of their deeds (v. 7). As I already mentioned in the introduction to this chapter, the people of Israel will go about seeking but will not find the words of Jehovah (v. 11-12). Indeed, the days were coming, and those days were dark. And … we need to spend a few paragraphs examining why and if there is a lesson for us today in those dark days for Israel – a lesson we can absorb and hopefully avoid.

Verses 4-6 reveal to us their true heart and why they are worthy of the darkness God will bring to them. For while they might give an outward show of worship, their actions of trampling the needy (v. 4), focusing on wealth (v. 5), and adjusting the scales so that they may cheat others with basically garbage wheat (v. 5-6) illustrate they are no better than those that Amos called out in the first section of his prophecy – Gaza, Tyre, Edom, Moab, and Damascus. And in many ways, Israel is worse, for they are God's Chosen Ones. God was holding Israel to a higher standard for their tactics of social injustice, as we should expect him to hold us to as well today.

For I ask you is it enough to do shoeboxes at Christmas filled with dollar store trinkets when the world is starving for physical bread as well as the spiritual bread that will give them eternal life? Being a light to the nations (both in Amos' day and today as well) requires a recognition that the stranger needs our help (Matt. 25), for perhaps the stranger was an angel unaware (Heb. 13:1-3). Yes, Israel was judged for worshipping false idols; however, their judgment was also because they forgot to love those whom God loved. They would never have worshipped the darkness of false idols if the darkness had not begun by first turning away from the words of Jehovah that informed them to love their neighbor as themselves.

I will not write a final section on chapter nine. However, I will write some final words as a missionary to the Jewish people in response to chapter nine. Many read the prophets – especially the minor prophets – and see only the destruction of the Jewish people. I read the minor prophets, especially the words of Amos and Hosea, and see hope for the Jewish people. Yes, God was angry with them. Yes, God was weary of their disobedience and seeming refusal to return to him. However, in Amos 9 and other places, including the minor prophets and elsewhere, we see the promise that God does not give up on the Jewish people.

They will be shaken, but they will not be destroyed (v. 8-9), and this is actually a promise for those of us who are not Jewish as well. God's unconditional covenant promises are ones that we can hold onto as well (Gen. 12-17). God's promises are ones that are forever, and this is something that we can hold onto as well, for God always will preserve a remnant of his people (Rom. 11 and elsewhere).

Does that mean that all Jewish people will receive salvation in the end simply because they are Jewish? No. They will receive salvation through Messiah Jesus in only the same way that we receive Jesus – by believing and receiving/accepting Jesus as we did. This is something that will be discussed in more detail in the chapter on Zechariah (and we will discuss Romans 11:17ff.). However, God keeps his unconditional promises to Israel even when judging them. This is the truth of Amos and the other minor prophets. This is the truth of Hebrews 12 as well. And this chapter will close with the final words of Amos to remind all of this hope that while it may seem dark … there is light for those who turn to God (9:11-15):

> On that day I will raise up the tabernacle of David, which has fallen down, and repair its damages; I will raise up its ruins and rebuild it as in the days of old; that they may possess the remnant of Edom, and all the Gentiles who are called by My name, says the Lord. Who does this thing? Behold, the days are coming, says the Lord, when the plowman shall overtake the reaper, and the treader of grapes him who sows seed; the mountains shall drip with sweet wine, and all the hills shall flow with it. I will bring back the captives of My people Israel; they shall build the waste cities and inhabit them; they shall plant vineyards and drink wine from them; they shall also make gardens and eat fruit from them. I will plant them in their land, and no longer shall they be pulled up from the land I have given them, says the Lord your God.

4. Obadiah: A Prophet of Few Words but Tremendous Power

Introduction

If you have not gathered in my illustrations by now, you will by the end of this book. I am a huge fan of Jack and Barbara Downey. My parents were amazing individuals. Each was born in anonymity – daddy in Honey Grove, Texas, and mama in Hamlin, Texas. If you do not know where these two locations are on the map, do not worry, as most Texans do not either.

My dad, for the first several years of his life, was known as Jack Bassing due to the fact that my beloved great-grandmother had left my great-grandfather (John Henry Downey) back in Tennessee due to his wandering eye and love of the bottle and married Mr. Bassing (he was always known as Mr. Bassing even though he was a good man to my grandpa and Grandma Bassing). It was only when daddy's parents left East Texas to move out west to become tenant farmers during the Great Depression that they had to secure Social Security cards and become known by their official, legal last name of Downey.

My dad met my mom when he was seventeen and she was nine at Calvary Baptist Church in Hamlin (which is in the middle of nowhere of West Texas). In fact, the tallest building in Hamlin today is the abandoned dog food factory, which, for a long time, was the economic mainstay of this town, and today, it has less than 1,000 souls. Anyway, and as mama told the story, she knew from the moment she met Jack Downey that he man for her, but do not worry, it did not happen for many, many years as it is not *that sort of story I am telling*.

Years later, after a stint in the Navy, daddy was 26 and mama was 18 and a high school graduate working at the drugstore in Hamlin as a pharmacist assistant. Daddy's mama (gramma) always liked mama and was glad no one had snatched up young Barbara and arranged for daddy to go down to the drugstore every time he came into town from his job in the big city of Fort Worth. Soon … 27-year-old Jack and 19-year-old Barbara were married in 1961 and stayed married until he died from a stomach aneurysm in 2000 at the age of 66. Mama's body joined his body in the Hamlin cemetery in 2020 (and they are now in Heaven together) because, in her heart, she was still his bride even for the twenty years they had been separated.

Now, what is the point of this story, you might be asking? Besides the point that I love the story of two people you will never hear of anywhere, but here, they mean the world to me. It is precisely because Jack and Barbara Downey were born, married, and died in obscurity to the vast majority of the world. Yet, to the lives they touched in their Christian ministry that spanned churches across five states and many decades they remind me in many ways of Obadiah. No one knows them, but their testimony is powerful, anonymous, and needed for, I believe needed today.

Who Obadiah Was and the Biblical Background
to This Small but Powerful Book

Who was Obadiah, whose name means servant of Jehovah? If anyone tells you they can write a biography of the prophet, they are not telling you the truth. For no one really knows who the prophet Obadiah was or even where he was from. The closest we come to a possible revelation is the one from the Babylonian Talmud by former Wheaton College Old Testament scholar C. Hassell Bullock.[40] In the BT *Sanhedrin 39b*, the rabbis argue that Obadiah was a steward in the palace of Ahab (of Ahab and Jezebel infamy) and was given the honor by God of delivering the oracle/vision because of his courage in hiding one hundred prophets from the clutches of those evil potentates.[41] Possible, yes. Provable, no.

The timing of the writing of this small oracle/vision is also a mystery. If one follows the Talmudic idea that he was a steward in the house of the evil Jezebel, that will place the writing around 850 BC/BCE. However, Bullock, who gave us the rabbinic tidbit, holds to the common guesstimate (and that is the best word in this setting) of the Obadiah vision somewhere around 586 BC/BCE, which would be after the fall of Jerusalem to the Babylonian Empire.[42] Ultimately, no one can pinpoint the date of Obadiah with certainty, and perhaps that is just as well. The timing of the vision is not as crucial as the timeless message, which also holds a warning for us today.

Theme of Obadiah – Worldly Wealth Is Like "Dust in the Wind"

My high school years were spent in Western Oklahoma – one of the five states that my parents touched in their ministry years. If you know anything about Western Oklahoma in the 1980s, Garth Brooks was king. If you know anything about me … I do not like Country Music.

---

[40] Bullock, *An Introduction to the Old Testament Prophetic Books*, 254.

[41] The Koren Noe Talmud Bavli (English from the William Davidson digital edition), commentary by Rabbi Adin Evin-Israel Steinsaltz, https://www.sefaria.org/Sanhedrin.39b?lang=bi, accessed 14 February 2024. This Talmudic edition also notes that some rabbis believe that Obadiah was an Edomite convert but again there is no proof or Biblical corroboration of this view.

[42] Bullock, *An Introduction to the Old Testament Prophetic Books*, 254. See also, Richard J. Coggins, *Nahum, Obadiah, Esther: Israel Among the Nations*, International Theological Commentary, gen. eds. George A. F. Knight and Fredrick Carlson Holmgren (Grand Rapids: William B. Eerdmans Publishing): 68 and Bartholomew and Thomas, *The Minor Prophets: A Theological Introduction*, 130.

I was desperate to find anything to listen to on the radio besides Garth and his love of finding "friends in low places." The music that I found and still love to this day is the sound of 1960s psychedelic and early 1970s music before Disco ruined the greatest decade of music ever. In fact, I have actual vinyl records in my house that have labels with The Byrds, The Kingston Trio, and Joan Baez. They are a treasure, and even now, I am humming, "Turn, Turn, Turn!"

As I was preparing to write this chapter on Obadiah, the 1977 song "Dust in the Wind" by the classic rock band Kansas came to my mind.[43] The idea that life and wealth are ultimately meaningless in the face of life and death is what I believe to be the theme for Obadiah. Others might spell a more profound and more complex theme for the book – and they would not be wrong. However, the future destruction of Edom, as prophesized by Obadiah due to the fact that they rejoiced over Israel's downfall, can be reduced to four words: "dust in the wind."

And if you have ever visited Jordan and the lost city of Petra … you would affirm these four words. God will not allow those who rejoice at the victimization of His people to go without punishment for long. They will experience the meaninglessness of temporal wealth, the meaninglessness of presumed invincibility, and the meaninglessness of false friends. Yes, Obadiah and his dusty vision are an excellent warning for today's world.

Sibling Rivalry Backstory
(General Overview of Obadiah; Especially Verse 3)

Throughout Obadiah's vision, you will see the interchangeable names of Esau and Edom and the judgment that God is casting down upon the people of the land. For while Edom was the name of the land during the period in question, the people themselves are the descendants of Esau. The backstory of both the land and the people takes us back to the story of Isaac, Rebekah, Jacob, and Esau (primarily Genesis 27 and 32).

---

[43] There are disputing views as to the concept behind the song. Some say it was Eccl. 6:20 and others say it was a book of Native American poetry that gave Kerry Livgren the idea for the song. However, according to sources, Livgren did become a Christian in 1980 and so the song apparently was a step in the right direction. See https://www.songfacts.com/facts/kansas/dust-in-the-wind, accessed 16 February 2024.

And without taking a great deal of space to repeat the tragic story of what happens when parents play favorites between their children, the longstanding rivalry between the children and grandchildren of Jacob and Esau did not ease over the decades or the centuries.[44] And one sees the bitterness continue into the oracle of Obadiah as the offspring of Esau are noted to be rejoicing over the decimation of Judah – most likely during the fall of Jerusalem in 586 BC/BCE when they are taken into Babylonian Captivity. The children of Edom's arrogance and glee over (v. 3, 11-14, 16) Jacob's lament would not be forgotten by God. They would result in judgment, as Obadiah foretold in this shortest but most powerful book.

The words of verse 3 should stand out as a cautionary tale for those of us who are reading Obadiah's words today (author's translation):

The arrogance/insolence of your heart has caused you to be deceived (Hiphil Perfect) You who live (Qal Perfect) in the cleft of the rocks – in the loftiness of your dwelling place who say in your heart (Qal Participle): "Who will cause me to be brought down (Hiphil Imperfect) to earth?

The Edomites assumed they were invincible because of their place among the rocks, which today is nothing but an interesting tourist destination called Petra. I have been to Petra, and it is breathtaking. It is a place that will leave one with awestruck wonder. Today, it is empty except for the unfortunate and impoverished families who live there among the cliff dwellings and function as supposed tour guides, camel drivers, and impish child pickpockets if one is not watching carefully.

However, the rocks of Sela/Seir (aka Petra) were not able to protect the Edomites, as Obadiah foretold. Their loftiness was brought down to earth due to their arrogance and their bemusement at seeing Jerusalem on fire. The question they asked in a mockingly rhetorical manner (v. 3) was definitely answered by God through the enemies of the Edomites.[45]

---

[44] There is a Talmudic Targum – *Targum Jonathan on Genesis 50* – that speculates that Esau (called "Esau the Wicked" in the Targum) sought to prevent his brother Jacob from being buried in the Cave of Machpelah but was ultimately beheaded by the son of Dan. In other words, grudges and rivalries are not long forgotten. For additional details, see https://www.sefaria.org/Targum_Jonathan_on_Genesis.50.13?lang=bi, accessed 19 February 2024.

[45] Coggins, *Nahum, Obadiah, Esther*, 71-72. Coggins notes that the Edomites were driven southward by the Nabataeans until they arrived in what will come to be known as Idumaea (birthplace of Herod the Great).

The application for today should be obvious – or I at least believe it is. Many Christians and churches (especially for those who live in America) presume they are immune from God's judgment as they believe the lie that the United States represents today the legacy of "a city set on a hill" (Mt. 5:14a) and that is a misunderstanding of the verse. We are not isolated from the problems or concerns of the world just because we are set apart from the rest of the world by two oceans. Neither are we any more special in God's eyes than any other nation or people or tongue. Yes, we have been blessed as a nation, but with that blessing comes a missionary responsibility that perhaps we have taken and are taking for granted. Therefore, the question must be asked and answered – Might we be headed for a future that looks more like the Petra of today than the America of many years ago?

Judgment on Edom – How and Why Were They Judged? (Verses 2, 4-16)

Whenever a verse begins with the word – BEHOLD – it is wise to pay attention. Not only because the word is almost always an interjection but also because something big is about to happen. In verse two, God declares (Behold!) through Obadiah that Edom will experience two results for their reaction to Judah's punishment. First – they will become small among all the nations (Gentiles). Second – and more likely an even worse punishment – they will become greatly despised and/or regarded with contempt by these same "goyim" (i.e., Gentiles).

You must understand it is one thing to be a small nation in a Middle Eastern culture, but to be despised or considered with contempt ... that is a wholly different level of disgrace. Verses 4-9 expand on the results of the "fall from grace": (1) God himself (v. 4 in the Hiphil Imperfect) caused them to come down from their lofty heights among the stars and where the eagles soar in punishment for their pride and hubris; (2) Edom can now be seen to be at the mercy of robbers who would not be stopped until nothing would be left – not even their hidden treasures (v. 5-6); (3) Former allies will not only deceive the nation descended from Esau but also destroy the leaders for God will allow it to happen to them (v. 7-9).

Now, verses 10-16 answer the "because" issue as to why God allowed all of what will happen to Edom to arise. However, and before we examine the "because," I think it would be wise to stop and consider these results. Consider the results from a historical and even a missional perspective in an **applicational situation for today**. What might cause groups, churches, and nations to fall under the judgment of verses 4-9, and what might happen when this occurs? For if we see the cause ... then the because might be preventable.

Many nations, many churches, and many Christian missional organizations have experienced what Peter Greer and Chris Horst discuss in their work ***Mission Drift*** – a toning down, a drifting away from their original Christian purpose or principles. Greer and Horst give examples such as the colleges of Harvard and Yale, which were originally established as institutions for the training of Christian ministers, or the Franciscan food banks of the Middle Ages that are today known as pawn shops.[46] Neither the food banks nor those colleges anticipated that today they would be known as places where an individual desperate for funds would sell precious antiques for pennies on the dollar or a place of higher learning where political correctness has become more important and more valued than the Harvard motto of *Veritas* (truth). Yet, both institutions, who operate on different ends of the socio-economic spectrum, seemingly have sold themselves for the master called "mammon" that the KJV mentions in Mt. 6:24 for Harvard's endowment today in 2024, which is valued at an estimated $49.4 billion.[47]

Instead, Greer and Horst ask instead if it is time for mission groups of all types to adopt what is called a "Mission True" definition – "Mission True organizations know why they exist and protect their core at all costs. They remain faithful to what they believe God has entrusted them to do. They define what is immutable: their values and purposes, their DNA, their heart and soul."[48] A few years ago, Tzedakah Ministries and the ministry board adopted this definition as our own, and we seek to consider this view when making every planning step for the ministry's present and future endeavors.

And while one might argue that this section is itself drifting too far away from the purpose of the original text, let us now consider the next few verses to see if this is a drift or not. Verses 10-16 begin with the conjunction "Because…" and then follow with almost a litany of charges against the Edomites for what they did and did not do. In other words, God did not forget, and hence, their crime and punishment were justified.

---

[46] Greer and Horst, *Mission Drift,* 16-21.

[47] Michael T. Nietzel, "College Endowments Saw An Average 7.7% Gain in Fiscal Year 2023," *Forbes Magazine*, 15 February 2024, https://www.forbes.com/sites/michaeltnietzel/2024/02/15/college-endowments-saw-an-average-77-gain-in-fiscal-year-2023/?sh=2bf9ab4260e5, accessed 21 February 2024. Incidentally, Yale University was third on the endowment list at $40.74 billion.

Suppose one is curious how pawn shops are doing today. In that case, they have been experiencing a downsizing from 2018-2023 but still managed to bring in $3.6 billion in approximately 8,500 shops in the United States alone. See the information available at IBIS World, Pawn Shttps://www.ibisworld.com/united-states/market-research-reports/pawn-shops-industry/#IndustryStatisticsAndTrendshops in the US - Market Size, Industry Analysis, Trends and Forecasts (2024-2029)| IBISWorld, accessed 22 February 2024.

[48] Greer and Horst, *Mission Drift,* 27.

Verses 10-11 and 15-16 appear to serve as the "because" bookends to what Edom did or did not do when Judah was facing destruction during the siege by Babylon. Verses 10-11 tell us that Edom that not only were they bystanders ("stood aloof") during the siege but also and actually were just as guilty as the Babylonians themselves –"you too as one as them." And for this bloodguilt, shame will cover them, and they will cut off ... forever. Verses 15-16 are not an exact repeat (chiasm in fancy theological terms) of verses 10-11, but it is, in essence, a restatement – especially the idea of the concept that they will "become as if they never existed."

Twice in four verses, Obadiah gives the warning to Edom and other nations that for standing by ("stood aloof") while the Jewish people were harmed, they will be harmed in an even greater measure. And the phrase "stood aloof" can be overlooked or passed by too quickly in reading this short book so that we can jump ahead to another portion of Scripture. The word in Hebrew for "aloof" in verse 11 is ***min neged*** or "away from." The Edomites literally were bystanders, or it can be translated as looked away while their neighbors were taken away to Babylon or murdered or starved during the siege, but after it was all over or even during – they profited from it (cf. Lam. 4:21-22; Ps. 137:7; Obadiah 12-14). One cannot help, or at least I have given my role as a missionary to the Jewish people and as a historian but think and make application to those who looked away in the not-so-recent past to when the Jewish people needed from European Christians or anyone to help them during the darkest days of World War II and far too many did far too little.[49] The American South cannot escape consideration of this issue as one examines the lack of church involvement in the Civil Rights Movement and how it took the Southern Baptist Convention over 150 years to apologize for the denomination's beginning over a belief in the right for one man to own another human being. Standing by while harm is done to anyone, whether it be the Edomites in Obadiah's days or the Jewish people in World War II, God will remember and judge.

Restoration of Judah – God Will Remember His People (Verses 17-21)

Due to the shortness of its length, Obadiah will be one of the few prophets who can cover every verse of the book. However, these five verses are important not only for the hope they bring to the people of Judah at the time of the Babylonian Captivity but also for the message they share with those of us who are watching and waiting and working today.

---

[49] Tzedakah Ministries has sought to answer this question for the Jewish people on our evangelistic website (www.exploremessiah.com) as best as we can -- https://www.exploremessiah.com/christians-not-fight-the-nazis/.

These last five verses of Obadiah – whether Jewish or not – provide us a message of God's faithfulness and the reality that Jehovah keeps His promises. Yes, God does judge the sins of the people he calls his own. However, he always (and this is a constant refrain all throughout the prophets, whether major or minor) holds close to himself a remnant of his Chosen People.[50]

This time will be holy, and as verse 17 and following promises to the House of Jacob, it will be a time when they will finally possess all that they have been promised (specifically v. 19). It is also a time of final judgment for Esau and his descendants (v. 18) due to their disobedience and joy at the suffering of God's people. God will judge his people for sinfulness, but he does not forget those who trample and rampage upon his children either. Judgment is swift and final and forever.

However, one of the most interesting verses in this section is verse 20. It relates to the idea of the return of the exiles from as far away as Zarephath and Sepharad and their possession of the Negev. Zarephath, a city in the area of Sidon/Phoenicia, is mentioned in 1 Kgs. 17:9, 10 for the refuge locale of Elijah. The widow of Zarephath and her faithfulness is a wonderful story that should not be overlooked. Yet … Sepharad is a more difficult place to locate on a map.

There are all sorts of opinions and blue and/or red map pins to the location of Sepharad. If you do an internet search, you will find anywhere from three to six. The Jewish people who settled in the Mediterranean areas of Spain, Italy, Greece, and North Africa were called Sephardic Jews as opposed to the Ashkenazi Jews of Western and Eastern Europe. Maimonides, the foremost Jewish scholar/theologian of the Middle Ages and whose influence still impacts Jewish religious thought today, held to the opinion that Obadiah 20 was a prophecy of Spanish Jewry returning to the Promised Land.[51]

Perhaps Maimonides was right. Perhaps he was wrong, but nevertheless, I have a magnet and some other souvenirs from my few days in Spain doing my dissertation research with Sepharad imprinted on it. And regardless of where Sepharad was when Obadiah wrote this verse, the point was and is that God will keep his promises to his people and bring his people back to the land – even from the most distant point of the world.[52]

---

[50] Most versions read "there shall be deliverance" in Obadiah but it can also be read as those who escape (those of the remnant).

[51] Amy Karen Downey, *Maimonides's Yahweh: Rabbinic Judaism's Attempt to Answer the Incarnational Question* (Eugene, OR: Wipf & Stock, 2019): 51. Yes, this is a book written by me. This was an edited version of my PhD dissertation and I believe it is a good read if you are interested.

[52] Please note the obvious but perhaps overlooked observation. Even during the days of Maimonides (1135-1204), this was pre-Columbian times and Spain was the end of the known world as far as anyone knew.

Obadiah held onto this truth and hope when he wrote this vision to the Jewish people in an exceptionally dark time. We can hold on to them as well. God will keep his promises. For the kingdom at Mount Zion will never belong to the powers of this world. The kingdom belongs to Jehovah … yesterday, today, and forever more (v. 21).

Section Three:
Truly Understanding the Day of the LORD
Zephaniah and Joel

Many Christians are not even aware that Zephaniah is in the Hebrew Scriptures. This is tragic! However, it could be understood because no one wants to be smacked in the face with these words from 3:2, as I mentioned in the introduction to the book – "She (Judah) has not obeyed *His* voice. She has not received correction; She has not trusted in the LORD, She (Judah) has not drawn near to her God." (NKJV).

Yes, this verse directly speaks to Judah in its context, but none of us, if we are honest, should go past this verse without feeling the stinging pangs of condemnation. For we all need to be humbled more often than we need to admit it. Our pride, our arrogance, and our image that we are greater than we imagine ourselves to be are things that need to be brought down a peg or two – whether by people having a "come to Jesus" chat with us or by God himself.

Yet, and entirely too often, we only want to be affirmed today in small groups and by our pastors. We go "church hopping" or engage in "pastor shopping" when the minister begins preaching sermons that step on our toes or bruise our egos. Zephaniah experienced this same struggle with the Jewish people and yet he still persevered even though he knew it would not be heard. This prophet had a challenging mission, much like Isaiah described for himself in 6:1-13, yet he did not stop in his work. Would we persevere like Zephaniah, or would we stop when the opposition grew difficult and the road grew rocky? Things to be considered in this 21st-century post-Christian world.

People do know about the book of Joel, but usually about five verses in this minor prophet – 2:28-32. You know those verses that describe old men who will see visions, young men who will dream dreams, and our sons and daughters who will prophesy? However, if you ask them what these verses mean as to relates to the phrase "Day of the Lord," the interpretations one will hear will vary from "I do not know" to eschatological charts to pan-millennialism (i.e., "it will all pan out"). For ultimately, no one understands the missional purpose of these verses much less the entire message Joel was seeking to share.

Yet, Joel is about more than dreaming dreams, "Day of the Lord," and those locusts that everyone wants not to discuss. Joel is about hope and, the future, and the present. Joel is about God controlling everything – even the locusts. Joel is about an all-encompassing message that needs to be read in its entirety and not in isolated verses that can be misinterpreted. Now … are you ready to find out about the locusts?

5. Zephaniah: Humbling the Smug in the Day of the Lord

Introduction

When I was a MATh student at Southwestern Baptist Theological Seminary in the early 2000s (and in the beginning days of my missionary years), I was the privileged one to be allowed to be the Sunday School teacher for Randy Holcomb. In fact, of all the people I have ever taught, whether it be in Sunday School or as a conference speaker in Tokyo, Japan, Randy will always be one of my favorite people of all time to teach.

Randy Holcomb, at the time, worked for the sanitation department in Fort Worth, Texas. And while studying for the next Sunday's class, I would design every Sunday School lesson around one basic question – how can this experience help Randy on a Thursday afternoon when he is knee-deep in "you know what"? For even though working in sanitation might not be the most glamorous of jobs, Randy loved his job, and I am thankful that I did not have to do it. Additionally, Randy always said "thank you" and "good class" after every Sunday School class, and there were other seminary students in the class who would often forget to say anything at all.

To this day, if you asked Randy what was my most memorable Sunday School lesson, I think he would still remember the title I gave the lesson – "Grandma Wants Me Dead." It was the story of King Josiah and his killer granny, Queen Athaliah (2 Kings 11). And while this chapter will not discuss Josiah and Athaliah except in the biblical background, Zephaniah himself has a connection to this story that is worth mentioning, and so Randy Holcomb deserves a mention as well, for I hope he would say to me after this chapter – "good job."

Who Zephaniah Was and a Little Biblical Background

Zephaniah was the great-great-grandson of Hezekiah. This means he was in the lineage of David and could claim royalty blood flowing in his veins. He could have had a lot of things going for him. However, he was chosen to be a prophet of God which in that day and age was not a popular thing to be (circa 640 to 609 BC/BCE). These were during the early days of King Josiah (a cousin of some sort to Zephaniah) when Josiah's grandmother (Athaliah) was still around, wanting her grandson killed. One could *imagine as well* that Zephaniah was probably also on her hit list, and if I were him or King Josiah, I would not attend any family reunions where she was in charge of the meal. And as someone who comes with a family history that includes a great-great aunt who might or might not have killed her husband (yes, this will probably be an illustration in a later chapter), I can say without reservations that some family therapy sessions would have been a good idea for King Josiah's dysfunctional family!

Theme of Zephaniah – Full of Woes and Warnings

As to the theme of Zephaniah's prophecy, there is a great deal of "woes" and "warnings" throughout this short but powerful book. Woes and warnings towards both Judah and the enemies of Judah — Nineveh, Ethiopia, Ammon/Moab, Philistines, and the inhabitants of Gaza, Ashdod, and Ashkelon. In fact, one could and might be very tempted to make modern-day application to what is happening in Gaza, West Bank, and Jordan today because of Zephaniah 2:4-11. If one does (and it is an interesting parallel but one that must be taken with great exegetical care and not simply by looking at the headlines on Fox News or CNN), then one also needs to consider what Zephaniah says about Israel as well.

The work of sending out the message that he did is an interesting responsibility for someone's name, which means "Jehovah Protects." Yet, Zephaniah, as well as all the other prophets we ignore to our detriment, took the responsibility of seriously protecting the Jewish people (whether they wanted it or not). Jeremiah warned the people and ended up in a well. According to tradition (cf. Heb 11:37), Isaiah was sawn in half for defying King Manasseh.[53] However, the question must be asked – would churches today react that much differently to a Zephaniah, Isaiah, Jeremiah, or Zechariah? Sadly, I am afraid that many churches would behave just as the people of Judah did in the day of the major and minor prophets.[54]

Are Warnings of the Prophet Only for the Distant Future? (1:7-9)

Hold your peace in the presence of the Lord God: for the day of the Lord is at hand: for the Lord has prepared a sacrifice, he has bid his guests. And it shall come to pass in the day of the Lord's sacrifice, that I will punish the princes, and the king's children, and all such as are clothed with strange apparel. In the same day also will I punish all those that leap on the threshold, which fill their masters' houses with violence and deceit.

---

[53] Obviously, and aside from the reference in Heb. 11:37 which does not mention who was sawn in half, the legend or lore that it was Isaiah is based on sources that cannot be proven categorically. However, the information should be noted – *Babylonian Talmud Yevamot 49b* and *The Martyrdom of Isaiah* 5:1-14, available online at https://ccel.org/c/charles/otpseudepig/martisah.htm, accessed 10 April 2024.

[54] Thom Rainer, "Five Common Themes in Churches with High Pastor Turnover," Church Answers, 10 May 2021, available online at https://churchanswers.com/blog/five-common-themes-in-churches-with-high-pastor-turnover/, accessed 10 April 2024.

Can one reading these verses of Zephaniah 1:7-9 not perhaps wonder if there could be a double fulfillment possibility to these verses. I believe a good understanding of what I mean by the idea of single vs. double fulfillment of prophecy is in order. In the evangelical world, there are those who hold to a strictly single fulfillment of prophecy argument (such as Walter Kaiser and Michael Rydelnick).[55] And who am I to argue against such great men? Especially since I know, like, and respect Michael Rydelnick and even like to think of him as an acquaintance friend. They believe that a prophecy of Scripture will only be fulfilled once and for all time.

However, there are other evangelical theologians who hold a double fulfillment of prophecy argument (i.e., former Dallas Theological Seminary president John Walvoord and David Jeremiah).[56] They believe that a prophecy can have an immediate fulfillment in time or place and then a future fulfillment. For transparency purposes, I hold to the particular idea that prophecies can but will not necessarily always have a double fulfillment potential. This is not because I always agree with Walvoord and Jeremiah in all matters, because I do not, but because of how I see Scripture itself unfolding itself in time and reality.

Let me give an example of one prophecy that I believe could have a double fulfillment, and it so happens to be one of the most important prophecies as well — Isaiah 7:14 ("Behold, a virgin shall conceive…"). I do not wish to get into the *almah/betulah* issue in these pages, but we find that Isaiah does have a son in chapter 8, which could be and quite possibly is a fulfillment of 7:14. **HOWEVER**, we also know there is more to the prophecy because of Isaiah 9:6 and Matthew 1 and Luke 1-2. Isaiah's son is NOT a distraction or denial of Jesus' fulfillment of Isaiah 7:14 but a completion of the prophecy in the immediate historical sense but not in the ultimate Messianic sense. **This is the definition of double fulfillment.**

Now on to the Question at Hand…

So … could Zephaniah 1:7-9 be another example of double fulfillment? I am still struggling with the question myself, but I do wonder, because of the text's language and verb tenses, that I will break down and apart now.

---

[55] Walter C. Kaiser, Jr., "Single Meaning, Unified Referents," *Three Views on the New Testament Use of the Old Testament*, Kenneth Berding and Jonathan Lunde, gen. eds. (Grand Rapids: Zondervan, 2008): 50-51.

[56] David Jeremiah, "The Principle of Double Fulfillment in Interpreting Prophecy," *Grace Journal* 13.2 (Spring 1972): 13-29, available online at https://www.biblicalstudies.org.uk/pdf/grace-journal/13-2_13.pdf, accessed for the second time 10 April 2024.

The phrase "day of the LORD (Jehovah/Adonai) is at hand" is most often considered as a reference to the eschaton/ultimate future and seen as a prophecy, and well, it should be. However, I am struck by the phrase, "for the LORD has prepared a sacrifice." Why would the LORD prepare a sacrifice on the **final** Day of the LORD?

I know many believe there will be sacrifices during the Millennial Kingdom period, and that is a topic for another day. However, I do not believe that is the point of Zephaniah 2:7. Based on the verb tenses and the language in Hebrew, this is a specific sacrifice for a specific moment.

For the sense of "Hold your peace" does not give the complete sense of what is being said here. It is more like "**BE SILENT!**" It is a command because you see it as an interjection(!). Additionally, The LORD is preparing a sacrifice (and apologies for giving all this Hebrew tense information, but it is vital for explanation). It is in the Hiphil Perfect and is better translated as "has cause to prepare." This is also true in the rest of the verse. Additionally, instead of "He has bid his guest," I would suggest that it should be translated as "He has cause to consecrate or set apart his guests*"* (Hiphil Perfect). The word "consecrate" or set apart is a better word choice than "bid" because the word in Hebrew is a form of *qadosh* or what we translate as "Holy."

I know that last paragraph was dense, but it was important because it shows my question — **why would the LORD be preparing a sacrifice in the Day of the LORD, and why would He be preparing His guests IF it was ONLY in the FINAL FUTURE** (i.e., a single fulfillment)? I am wondering if Zephaniah saw or foretold a vision of Jesus' crucifixion (sacrifice) as well as the ultimate Day of the LORD in Zephaniah 1:7-9 and even going into verses 10-13. The verses read as if God is preparing a sacrifice for those who have been set aside (consecrated) to receive the sacrifice — hence the Hebrew tense of Hiphil Perfect. Those who will reject the sacrifice are to be judged for their rejection in verses 8-13. This does happen in the final DAY of the LORD, it also happens then in AD/CE 70 when the Temple was destroyed by the Romans and sacrifices were no longer possible and now both physically and spiritually (again a reality of the Hiphil Perfect).

I am still searching and praying about what I believe the prophetic significance of these verses to be — single or double. I have my questions, and I am searching for answers. Who is right – Walt Kaiser or David Jeremiah? I am not certain about this particular passage. However, I do know that they show a reality and a warning for all who reject the Lord's sacrifice. If so, is this why Zephaniah is not on the schedule to be in the read in the Jewish synagogues today? If so, is this why they are not read and preached about in today's churches as well?

So the question must arise ... what are we to do about this passage in our churches today and in evangelism work? I cannot help but consider the parable from Lk 14:15-24 where Jesus tells the story of a man who invited many to come to a dinner. Many ignored the invitation or came up with excuses as to why they could not come. Ultimately, the man of the house decided to invite the poor, the lame, and the blind of the community to the dinner in place of the "esteemed and invited guests" to the dinner. When there was room still available, we find in verses 23-24 those great inclusive **and** exclusive words from Jesus, *"Go out into the highways and hedges, and compel them to come in, that my house may be filled. For I say to you that none of those men who were invited shall taste my supper."*

As I consider the passage from Zephaniah and Jesus' parable, I cannot help but see some parallels. In Zephaniah's day, the punishment was reserved for those who were leaders but yet had defiled themselves with "foreign apparel." These would be leaders and their children who had become like the world to the point that they were unrecognizable from the world. This solidarity with the world is evident because they have become violent and deceitful. And in Jesus' parable, they would be the ones who would not have wanted to attend the dinner because it would have required a change in apparel, a change in behavior, from what they have become. Therefore, they had to create excuses not to show up.

But, and ultimately, the dinner was not for them anyway either in Zephaniah or in Luke. It was for the downtrodden and the weak and for those whose apparel was anything but special. They are the truly holy ones. They are the truly consecrated ones. They are the ones many times that people never expected and many churches never want.

My dad's first church ministry after graduating from Bible College was at a First Baptist in a small town in Kentucky in 1975. He was the children's and evangelism pastor for a very proper and dignified church in which the starch in the pastor's collar seemingly had starch. The pastor's wife was so proper that I do not believe she had smiled since Jackie Kennedy was last First Lady in 1963.

Daddy was asked to go into the community and bring children into the church that had never seen the inside of a church building. Anyway, the church begins to grow not only with children but also with their mom's. And you must remember it was the 1970s when the mini-skirt was still fashionable and some of those young mothers (some of whom were not white) wore their skirts very high. Many of the church were excited and challenged by the changes but others were not – including the pastor and his wife – who were worried that the white walls and pews would never be the same. If you catch my drift...

After about eight to ten months at the First Baptist in Kentucky, and while we were on vacation, the pastor called and informed us that daddy that his services were no longer needed as evangelism and children's pastor. We returned from our vacation, and several in the church were distraught, angry, and ready to call one of those infamous Baptist business meetings. Daddy refused the offer and we moved to Texas and the next ministry calling. The children and those mini-skirt women never returned to FBC, and I believe the spiritual dinner God had planned for the church never materialized or was eaten at another venue.

Too often today, Christians and churches try to help God with his guest list based on color, wealth, perceived value, apparel, and an assorted laundry list that has nothing to do with a person's eternal soul. We are afraid of the scuffs on the wall and the pews being damaged, not whether a soul might need to be forever changed. Zephaniah does have something to teach us, regardless of whether this is a single or double-fulfillment prophecy.

Command to Seek! (2:1-3)

Gather yourselves together, yes, gather together,
O undesirable nation,
Before the decree is issued,
Or the day passes like chaff,
Before the Lord's fierce anger comes upon you,
Before the day of the Lord's anger comes upon you!
Seek the Lord, all you meek of the earth,
Who have upheld His justice.
Seek righteousness, seek humility.
It may be that you will be hidden.
In the day of the Lord's anger.

This passage of verses was written to the nation of Judah, which, even though it had a righteous king (Josiah) at the time, was only a few years removed from the evil king Manasseh and a few years away from being uprooted by Babylon and taken into captivity. Judah was a self-righteous nation that assumed it was exempt from judgment like its brothers Israel, who had already been taken captive by Assyria.

Why – did they not have the Temple and did they not have possession of Jerusalem? However, nothing could be further from the truth and the prophet Zephaniah was one of many prophets seeking to warn them of their destruction and how to avoid it.

The answer is simply to SEEK, but there is more than just "seeking" in that Hebrew word. The word (transliterated as **bawkash)** is SEEK TO FIND and is in the intensive command. In other words — do not just try but do it.

The people of God who are **still** meek and have **still** upheld His justice are told to do three things in verse 3 — seek to find the LORD (the holiest name of God), seek to find righteousness (tzedakah) and seek to find humility so that *perhaps* they will be hidden in the day of the LORD's anger. Yes, God's anger is coming, for God's anger is deserved towards the Jewish people, but if they seek to find the LORD and His righteousness and continue to live humbly … they can escape.

It is a tough message but something we need to consider today as well. For what are we seeking today, and how are we living? Are we living humbly or brashly? Are we seeking His righteousness, or are we seeking political power? Are we living a life of the Beatitudes (i.e., Matthew 5:1-12), or do we want to push our way to the top? Do we want human justice, or do we turn the other cheek in order to reach the world for the Gospel? Do we push or pull the world closer to Him? What are we seeking to find – self-glorification or His glorification?

God Is Just – Lord Help Us! (3:1-7)

Woe to her that is filthy and polluted, to the oppressing city! She <u>obeyed not</u> the voice; she <u>received not</u> correction; she <u>trusted not</u> in the LORD; she <u>drew not near</u> to her God. Her princes within her are roaring lions; her judges are evening wolves; they gnaw not the bones till the morrow. Her prophets are light and treacherous persons: her priests have polluted the sanctuary, and they have done violence to the law. The JUST LORD is in the midst thereof; he will not do iniquity: every morning doth he bring his judgment to light, he faileth not; but the unjust knoweth no shame. I have cut off the nations: their towers are desolate; I made their streets waste, that none passeth by: their cities are destroyed, so that there is no man, that there is none inhabitant. I said, Surely thou wilt fear me, thou wilt receive instruction; so their dwelling should not be cut off, howsoever I punished them: but they rose early, and corrupted all their doings. Zephaniah 3:1-7 (KJV — Public Domain)

There is a quote/phrase that has been used by others – but it is simply too appropriate not to use it again. As the Pevensie children from C. S. Lewis' *The Lion, The Witch, and The Wardrobe* are hearing about Aslan for the first time, they ask a simple question about this mysterious lion:

"Is he—quite safe?" I shall feel rather nervous about meeting a lion" – Susan

"If there's anyone who can appear before Aslan without their knees knocking, they're either braver than most or else just silly." – Mrs. Beaver
"Then he isn't safe?" – Lucy
"Safe? ... Who said anything about safe? Course he isn't safe. But he's good. He's the King I tell you." – Mr. Beaver

As I consider the first seven verses of Zephaniah 3 — the sins of the people (from the political leaders to the religious leaders to people on the street) and then the reaction of the LORD, I tremble and wonder to myself if Lewis considered the words of Zephaniah because Jehovah Adonai indeed is not safe, but He is good and just and righteous. **And, LORD, help us!**

I believe this is why we often avoid the minor prophets in our churches, Bible studies, personal devotional time. Zephaniah, Joel, Nahum, Obadiah, and the others make us uncomfortable. They do not write a lot of words, but what they wrote should cause us to squirm in our chairs and make us long for the out-of-context verbiage that we look for in other places in Scripture. Yet, it is the words of Zephaniah that we need so greatly today, for this great-grandson of King Hezekiah seemingly holds a mirror from long ago to the churches of today and to the leadership of many of our churches — if only we will take a look at our own reflection. Shall we dare to glance the words at Zephaniah 3 together?

FIRST – The prophet Zephaniah is speaking directly to the people of Judah; however, I believe there is an application for us today as well. After the interjection of WOE in verse 1 (and I underlined the sins in the verses above), we see the four errors/sins in verse 2.

(1) Judah heeded no voice;
(2) Judah accepted no instruction;
(3) Judah did not trust in the LORD; and
(4) Judah did not draw need to God.

Let me simply ask you whether we, as Christians and churches, are really any different today. Do we heed to the voice of God? Do we accept instruction if we do not like what is being told to us? Do we really trust in the LORD (or do we trust in politicians and power)? Do we draw near to God? If we are honest with ourselves, I believe we know the answer.

We believe a political candidate will solve the issues of the world because we are interested in instant gratification—instant oatmeal and not a real breakfast that is filled with protein and true sustenance. We believe power will resolve the sins of the world and not a true surrender to the will of the Father that often requires sacrifice and even, dare I write, suffering. We simply do not trust the LORD God of the Universe to solve the simple problems of today, and then we wonder why things are so horrible tomorrow.

This is why Christians and churches have lost our influence in today's society, just as the false prophets and immoral priests in Judah profaned the sanctuary and did violence to the Law/Torah (v. 3-4). We hide our light under a bushel (see Matthew 5), and our light goes out. When this happens, and it is happening, our country will cease to be what it has been — the mission agency to the world. We are being replaced by Korea and nations that are oppressed but live their light even in the midst of darkness and death, like Iran and China and North Korea.

However, and it is important that I write this sentence/paragraph, the United States and the Christian Church will never and never could replace the Jewish people as the Chosen People of God. However, we are a type of what happened to them when they abandoned their call of God on their lives. Zephaniah warned them approximately 600 years before Jesus, and he is warning us today as well. The Jewish people did not listen, and we are not listening either.

And God is just ... LORD help us. And as I close this section, I want to remind you of a TV series entitled *Life After People*. It imagined what would happen to the planet if people just disappeared one day. The world would continue, but the buildings and the structures that people built would eventually rot and decay because they were basically unimportant (v. 6-7). And that is what would happen if American Christianity disappeared as well; the Church of God would continue because Matthew 16:18 is still true, and the gates of Hell would never prevail against the Church of God. **God does not need America, but we need Him — LORD help us.** Repent! Heed His Voice! Accept Instruction! Trust in the LORD! Draw Near to God! RETURN! For He is Good, but He is not Safe!

6. Joel: The Locusts Are Coming! The Locusts Are Coming!

Introduction

My grandpa (daddy's dad) was a farmer. My Uncle Don (daddy's brother-in-law) was a farmer. My other grandpa (mama's dad) wanted to be a farmer but his wife would not let him be what he wanted to be all his life but he was a master gardener. In fact, everyone in the neighborhood would go to Clarence Butler before even *The Farmer's Almanac* if they had any questions about what time to plant anything. However, I never wanted to be a farmer or the wife of a farmer. Why ... farming is one of the most difficult lives that could be imagined, and my respect for those who are farmers and the families of farmers today is immense. I do not have the physical or mental stamina to be a farmer or a farmer's wife, and I know it.

Grandpa Downey was a tenant farmer before, during, and after the Great Depression in West Texas. He tried to do other jobs – especially during the Depression years of the 1930s and the war years of the 1940s, but the dirt and the land kept calling out to him. In fact, my dad, along with his family, even made a trip to California, reminiscent of the Judd family in *The Grapes of Wrath* by John Steinbeck. However, the dusty farms of West Texas called them back home after only four months of picking fruit along the California coastline. However, you need to know that being a tenant farmer, especially during the 1930s, was an incredibly difficult life for anyone who dared to undertake the life. However, it was at least better than being a sharecropper.

To explain these terms briefly, a tenant farmer paid "rent" every year to the landowner (and sometimes rented out the tractor and other farming equipment from the landowner) with the hope that he could one day own the land he was farming. In many ways, being a tenant farmer was like being an indentured servant with the hope that you could buy your freedom one day. A sharecropper lived on and farmed the land that the landowner owned, and a portion of the crops was also paid back to the landowner at the end of the year. The sharecropper never had a chance to own the land he farmed and often would go and work for a tenant farmer like my grandpa for extra income during harvest season(s) – especially if the crops were not doing well that year. Otherwise, his family would starve during the winter months.

My dad could remember working alongside the sharecroppers and their whole family – especially during cotton harvest season – while my grandma was responsible for feeding all the workers on the farm. Indeed, farming was/is hard work that depended on the weather (never wanting too much or not enough rain) and praying that the dreaded grasshoppers and/or locusts would not come, especially when there was a bumper crop in a given year. For if there were locusts, people could and did starve during the winter. Locusts were to be feared. Locusts were from the devil. Locusts were evil incarnate according to the farmers – especially during those Great Depression years – when no one could spare a dime for anyone.[57]

Who Joel Was and the Biblical Background to the Prophet

Who was Joel? Good question because this prophet of God, and unlike Haggai, as you will see in chapter 11, who shared the date, time, and place of when he was prophesying, shares almost nothing. What we do know about Joel is limited primarily to knowing that his name means "Jehovah is God" and that his father was named Pethuel, which possibly means "vision of God." However, there is a question as to exactly what Pethuel actually means. One can only assume that the readers and hearers of Joel's original message knew and trusted the prophet.

As to any ability to establish a date for the writing of Joel. I honestly can write … your guess is as good as anyone's. Various scholars have placed the timing for Joel anywhere from the 8th century before the fall of Samaria to the Assyrians to after the return of the remnant from Babylon to even around the rise of the Greeks and Alexander the Great. Estimates truly do run the gamut for when Joel was written, and some will not even try to guess the date when Joel was written. A well-known Southern Baptist Old Testament scholar even provides a chart with several options for when Joel could have been written and spends eight pages presenting the various views.[58] Eventually, Duane Garrett provides what can only be called a guess when he writes that the 7th century before the birth of Jesus is probably the best time for when Joel was written. But again … who today knows?

---

[57] Yip Harburg and Jay Gorney, "Brother, Can You Spare a Dime,?" story of the Depression era song available online https://www.kennedy-center.org/education/resources-for-educators/classroom-resources/media-and-interactives/media/music/story-behind-the-song/the-story-behind-the-song/brother-can-you-spare-a-dime/, accessed 1 May 2024.

[58] Garrett, *Hosea, Joel*, 286-94. Garrett cautiously holds to a 7th century position for the writing of Joel but does not believe that any view creates a view that that would be problematic to interpretation or an argument against inerrancy.

Therefore, it is impossible to know whether Joel was a prophet to the Northern Kingdom, the Southern Kingdom, and the people of Israel after they returned from Babylon as a humbled remnant or perhaps even before the kingdom of Israel was divided. What we can know is that Joel saw that judgment was coming for Israel, judgment was coming for the nations that came against Israel, and that in the future (the Day of the Lord), there would be a day of great revival that would come upon the people of God. And it is in the context of the Day of the Lord that Joel draws the people's attention to … in the future … but he also wants them to know that before that day comes – the locusts are coming as well.

Theme of Joel – Locusts, Locusts, Locusts???

I am being a tad bit sarcastic in the heading to this section. For while we will discuss the idea of locusts a great deal in the prophecy of Joel, I do not believe those nasty little critters are the overarching theme of the book. In fact, and much like any effort to nail down a biblical time frame for Joel, discerning a thematic structure for Joel's prophecy is difficult as well.

Why? Joel discusses many important issues, and while it might be easy to just write "Day of the Lord" for the theme, I would argue that "Day of the Lord" is more of a result and/or outcome of the theme than the subject itself. So, just what is the overarching concept of the prophet's narrative? I would present that we can find it in the meaning of the prophet's name—"Jehovah is God."

Joel was seeking to remind the people that even when the locusts come (and whatever the nature of the locusts may be) that Jehovah is God. Joel wanted the Chosen People to always recognize that in their worship – whether it be in a traditional Sabbath observance or a solemn assembly – Jehovah is God. Joel wanted the Jewish people to see that there was no reason to be afraid or to be in shame on the Day of the Lord if they truly returned because … Jehovah is God. And ultimately, Jehovah is God, as Joel tells us because there will come a day when God judges the nations. Indeed, Joel is right about who God is, and his name is Jehovah.

Jehovah Is God … Even When the Locusts Come (1:2-12)

As in so many of the prophets, Joel begins in verse 2 with the imperative command to simply "Hear." The first who is given the command are the "elders" or the ones who have hair on their faces (aka beards). The ones who are supposed to be leaders among the people. The ones who were to guide the younger ones in the Torah and the ways of God but obviously failed because judgment is coming and the fault lies first at their door.

And, yes, there is a lesson for us today in the very first part of verse 2. Look around the churches today and ask what the median age is of our churches and/or our pastors. I looked at two different articles – one from *Christianity Today* and one from *Lifeway Research* – to decipher the future direction of just American churches. Both articles tried to put as positive of a spin as possible on the issue; however, the truth is American Christianity is aging:

- The average age of evangelical pastors is 53.8 (median age of 55), and the average age of mainline pastors is 54.8 (median age of 56).
- The average church is aging as well as they are twice as likely to be 65 or older than other age groups (33% to 17%).
- 1 out of 4 pastors are hoping/anticipating retiring within the next nine years and are uncertain as to who will replace them as the number of M.Div. students in ATS accredited schools is declining as well.[59]

The next example can only be described as anecdotal and comes from a trip that I took to Japan to speak at a Jewish evangelism conference in Tokyo. I was able to speak with several of the Japanese pastors and even one of the missionaries who had been there for over three decades. Each one of them pastored more than one church, and at least two of them pastored three or more churches. Additionally, the pastoral work that they engaged in was not of the circuit-riding variety that American pastors engaged in in the 19th century when a pastor traveled and preached at one church one Sunday and another church the next. No … these Japanese pastors traveled for hours each Sunday to minister to each individual church he pastored. The reason for this backbreaking schedule is that there are not enough young Japanese men to take over the work for these faithful men of God. Some come to America for theological training and do not wish to return to Japan, and others do not wish to commit to what is considered a "thankless and financially poor" career choice.

---

[59] Aaron Earls, "Pastors' Age Stable Over Past Decade," *Lifeway Research* (30 August 2023), available online at https://research.lifeway.com/2023/08/30/pastors-average-age-stable-over-past-decade/ and David Roach, "1 in 4 Pastors Plan to Retire Before 2030," *Christianity Today* (28 April 2023), available online at https://www.christianitytoday.com/news/2023/april/pastor-succession-church-next-generation-leader-barna-surve.html, accessed 1 May 2024.

Please know that I am not being critical of our faithful leaders who serve and are serving today. I am simply asking – who will follow them? My pastor would be considered a young man and he is in his mid-forties. Where are the truly young men to follow after him? I am 54 years old and one of the younger leaders in the world of Jewish evangelism. Who will follow me? This is not a Boomer vs. Buster vs. Millennial question. This is a question we all need to ask: What will American Christianity and world missions look like in the next decade and beyond when there are fewer and fewer people who are willing, able, and trained to share the Word of God?

Let us now return to the text and what Joel had to tell the people about those locusts in chapter one (v. 4). Some will argue whether there were four kinds of locusts or one type of locust in four stages. I personally hold to the view that it was four kinds of locusts, for in the Hebrew, you will find four different names and roles for the locusts – *gazam* (chewing), *arbeh* (swarming), *yaleg* (crawling), and *hasil* (consuming). And given that I am not a fan of any type of bug or crawling thing, all I can do is shudder at the thought of all these locusts!

The purpose of these locusts was to ensure that there was nothing left of the crops (the economy) of Judah. It was an onslaught that probably seemed as if it was never going to end – probably much like we all felt like during those never-ending months of COVID beginning in March 2020 but much, much worse. Everything in Israel/Judah had been destroyed that could be produced for income, food for the people, sacrifices for the Temple. The only thing and the one thing that could be done is mourn for the losses, and that is what God tells them to do – but not for the personal losses but for the fact that they brought this loss upon themselves (v. 5-12).

Jehovah Is God ... So Worship Him (1:13-20)

Verse 13 begins with four imperative (command) verbs – gird, lament, wail, and come to lie all night in sackcloth – and they are directed towards the priests who are in charge of the sacrifices at the Temple. Why, you might ask – because the locusts have devoured and/or eaten all the possible grain and wine that can be used for sacrifices. Why, you might ask – because the leaders (aka the bearded ones, including THEM) have failed to teach the people, and God allowed the locusts to invade the land. God's solution is simple – ask forgiveness of me (v. 13) and then direct the people to worship me.

I have to admit that my favorite of these four imperative verbs is the word gird (*chagar*). It is the idea of "suck it up" and get yourselves ready for battle and it is the same word that was used for to inform soldiers that it was time to prepare for actual battle throughout the Hebrew Scriptures. God was informing the priests in the Temple that it was time to prepare for spiritual battle by first preparing themselves via the act of regret and shame as symbolized by spending a night wrapped in sackcloth. For before the nation can repent, the spiritual leaders must repent first and I would argue the most loudly.

Another lesson for today, if I may have a second rabbit trail moment … I have to admit that I grow a tad bit weary of those memes proclaiming 2 Chron. 7:14 all over social media. First, because I believe this verse is taken out of context. Second, because I believe that repentance needs to begin with our spiritual leaders who have abdicated the responsibility for the easiness of Name/Claim and Health/Wealth because their offerings and human praise are so much greater. However, the people of their congregations are dying for lack of true Biblical knowledge.

This is why Joel called for the priests to gather all the leaders of the people for a fast and a solemn assembly (v. 14). I would argue that today, we need to gather ourselves together for a consecrated fast – not necessarily an abstaining from food but perhaps a fast from social media – as well as a solemn assembly. However, this solemn assembly was not in Joel's day (and it would not be in our day either) just another worship service.

The "Solemn (or Sacred) Assembly" was an additional service in which no work was done, and they restrained themselves, actually what the word is in Hebrew, from doing any work except to devote one's heart to God. Leviticus 23 is filled with examples of the idea of the solemn/sacred assembly for Leviticus is filled with the idea of "be ye holy, as I am holy." And Joel wanted the people to return to the idea of the holiness of God.

Joel then spends the next few verses (v. 15-20) explaining to the people why it is so urgent for the people to devote themselves to this vision of holiness – the Day of the Lord is coming. They need to be prepared for famine is also coming and this is not related I would argue to the locusts that invaded their land in earlier verses but something that would make those nasty bugs seem tame in comparison.

We, as well in the 21st century, need to prepare ourselves both missionally and congregationally and evangelistically for the Day of the Lord is at hand. And there is coming a day that will make COVID seem tame in comparison. It might not be another plague, but it could be. It might not be a war, but it could be. Whatever it might be, we need to be prepared to reach the world with the truth of Messiah, for this is the greatest act of holiness that could be done.[60]

Jehovah Is God … When the "Day of the Lord" Arrives (2:1-32)

There could be a temptation to separate verses 28-32 and analyze them independently from the rest of the chapter. However, to do so would be to take these verses out of the context of the chapter and the meaning of the whole chapter. So … I cannot do it even though we want to experience those dreams, visions, and prophecies, but we cannot without seeing it through the "Day of the Lord" and the fact that more locusts of some variety had to come first.

"Day of the Lord" … Worship Equals Utter Despondency/Utter Need (2:1, 12-17)

Indeed, these "locusts" are more fearsome than the ones found in the first chapter of Joel, and the arrival of these fearsome creatures (human army) is accompanied by the command (imperative) to blow the shofar (translated as a trumpet in English versions) and the announcement that the "Day of the Lord" has arrived. In fact, we find the command to blow the shofar twice in Joel 2. The first time in verse one is for the warning of the oncoming attack, and the second in verse 15 is to call the people to worship because the attack has happened.

This is an interesting juxtaposition or contrast, is it not? Today, we often have a call to worship before something bad happens, and God is calling the people to worship **after** a horrific event happens. Yes, I know people went to houses of worship in droves after 9/11, but that did not last very long. People attended Zoom worship services in great numbers for a couple of weeks when COVID-19 first began, but many churches closed before, during, and after COVID-19.[61] For when humans have chosen to rush to God after a tragedy, the impact never seems to last, but God calling us to worship him after heartbreak … seems to have more influence.

---

[60] Baker, *Joel, Obadiah, Malachi*, 64-67. Baker does not get as specific as I just did; however, he does include a "contemporary Significance" section in his commentary that glosses over some of the issues that I raise. If you had a chance to look at his commentary, I do not believe that you would be disappointed.

[61] Adam Gabbatt, "Losing Their Religion: Why US Churches Are on the Decline," *The Guardian Online* (22 January 2023), available online at https://www.theguardian.com/us-news/2023/jan/22/us-churches-closing-religion-covid-christianity, accessed 13 May 2024. Gabbatt reports that American Protestant churches are at only 85% of attendance levels as compared to pre-pandemic levels.

God's call to worship (aka another Solemn Assembly) in verses 15-17 was for the purpose of gathering and sanctifying and weeping and is tied to verses to the call of returning to God in verses 12-14. And often, we want the God of verses 12-14 that is gracious, merciful, and kindness without doing the actions that he requires in verses 15-17. Sorry … it does not work that way. Verses 15-17 are required and painful and necessary. These verses (15-17) were also for the purpose of telling them what to say … to God himself.

God wanted/needed/commanded the people to repent for their sins during the times of their greatest sorrow. God told them to say (v. 17), "Spare/Have compassion upon (*husah*) your people, Jehovah." This plea for compassion, which I believe is a better word than spare, shows a group of individuals who are at the bottom of the pit and have no way out but God alone. And sometimes, this is where God allows us to go because he knows this is where we need to get before we will turn to him. Utter desperation is a horrible place to be unless one knows that God is waiting to hear from us.

As I was thinking about these verses (and we will get to the concluding verses of this chapter shortly), I thought of a wonderful pastor of mine (not my dad this time) who shared a very personal story about one of his children who had wandered far away from God. During the height of his child's rebellion, a church member seeking to encourage my pastor told him that he was praying for the family and especially the prodigal's protection – who was homeless and on drugs. My pastor asked the church member to stop praying for God's protection over his child and that his child would reach such levels of depravity that he/she would have no choice but to call out to God for deliverance. The church member was appalled by such a request and ended up leaving the church; however, today my former pastor's child is serving God in a ministry very similar to what he/she once experienced because God delivered this soul from depravity that none of us could ever imagine.

This "tough love" that my pastor loved and struggled enough to give to his child is very similar to Joel 2:1-17 in many ways – and we will examine verses 2-11 in the next paragraph. God had to bring his covenant people to a level where they would beg/plead for the compassion that they had every right to call out for because they were/are his covenant children. Painful? Yes. Difficult to experience? Yes. Did the writer of Hebrews 12 write something very similar? Indeed, he did.

Human Locusts of Joel 2:2-11 … Who Are They?

Who was the army that Joel saw in his prophetic work? An army that could be described as locust-like in their destructive power. Let us look at how Joel describes this army in these verses. Verse 2 describes them in a way that fills the imagination with the sense of vastness that they fill the sky with such sheer size that the day becomes dark and gloomy, as the prophet writes. He also writes that no one will ever see such an enormous army again for many generations to come.

As I read and re-read these verses, I could not help but have my heart stop for a moment, which is not good for someone who has already had one heart attack to try to imagine what Joel must have seen in the vision that God gave him in these verses that we will continue to examine. However, I must stop for a moment to ask you to consider something (**important rabbit trail thought**). Daniel had visions similar to those of John in Revelation, and I can only imagine that the sights they saw must have been overwhelming for them. So … why do so many people believe they need to seek other sources such as Nostradamus or even themselves (i.e., "I had a revelation about the future") when God, by necessity, limits them for our own protection? My question is not one designed to begin a debate about whether prophetic gifts are available today or not because they are not. My question is to ask us to consider the purpose of seeking to know more about the future than what God has already revealed to us in his word.

Joel, Daniel, John, and the other prophets were given a mission to inform for a purpose in their day and time. We were given a mission (Matt. 28:18-20; Acts 1:8; Rom. 1:16; and elsewhere) to share the Gospel and to disciple for a purpose as well – to reach the world with the message of Messiah Jesus. Yes, a part of our mission is to share the truth of Joel and John and the truth of the Second Coming of Jesus but that should not be the end goal or even the primary goal of our efforts. Yet, conferences on eschatology will be attended in immensely greater numbers than conferences on evangelism and missions … and that should not be the case. For as my daddy once preached in a sermon from Acts 1:1-10, we need to stop looking up for the return and begin looking out and going out to reach the world with the Gospel.

Now, back to the text … If you are a student of the Civil War or perhaps you watched the classic 1939 film *Gone with the Wind* with Clark Gable and Vivian Leigh, the fiery imagery as described by Joel in verse 3 must strike a chord with you. General Sherman's "March to the Sea" in 1864-65, when he utterly devastated the farms and plantations of Georgia to bring the South to its knees, is a perfect picture of what Joel described in verses three and beyond. Sherman was relentless and brutal, and the army, as described in Joel 2, was as well.

It would be so easy to allegorize and to draw historical allusions to other brutal historical leaders – Nebuchadnezzar, Alexander the Great, Julius Caesar, Suleiman, Genghis Khan, Napoleon, and Hitler – with the mental imagery that Joel creates in his prophetic writing. However, and because we do not have a date certain for the time of Joel's authorship, the leader of this horrible army is unknown and perhaps left open to our imagination on some level. We know that they are disciplined, brutal, and seemingly unbeatable – except by God himself, who allows their temporary victories, as we see in verse 11.

For we must deal with verse 11 even if these words are incredibly difficult to read and understand in our own finite minds. Why would God allow his people, the people of the covenant, to undergo such a horrific experience, as is described in Joel? Why would God allow the Jewish people to go through the Crusades, the Inquisition, Pogroms, and the Holocaust? Such unanswerable questions in so many ways, and yet I am forced to answer this question as a missionary to the Jewish people more often than you can even imagine. Tzedakah Ministries at **www.exploremessiah.com** has an entire section to the question "Why the Holocaust?" and I earned a PhD in Theology and Apologetics solely to be better equipped on how to be more adequately trained on these unanswerable issues. Trust me … they are tough.

So why would God say in Joel 2:11 that this was his army and that the "Day of the Lord" is great and terrible, while in other places, this day is described in wonderful terms? Sadly, David Baker, in his commentary on Joel, says it is much more elaborate wording than I will, but the concept is the same: sometimes God has to grab us by the "scruff of our neck" to get our attention.[62] Nothing else would do it but a horrible and drastic "Day of the Lord," as Joel described.

Please do not read me wrong here. I am not writing that the Holocaust and the death of six million Jewish people was God's will, for I do not believe it was. However, God did not prevent it from happening even though he could have. It is beyond our human comprehension to understand why he did not prevent it from happening much like there are an innumerable events in the history of time that we could bring to God's attention that would have the same answer. We sometimes have to return to Job 38-42 and realize that we will never know the answer, but God is in control of the question and answer.

Please note that I will seek to discuss the reality of evil and who is responsible for it in chapter 10 (even though you might not like the answer), but even then, it is only my limited understanding of the question. I do, however, know that there are times when **our evil** sometimes "forces" God to grab our attention and to tell us to "repent already" for our own good. This is what he did for his covenant people in Joel 2, and this is often what he does for us today if we only do so for our own good. This is why this section began with repentance before we got to the punishment section of the chapter.

---

[62] Baker, *Joel, Obadiah, Malachi*, 78-79.

Then ... Jehovah (2:18-32)

One of my favorite words in all of Scripture is the word "but." I know this might sound odd to you, but think about a couple of instances where the word "but" signaled a significant change for everyone. The first instance is in Genesis 6 reveals that God is disgusted with humanity as they have fallen so far from the perfection that was the Garden. God decided to destroy everything that he had created in verse 7, and then ... we have the great word "but" in verse 8 – "**But** Noah found grace in the eyes of Jehovah." The second example I will show is perhaps the greatest one of all – Ephesians 2:4-5 – "**But** God, who is rich in mercy, for his great love wherewith he loved us, even when we were dead in sins has made us alive together with Christ/Messiah (by grace you are saved;)."

I have decided after this careful study of these wonderful prophets that my next second favorite word has become "then." For most of the time when we have this "then" transition in the prophets with this usage of the word, things are about to get a great deal better for God's Chosen People. This reality is also true in verse 18 through the rest of chapter two.

For after repentance in verses 12-17, we find a Piel verb which is an intentional verb of zealousness and then a display of compassion/pity for God's people taking place. The crop devastation and the drought (v. 19, 22-24) are removed from the land, as well as the marauding army from the north (v. 20). In fact, the people are told that the malicious army will not only be destroyed but they will be driven away to a barren land of their own making because they have done monstrous things. And again, while there is a great temptation to read historical or even modern-day headlines into verse 20 (i.e., what has happened to every nation that has tried to come against Israel), we should only see that God protects his covenant people when they return to him.

By the way, I am telling myself to do the same thing even while I am writing out the same instructions to you. And why am I telling both of us to do such a difficult task? It is because I believe this is another example of a double (or even a multiple) fulfillment of prophecy. This is not something that God has done once or even twice, or even three times for Israel. For ultimately, and what will be seen in chapter 12 (Zechariah), God will do ultimately in the final "Day of the Lord" for Israel and those who are faithful to God's promises.

This is the true and ultimate reality of verse 27 and throughout the rest of the chapter. For it all begins with the awesome word "then," for Israel has been put to shame since the prophecies of Joel. However, there will come a day when all those sorrowful events will end, and they ("the remnant" of verse 32) will realize that Jehovah truly is God ... and just who is Jehovah God in all His reality.

Now, here is the question that we have all been waiting for – what does Joel 2:28-32 actually mean? What are the visions, dreams, and prophecies all about in Joel's days and our day as well? Who was the promise directed towards? And finally ... when will it or will it be realized?

First, I am going to examine each of the words – prophecy, dreams, and visions – individually. Let us begin with prophecy, which has an implication today in foretelling future events. However, this is not the only or even primary meaning of the word. Prophesying, especially in the latter days of the Hebrew Scriptures, had come to mean giving forth "instruction" with only "occasional" predictive messages.[63] The BDB, as the Hebrew lexicon I used for this information has come to be known, has no agenda or bias but recognizes that the prophets primarily delivered messages, whether good or bad, from God that were interspersed with prophetic promises and not the other way around.

Or as my Baptist preacher father used to explain, the word prophecy had a two-fold purpose in Scripture – one was to foretell a message from God, and the other was to forthtell the Gospel of God. Therefore, we need to be careful to understand which prophecy is being used in which context, but never forget that the message of prophesying the Gospel of God is our primary message today. I would argue that is the point Joel was also sharing with the people of God as well as the other people who would be given the gift, as we must never forget that Joel promised that this gift would be given to "all flesh" as well as to manservants and maidservants. This is the point Isaiah also constantly makes when he reminds the Jewish people that they are to be a "light to the nations." It was not because they could foretell the future but because they were to tell forth who the God of the universe was. This also was the message that Peter carried over to Acts 2 because the story was completed in Messiah Jesus.

So ... what about dreams and visions? Does that not mean something supernatural? Maybe or maybe not. Jacob and Joseph both dreamed (*chalam*) in Genesis, but Hezekiah begged God that he would recover (*chalam*) from his illness in Isaiah. The concept of old men dreaming must be read in the context of what is occurring in the overall section. People are forth telling the message of God. People are calling on the name of Jehovah and being delivered/saved (i.e., the same words that Paul uses in Romans 10). Do the "old men" need to dream, or do they need to "recover" in order to be a part of the experience of sharing the truth of God with the whole world? You can decide for yourselves, but I know what I believe is the best answer to this question. But ... I will leave you with a question – do we need dreamers or missionaries today?

---

[63] Samuel Rolles Driver, Francis Brown, and Charles Augustus Briggs, "נָבָא," *Hebrew and English Lexicon of the Old Testament* (Oxford: Oxford University Press, 1906).

The word "visions" for the young men is fairly straightforward. They are given a word from God to share, a message, a prophecy. However, and as has already been discussed, is a prophecy the idea of prophecy that we often see today? Or is it simply the message of God for the world?

Peter in Acts 2 uses this passage on Pentecost (the Jewish feast of Shavuot) for a specific purpose. The Holy Spirit arrived during this feast, as all Jewish men were commanded to be in Jerusalem and at the Temple. This was also the feast that the Gentiles who were God-fearers were allowed to be included in the observance, for even today, Ruth is often included in the reading in the synagogue (see Ruth 1:22).[64] The Gospel message of God is to be expansive. This is the message of Joel 2:28-32, and it is so much more than just a really good dream – it is the message of missions.

Jehovah Is God … Whenever and Wherever He Chooses to Judge the Nations (3:1-21)

As we come to the close of a chapter that has become a great deal longer than I anticipated, I have come to admire this almost anonymous prophet a great deal more than I ever have. Indeed, he was a brave man for writing words that could not have been popular among an agrarian population that depended on their crops for survival. He was a truthful man for warning them that God was not satisfied with their worship, and he was an interesting man because he saved the "good news" for last.

Amos opened his prophetic work with the judgment on the other nations, but Joel saved those words for last. It was an interesting choice, but I believe I understand why he did it (aside from God telling him to do it). I believe Joel did so because he wanted the people to be aware that mercy is not possible without justice. We also forget that lesson. We want a God of mercy but not a God of justice. Well … it does not work that way.

The final words of Joel offer the reprieve that I am sure that the people were longing to hear, but this comfort was not going to happen perhaps as soon as they wanted or hoped because Joel begins in verse 1 with the phrase – "in those days." The judgment will happen upon those peoples and nations that oppressed the covenant people of Israel. Among those specifically named in Joel 3 are the cities of Tyre and Sidon and the people of the Philistia coast (v. 4), the Greeks (v. 6), and by possible implication, the Babylonians (v. 5). The sins of those people are stealing from God and enslaving the people in order to be seduced by "wine, women, and song." However, it will happen "in those days," for that is the perfect timing of God.

---

64 Ronald Isaacs, "Why We Read the Book of Ruth on Shavuot," *My Jewish Learning*, available online at https://www.myjewishlearning.com/article/why-do-we-read-the-book-of-ruth-on-shavuot/, accessed 16 May 2024.

The other irregularity one might find in this chapter is the location for God's judgment upon the people – the Valley of Jehoshaphat. For if you have been to Israel, and I have been to the land four times, you cannot go to a place that is officially designated as the Jehoshaphat Valley. There is no sign or marker, or giant X marks the spot for the locale. And while people have tried to locate the place, as somewhere in the Kidron Valley,[65] the actual location is known only to God. The name Jehoshaphat means "Jehovah has judged," and God judges when and where he chooses, and we are only to wait for "that day."[66]

For in that day, we find once again this reminder (v. 10) that this will be a time when people will go to war never again and the weak will find that they are finally strong because God is ruling on the throne. We also find another promise in verse 17 that gives those who are not Jewish a promise that I believe that Paul connects to in Romans 11 – those who find hope in Messiah Jesus (cf. Joel 2:28-32; Acts 1) because we are grafted into the promise of Abraham's covenant as well.

Today, and I do not believe this is an actual rabbit trail, too many people seek to find a reason to replace this group or that group and, especially, the Jewish people from the covenant promises of the Hebrew Scriptures. And while the hope of eternity with God is available only through Jesus the Messiah (John 14:6; Acts 4:12; and elsewhere), the covenant promises of being the Chosen People continues to this day for the Jewish people. This is not about a particular view of the end times or anything else. This is about an understanding of Scripture based on the words alone. This is the reality of the remnant that is discussed all throughout the prophets called minor. This is the conclusion of the promise of Joel 3:18-21. This is the hope of "in that day."

The best way I can bring this truth down to a human level is to end where I started this chapter and that is with a discussion of the Great Depression and my Grandpa Downey. Grandpa, as a tenant farmer, would often use the winter months during the depression to "hop the rails" with my great-uncle Al to look for extra jobs to provide for my gramma, daddy, and daddy's sister Fayma. Grandpa and Uncle Al had many adventures as they traveled the country as nothing more than hobos. However, one of their favorites serves as a perfect illustration of what I am trying to explain in relation to the Jewish people and their role as a remnant people.

---

[65] "Jehoshaphat, Valley of," *Zondervan's Pictorial Bible Dictionary*, Merrill C. Tenney, gen. ed. (Grand Rapids, MI: Zondervan Publishing House, 1963): 408.
[66] Bartholomew and Thomas, *The Minor Prophets*, 77.

One day, during their adventures, the trains were not running, so they hitchhiked on a truck filled with bananas. The truck driver told them that he doubted whether he could deliver all the bananas to their locations on time and so they could eat all they wanted if they were hungry. Well … hunger and the Great Depression were a common refrain for most people and grandpa and Uncle Al began eating and eating and eating.

I do not know if you are aware of what happens to a body if one eats too many bananas in one sitting. However, it was not a pleasant experience as that moment of bloating and "excessive air" in the body began to happen to both of my dear relatives. After what happened to my grandpa and Uncle Al in the 1930s, neither one of them ever wanted to eat a banana again – and my grandpa died at the age of 91 in 2001. However, in the 1930s, it was either starvation or "excessive air," and they chose not to starve to death.

The Jewish people today are in the banana truck (and always have and will be because they are the covenant people of God). They have access to the bananas just as we did and do – they only need to eat as we did and are. However, many Jewish people do not realize that those bananas are for them as well. They are still waiting for their bananas (i.e., the Messiah). Some have given up on their bananas coming either because they have no hope or a belief that they can create their own bananas themselves. They are sitting, waiting, and starving to death because we who are eating have not told them about those wonderful bananas (Romans 10:11-15). Isn't that just bananas because nothing goes better with a banana than a glass of milk (Joel 3:18)?

Section Four:
Divorce is Ugly – Even God Understands and Hates It
Hosea and Malachi

Of the two prophets we will be examining in this first section, I am going to argue that both Hosea and Malachi are misunderstood by most Christians and churches who even dare to read these masterful works of prophecy. Hosea has been emasculated in recent years by a well-meaning but ultimately incorrect work of Christian fiction. Malachi is often relegated to sermons during "Stewardship Month" by churches. However, I would argue that to see these as just a work of romance or tithing is an injustice to Scripture and to the message of what these prophets were seeking to share with Israel during a time of search and loss.

As I read Hosea, I was struck by how different it is from how we want to read it (especially by women) today. I have read Francine Rivers' *Redeeming Love*, and I understand and empathize with what she is trying to convey. However, the well-meaning author gets the story wrong on so many levels.

There are several statements that must be understood when one begins to read the words of Hosea, the prophet. God is heartbroken. God is angry. God is in many ways … divorced from the people of Israel because of the harlotry and infidelity they have committed against Him. And God commands His prophet to act out an actual metaphor before the people so they can see the pain in perverse, ugly, and dare I say living color. And before we go any further, yes, you need to recognize that I believe that the highly dysfunctional marriage of Hosea and Gomer was actual and real and heartbreaking.

And while there is redemption and restoration in Hosea, it is not the love story portrayed by Christian fiction. It is not easily "fixed" by the end of a few hundred pages. There are emotional scars. There are spiritual scars. There are lingering scars still to be reconciled by the end of the Hosea. This is why Hosea must not be forgotten in the section labeled as minor or allegorized by fiction writers. Hosea is a prophetic type of love and restoration that we cannot even imagine … especially when we approach the verses of when he purchased Gomer for the price of a slave.

Malachi I believe is also misunderstood. It is misunderstood by those who sit in the pews because so often, they only hear about this book in the Bible when the pastor wants to preach a sermon about stewardship. Therefore, they think this is a book only about tithing. Pastors often only utilize Malachi to preach sermons about stewardship – even though they know it is so much richer and deeper than just about giving. In fact, I have only had one pastor (Bruce Zimmerman) actually preach through the entirety of Malachi in a sermon series in my 50+ years of living.

For while Hosea indicts the people before captivity, Malachi accuses them post-captivity. Yet, we find them reverting back to the same sins that caused them to lose their freedom and their homeland for so many years. The people seemed incapable of learning their lesson. And you know what? So do we.

Therefore, Malachi should be read more than when the church needs a boost in giving or when a mission organization is starting a capital campaign fund outreach. Malachi should be read because it reminds us of what happens when people forget. It reminds us that silence could be the punishment for forgetfulness. Malachi reminds us that God hates divorce even though, at times, as Hosea tells us, he is tempted to file the papers.

7. Hosea: The Non-Love Love Story of Hosea & Gomer

Introduction

One of the best parts of visiting my gramma's house while growing up was her collection of Grace Livingston Hill books. Grace Livingston Hill was perhaps the first Christian romance writer — even though I do not know if Mrs. Hill would have seen herself in that genre, but she was.[67] Anyway, and when gramma died, everyone knew that no one deserved to have those books except me. For it was this granddaughter, who read the books along with her and who loved talking with her about the characters and the storylines. And it is I, to this day, who possesses all of gramma's Grace Livingston Hill's books. I treasure them, and they are a part of my overwhelming book collection. Yes, I confess I am addicted to books.

Now, I am not today a large reader of fiction and especially not Christian fiction and **certainly not Christian romance** (except for those GLH books). The genre, as a whole, drives me more than a little crazy. However, I have read the book Redeeming Love by Francine Rivers. She is one of the few modern Christian fiction writers that does not drive me insane. Her characters, for the most part, reflect the flaws and foibles that all people possess. No one in her books is solely all good or evil but contains the shades of gray that we all hold. And if she sees this introduction, I hope she realizes that I am bestowing upon her great praise because I really do not like Christian romance books.

And while ***Redeeming Love*** as a work of fiction is better than 99.4% of today's modern Christian fiction that is out there, I believe that the work itself has misconstrued the true message which God through Hosea would like to share with today's world. *The book of Hosea is both a love story between the people of Israel and God and yet, at the same time, it is a non-love story between Hosea and Gomer.*

Now ... and I hope you are scratching your head about now by the last sentence of the paragraph above because I meant it to be shocking. I want anyone to read the book of Hosea and point out the LOVE between Hosea and Gomer, and then I would like anyone to read the book and point out where there is NO LOVE between God and the people of Israel.

---

[67] Actually, and according to the website dedicated to her life, Grace Livington Hill, did acknowledge herself as a Christian romance writer. However, she viewed her writing as having a purpose that was more than just writing a love story. She wanted to be someone whose life and stories would bring someone to Jesus. Grace Livingston Hill Homepage, accessed 18 January 2024, https://gracelivingstonhill.com/.

And while there are those who seek to see the marriage of Hosea and Gomer as nothing but a fictional metaphor, I am not one of those. I believe the marriage was real, and it was difficult, and it was painful for both of them. It was painful for Hosea to marry a woman who preferred to sell herself to others. It was painful when God told Hosea to take her back again and perhaps even again. It was painful for Hosea to know that more than likely, two of the three children were not his, but he had a responsibility to care for and provide for them.

It was also painful for Gomer to know that Hosea saw her as a responsibility, an obligation – for even "women of the night" have feelings. I can imagine that it was painful for Gomer to have a husband who did not love her until he was ordered to do so and to realize that she was nothing more than a metaphor in some grand story. I can imagine that it was painful as I read the chapters in Hosea that it was painful for Gomer to be nothing more than a showpiece on God's eternal stage … just because she was a harlot. And while we know nothing of Gomer's backstory, we are allowed to wonder why she was a prostitute to begin with and that is what Francine Rivers' wondered as well. But to lose ourselves in curiosity as to Gomer's backstory is to lose the message of Hosea.

However, the message and the point of Hosea and what must be studied and applied in today's age is a love story between God and Israel and not between a man and woman. Let us not be misdirected or misguided by anything else.

Who Hosea Was and a Little Biblical Background

What little we know of Hosea specifically is found in the first verse of the book itself. The biography of the man is brief. He is the son of a man named Beeri, which is not common and is only found one other time in Scripture (Gen. 26:34) when Esau married Judith, and her father Beeri was a Hittite.

This does not necessarily mean that Hosea's father was descended from the Hittites. And we should remember that Bathsheba's husband Uriah, who was murdered by order of David, was a Hittite. It is just a thought we should consider and hold onto as we examine the book itself and as we remember that the name Beeri is derived from a word that means "pit," and Hosea has the meaning of "deliver." For as we should remember, the meaning of names for people in Scripture is not accidental. Incidentally, Gomer's name gives one the idea of completion but, not just any ending but a finality that ends in failure.

114

The time frame for the period of Hosea's prophetic ministry is very specific. The kings of Judah are from the days of Uzziah to Hezekiah and King Jeroboam II (the son of Joash) in the Northern Kingdom (c.785-722 BC/BCE).[68] And what do we know of these kings and their reigns? The Northern Kingdom never had a godly king, and so Jeroboam was a failure in the eyes of God. Uzziah did what was right **until he was struck down by the sin of pride** – which will destroy even the best of us. Jotham did what was right in Jehovah's eyes, but he failed to remove the idols in the high places, which allowed the people to continue to engage in false worship. Ahaz did not do what was right in Jehovah's eyes, and it is stated in 2 Kings 16:2 **that he made his son "pass through the fire" (aka child sacrifice).**

And what about Hezekiah, who is considered one of the greatest and most godly of Judah's kings? His pride and hubris in Isaiah 39 lead to one of the most tragic prophecies in Isaiah 39 – the promise of the destruction of the Temple. His reaction can only be described as, "Oh well, I will be dead by then." Five kings during the prophetic ministry of Hosea who failed the Jewish people. No wonder both Hosea and God were burdened by a relationship that was so dysfunctional and broken.

Theme of Hosea – Love(?) and Marriage, Divorce Court, and What Does This Say About God?

I believe in many ways, the introduction and background sections have already revealed the "theme" of Hosea. We have a loving God who is in a covenantal marriage to an emotionally and spiritually broken people. And while in today's world, there is rarely a marriage that can be determined as 100% one person's fault, we can look at not only the book of Hosea but also throughout the Hebrew Scriptures and point the finger at the Chosen People and say – the problem is with you.

Yet, God, throughout this wonderful book of love, marriage, divorce court, and reconciliation, does not give up on the relationship. For while there is a point in the scroll that God, in a sense, does file the divorce papers (chapters four and five), God cannot give up on his scarred, damaged bride, and neither will he allow Hosea to give up on Gomer either. For this living metaphor that God asks Hosea to re-enact is one that we should be thankful is one that God re-enacts every moment with not only the Jewish people but also with those of us He also calls His spiritual bride.

---

[68] J. Maxwell Miller, "Judah, The Kingdom of," *The Oxford Companion to the Bible*, eds. Bruce M. Metzger and Michael D. Coogan (New York: Oxford University Press, 1993): 391. Miller provides a clear overlapping chart of the various kings of the two kingdoms. And while it is doubtful that Hosea was a prophet for 63 years, hence the usage of the abbreviation for circa. I included the rough beginning dates for King Uzziah's reign and gave an end date of 722 BC/BCE as this is an established date for the fall of the Northern Kingdom.

An Uncomfortable Marriage/a Difficult Analogy (1:2-2:23)

I met Clark (not his real name) during my freshman year in college. When I first met Clark, he seemed like he was a good guy, but that did not last long. He decided that he wanted to compete with another guy on campus about who could date the most girls during our freshman year. I am not sure who won that unspoken competition and I actually do not care. What I soon learned about Clark was that first impressions can truly disguise what is in the heart.

Clark and I had encounters over the years because apparently, "I was the one that got away" in his mind, and I am so grateful I was. Sadly, Clark had a difficult life and problematic relationships with many women, and my heart broke for him, but I am glad that "I was the one that got away." Truly … very grateful!

And I do not know what I would have done if God had ever come to me and said, "Amy, I want you to marry Clark because I need your marriage to be an example of XXX." Seriously … I might have told God, "Absolutely not!" I do not believe I could have had the trust, faith, and ability to believe that all things could turn out for the best – regardless of what the best might turn out to be – like Hosea did. Yet, Hosea did because he was a better person than I am, and now we have this analogy/metaphor/illustration of God's love for Israel … regardless of the circumstances, regardless of Israel's adultery, regardless of whatever.

How bad was this marriage between Hosea and Gomer in the beginning? Let us examine the first two chapters along with a brief glance at 4:1-5:15 of what can only be described as the "separation/divorce agreement" between God and Israel to see how bad it really got. And then you will truly see how much better of a man Hosea was than I could ever be.

Go! Take! What…? Why…? (1:2-9)

Yes, we know the story but we still need to take a deep look at the setting of the non-love story of Hosea and Gomer. The verbs in verse 2 are in the imperative (command) and the word "take" is the word *laqach* which gives one the idea of capture or seize. But why was Hosea supposed to do with this odd command? Because … Israel is committing *zanoh tizneh* or double harlotry in Hebrew, and God was utilizing Hosea and Gomer to illustrate Israel's sins.

It is significant that we see the double usage of a word in which the root word is harlot or whoredom – which is the more accurate word. Incidentally, there is no concept or usage of the exclamation point in Hebrew, and so when God or the writer of Scripture is seeking to make a strong point, we will see a repetition of a word such as "Holy, Holy, Holy" in Isaiah 6. And on a side note that I feel compelled to include, my review check tells me that the word "whoredom" could be offensive to the reader. If it is, I cannot apologize for using it. However, I hope you can understand because I want you to realize how much more our sins and the sins of Israel were offensive to God.

And because Hosea is a better person than I could ever hope to be, Hosea went and "took" Gomer for his wife. She conceived and gave birth to her first son Jezreel ("God will scatter"), as his name symbolized the end of the kingdom of Israel. Gomer gave birth to two more children – the daughter Lo-Ruhamah ("no mercy/compassion/love") and the son Lo-Ammi ("not my people").

There have been questions as to whether or not the last two children belong to Hosea, but those questions can only be answered speculatively and are beside the point.[69] The greater point is the symbolism or the metaphor that these children and Hosea had to carry before the people of Israel. The weight of Israel's sins was placed upon children via their names.[70] A burden no one, regardless of their age, should be asked to bear but because of the sins of others, a weight that someone was forced to carry ... much like Messiah Jesus did hundreds of years later.

Verses 10-11 of chapter one illustrate the mercurial or changeable nature of what we can read and find in Hosea. There is emotional pain in verses 2-9, and then we see God affirming that the people of his covenant marriage – the Jewish people – will return and be as numerous as the sand on the sea. Is this not a perfect illustration of a marital relationship playing out before our eyes not only in 1:10-11 but all throughout the prophecy of Hosea? Vicious anger (2:1-5). Love – both requited and unrequited. One spouse is ready to walk out the door. One spouse fights to hold the marriage together regardless of the pain it takes to do so (2:6-23).

The best way that I can describe this is to share a little about my parents' marriage with you. They had 39 years of marriage before daddy died in 2000 and were an example of what a godly union should be. However, it was not always easy for either one of them. My mom came from a difficult childhood in which unconditional love was not shown or given in her childhood home. For while my grandpa was a wonderful man, my grandmother was a difficult woman to say it nicely. The first couple of years of their marriage were dedicated to my dad living out the example of a husband who would always love his wife, Barbara, unconditionally and not walk away when her insecurities raised their ugly head.

---

[69] Duane A. Garrett, *Hosea, Joel* (vol. 19a), The New American Commentary, vol. 19a, gen. ed. E. Ray McClenden (Nashville, TN: Broadman & Holman, 1997): 69 and Jack P. Lewis, *The Minor Prophets* (Grand Rapids, MI: Baker Book House, 1966): 26.

[70] Arno Gaebelein, *The Annotated Bible: The Holy Scriptures Analyzed and Annotated – Daniel to Malachi* (vol. 5), (Travelers Rest, SC: Southern Bible Book House, n.d.): 54-55 and Bartholomew and Thomas, *The Minor Prophets: A Theological Introduction, 46-47.*

My dad was born with a cleft palate during the height of the Great Depression, and while my grandparents did what they could to have it repaired, it was impossible to fix it perfectly. My sister and I never noticed it for we just saw daddy as the cute, bald Teddy Bear that he was. However, my dad was always self-conscious of his "hair lip," as they called it in those days, and was convinced that no one would ever love him because he was not handsome or normal. My mom loved him without reservation because Jack Downey was her knight in shining armor who rescued her from an emotionally abusive life.

Jack and Barbara were two amazing people who served God during their entire lives, but they had baggage they had to overcome, and they did so together, giving 100% every day. This is what a covenant marriage does. However, Hosea had to do the heavy lifting in his marriage alone, just as God had to do the work in his covenant relationship with Israel. The difficulty at times seemingly was impossible and hence why we see the changing, rollercoaster emotions in the book of Hosea. When we recognize it as the ebbs and flows of marriage, then we can understand why there are so many changes at times – even what we might call a separation or divorce agreement against Israel (4:1-5:15).

Or, as my mother once said to me when I asked her if she still loved my dad after overhearing an argument, "Amy, I might not always like your dad, but I always choose to love him." Excellent advice if you stop to think about it for a second. However, I believe her wisest advice to me is something I still often write to newlyweds – "May your wedding day be the least happiest day of your life together." Or as my mom explained to me, "For if the wedding day is the best moment together, the marriage will not last."

"Love, Her Anyway" … for a <u>Couple</u> of Prophetic Reasons (3:1-5)

This is a personal admission as consideration begins in chapter three; I have struggled with this chapter in several different areas and for a long time. I have considered this chapter. I have even set this chapter to one side for months (perhaps even years) when I first encountered these areas. Yet, I have come back to what the verses have to share. I have done the grammar homework, and I have searched through a plethora of commentaries. So … what I am writing here is not done carelessly or without a great deal of trepidation. I actually believe we have been missing is something in Hosea's words that should not be overlooked. It is prophetic, but even more so, it is invaluable for us as we consider God's love in so many ways, as Francis Thompson described to us from the streets of London of the late 19th century, "the hound of Heaven."[71]

First Area: Take Gomer (Back) … but in a Different Way than Before

In Hosea 1:2, God instructs Hosea to "take" Gomer as his wife. In 3:1, God again directs Hosea, and the verb is the same in the sense that it is in the command form (see below), but this time, Hosea is told to "love" Gomer.

Go (Qal Imperative) **again love** *(Qal Imperative)* **a woman/wife loved by her husband yet an adulteress** *(Piel Participle)* **even as Jehovah loves the sons of Israel though they turn to other Gods and love raisin cakes.** *(personal translation and abbreviated grammatical analysis)*

This command of God is made more complicated by the fact that Gomer is still an adulteress and, as the verb shows us by its Piel Participial form – intentional and ongoing despite her "salacious activities." We can gather from the verse that she has no shame about her activities, just as God wants Hosea (and the reader) to see that Israel has no shame about their ongoing and intentional love of other gods and those scandalous "raisin cakes."

Now … you have to know that I have never been a fan of raisins in any form. I have never liked them in cereal, cookies, and, most definitely, by themselves. I am, if you remember, Dr. Suess and ***Green Eggs and Ham,*** the Sam I Am of raisins. I would not say I like the texture, the shape, or the taste of raisins. And the reason is simple – to me when I was a child, they resembled something that came out of the backside of a rabbit, and I did not want to eat anything that came out of the backside of a rabbit.

---

[71] Francis Thompson penned the poem "The Hound of Heaven" while recovering from a drug addiction at Our Lady of England Priory. The poem was published in 1893 and then again in 1917 in the *Oxford Book of English Mystic Verse.* For additional information, see https://www.youtube.com/watch?v=Qe62b5NMXfken | Catholic Culture, accessed 10 February 2024. A documentary on the life of Francis Thompson is also available on YouTube at https://www.youtube.com/watch?v=Qe62b5NMXfk, accessed 10 February 2024.

Perhaps this visual illustration was a little too much for you, but I hope it will set the stage for why we should resist the lure and sensual temptation of spiritual "raisin cakes" when they are offered to us. Raisin cakes—either literal or figurative—in this particular passage represent indulging in temporal pleasure more than real worship.[72] Indulging in the world's oldest profession, either as an employee or a "John," also only offers a temporary experience rather than a real and lasting experience that can be called a relationship or love.

So … God is telling (imperative command here) Hosea to not only take Gomer back but to love her. And the word in Hebrew is love in all its beautiful shape and form and relationship implications. Gomer, who we can realistically imagine knows how to appeal to the sensual and temporary, is now supposed to understand, recognize, and respond to true and everlasting love. How is this possible? Yet, God commands this of Hosea because this is the spiritual chase that He (God) himself has and is engaged in with the people of Israel.

Israel does not understand, recognize, or know how to respond to true spiritual love because the false gods' deceitful raisin cakes have deceived them. Yet, God will not give up because his love, while not as beguiling as a raisin cake, is far more eternally healthy and good for Israel than they will ever realize.

As I was writing this section, I thought of an illustration that might summarize it better than I have been doing so far. In the TV show *The Big Bang Theory*, the beautiful Penny finally realizes that the nerdy Leonard is the one for her, but he does not want to be the "bran muffin" she settles for because it is good for her. He wants to be the "pop tart," which is exciting. Penny finally tells him that she wants him that he is – her healthy but essentially "healthy" pop-tart. God is Israel's healthy pop-tart, and they do not recognize it. The question we need to ask today is, are we chasing those "raisin cakes" so desperately that once we catch and taste them, are they really nothing more than what I thought they were as a child, or should we savor what God wants for us – the healthy pop-tart he has been offering all along.

---

[72] Garrett, *Hosea, Joel* (vol. 19a), 100; C. F. Keil, *Minor Prophets*, Commentary on the Old Testament in 10 Volumes, vol. 10, ed. C. F. Keil and F. Delitzsch (Grand Rapids, MI: William B. Eerdmans, n.d.): 68.

Second Area: Have We Been Missing a Hidden Prophecy All This Time?

A few years ago, I read verse 2 – "So I bought her for myself for 15 shekels of silver and a homer and a half of barley" and became curious as to how much a homer and a half of barley would cost in Hosea's day. I did a little price checking and discovered that the going rate for that much barley in Hosea's day would run another 15 shekels of silver. Now, I do not know if that was a good price for barley or not, but I can add: 15 + 15 = 30 shekels of silver. When I did the math for verse two, a few other verses came to mind, such as Zech. 11:12-13 and Mt. 27:9 (i.e., the prophecy and the fulfillment of Jesus being betrayed for 30 pieces of silver).

Now, I recognize we must be careful not to see prophecies, allegories, metaphors, typologies, and other such devices in such detail that we might want to insert what we long to see for **our** interpretation. However, I do believe the **30 Shekels of Silver** is sitting there in big, bold Hebrew letters for an important reason in chapter three. And, therefore, the rest of chapter three is perhaps just waiting for us to read it for a true and maybe a new understanding to be developed – both then and now.

So … in verse two, Hosea purchases, because he had no choice due to the level of her personal degradation, his wife Gomer, who had turned back (or perhaps had never left the life but had just now truly hit rock bottom) to her life as a prostitute for the price of a slave who just happens to be 30 pieces of silver (Ex. 21:32). However, Hosea is commanded (the word for love is in the Piel in Hebrew) by God not to treat her as a slave but he is to love her as his wife as God loves Israel (3:1).

If we then go to the overt/obvious prophecy related to the Messiah Jesus being betrayed for "30 Pieces of Silver" in Zech. 11:12-13, one can see that thirty pieces of silver are given for "the potter" (i.e., Jehovah) before the bonds of brotherhood are broken in verse 14. This prophecy is then fulfilled when Judas betrays and then recants his betrayal of Jesus for thirty pieces of silver in Matthew and Acts.

The Messiah of the Jewish people is betrayed for the price of a slave, yet Jesus' unconditional love for the Jewish people (and all of humanity) is such that he goes willingly to the cross for their (and our) sins. For just as Gomer had sunk to such a point of degradation (i.e., rock bottom) that Hosea had to buy her back from what we would today call her pimp or trafficker, Jesus had to redeem us from Satan because of the level of degradation and sin and death (Rom. 6:1-4; Eph. 1:7) we were in before Jesus purchased us. Alister McGrath says it so much better than I can when he wrote in *What Was God Doing on the Cross?*, "God does not redeem us in some arbitrary and haphazard manner, but in a way which both accords with and declares his righteousness."[73] From Exodus to Leviticus (see fn. 3) to Hosea to Zechariah to the Gospels, I would suggest that the prophecy is there to be found and realized.

Now, you might expect all the commentaries to be making the connection that I am seeking to make on these pages. You would be wrong. I have done my due diligence, including the president of the board for Tzedakah Ministries in 2023 (Chris Price), who helped me on my search as well, and we were only able to find one other pastor who wrote a blog, making the link here.[74] As to why commentaries did not make the connection, I cannot tell you, but I believe that not making the connection misses a key component in the story of Jesus' atoning sacrifice – the story of redemption, and that is a story we are missing today as well.

Third Area: The Obvious Prophecy and Its Promise for the Future

A marriage that has been broken, whether it be because of adultery or any issue that might cause a loss of trust, cannot begin again as if nothing has happened. When the loss of trust has occurred, reconciliation must happen before intimacy – whether it be sexual intimacy or not – begins again in a marriage.

---

[73] Alister E. McGrath, *What Was God Doing on the Cross?* (Grand Rapids: Zondervan Publishing House, 1992): 55. Additionally, Leon Morris, in his work *The Atonement: Its Meaning and Significance* (Grand Rapids: InterVarsity Press, 1983): 110-19, considers the Jewish background of the redemption concept and even points out that Lev. 25:48-49 allows for a close relative to purchase back (i.e., redeem) someone from slavery. Ergo, Hosea was allowed by the Torah/Law to purchase Gomer from her trafficker and, consequently, Jesus would be allowed to purchase his people as well.

[74] Phillip Way, "Redeeming Gomer: The Price," TIME in the Word Ministries, accessed 23 January 2024, Redeeming Gomer: The Price | TIME in the Word Ministries. I contacted Pastor Way personally, and he directed me to two commentaries that he was able to find that made an indirect reference/linkage. I searched those commentaries for myself, and while they did not follow the connection to Judas/Jesus, they did make the reference to Ex. 21:32 – Keil, *Minor Prophets*, 69 and Joseph S Exell and Henry Donald Maurice Spence-Jones. "Commentary on Hosea 3," *The Pulpit Commentary* (1897), accessed 23 January 2024, https://www.studylight.org/commentaries/eng/tpc/hosea-3.html.

A few years ago, I had a friend (and I am keeping names and specific details anonymous for privacy's sake) come to me because of a situation in her marriage. Her husband was addicted to pornography but denied it was adultery when she confronted him about it. He also became angry when she refused to be intimate with him until he dealt with his pornography addiction and she was considering divorce.

Many of her other friends did not consider porn to be actual "adultery" and told her she was overreacting and that the sin of divorce was worse than his sin of pornography. She asked me what I thought of the situation, and I asked her if her husband had ever brought what he saw into their relationship. She said he did, and it made her feel cheap and dirty. I then told her what my dad would have told her in his role as a pastoral counselor (because I had talked to him about this situation years earlier).

Daddy, because Southern women are always allowed to call their father's daddy regardless of their age, would have called pornography addiction adultery because he was bringing other women into the marriage and into the bedroom. Daddy also told me years earlier that adultery does not have to be an actual physical affair; it can be a relationship that is just too close for comfort – and this was years before the idea of emotional affairs was even considered adulterous. Daddy's advice to my friend would have been, and the one she took, was to separate from her husband until he was ready to face his addiction and become the man and the husband she married in the first place.

And this was my dad's most important piece of advice: absolutely NO SEX until the marriage is once again on solid footing. If you are wondering why, the answer is simple. What motivation did my friend's husband have to work on his addiction and marriage if he was going to be still intimate with his wife? The answer is absolutely none.

This long, introductory illustration takes us to what God instructed Hosea to do in his relationship with Gomer after he purchased/secured/redeemed her back from slavery. And while I recognize the introduction was rather long and perhaps too detailed for some who might be reading, I hope I can show that it was necessary because of the serious nature of sin and how seriously God takes sin – not just in the Hebrew Scriptures but also today. To borrow from Alister McGrath again – "Sin amounts to a violation of the moral ordering of the creation, established by God himself at the foundation of the world. *Sin is an offence against the moral fabric of the creation, not just some personal insult to God*."[75] And for far too long, we within the church itself have seen sin as an insult and not as offensive to God, and the result is what we see in the world today.

---

[75] McGrath, *What Was God Doing on the Cross?*, 55. Emphasis added.

So let us now examine the rest of this short but powerful chapter – both as it relates to Israel/Gomer and how it can apply to us **and** Israel today on a prophetic level, for the passage indeed is a prophecy that applies to Israel first before it applies to anyone else.

In verse three, Hosea says to Gomer after "buying her back," three important statements: (1) you will dwell with me for a long time; (2) you will be faithful to me (i.e., no longer play the harlot); and (3) "nor shall you have a man so I will also be toward you." The first two statements are easy to understand – stay at home and be loyal. The third statement is much harder to grasp the full implication. Was he repeating – be faithful to me? No, Homer was saying what my dad's advice to those married couple who were trying to rebuild a marriage after one spouse had committed adultery – we are back together, but I will not be joining you in the bedroom.[76]

The reason why Hosea's reaction is explained specifically in verse four, as it relates to the analogy/metaphor regarding Israel but brought to full magnification in verse 5, is that Israel would have to dwell without royalty and without a place to offer sacrifices for many days due to their disobedience and sinfulness against God. Now, this would normally be the place in a book where the writer might spell out their eschatological (i.e., view of the end of the world) leanings. However, I am not going to do that because this is not the point of this book and because I do not my personal views to distract anyone from the idea of "missions in the minor key."

Instead, I am only to point out the historical truth that Israel (the Jewish people) was scattered – the fancy theological/historical term is Diaspora – 2.5 times in history. The half-time is when the Assyrians captured the Northern Kingdom in 712 BC/BCE. The first full time for the Southern Kingdom happened in 586 BC/BCE with the Babylonians and Nebuchadnezzar. The second time was when the Romans under General Titus captured Jerusalem and Judea in AD/CE 70 and then again when the Bar Kokhba Rebellion was crushed in AD/CE 135.

---

[76] Duane Garrett, *Hosea, Joel* (vol. 19a), 103. See also, Keil, *Minor Prophets*, 69-70.

Now, there are questions as to what has happened to the "lost tribes" of the Northern Kingdom, and I will only say they are not lost to God and appear again in some manifestation in Revelation—regardless of your interpretation. As to the historical return of the Jewish people to the covenant land of promise (Genesis 12, 15, 17), one legitimately can point to 14 May 1948, when the nation was restored once again in one day.[77] However, is this the only interpretation of Isaiah 66:8 – *"Who has seen such things? Shall the earth be made to give birth in one day? Or shall a nation be born at once? For as soon as Zion was in labor, She gave birth to her children."* – that should be seen? For while I disagree with those such as Albert Barnes who see this verse as a generic evangelistic outpouring,[78] I can affirm the view that it applies specifically to John Gill, who sees it as an evangelistic flood of salvation results coming to the Jewish people.[79] So the question can and should be asked – can it be both? Can it be historically applied to that of 14 May 1948 as well as to Jewish missions and evangelism? Of course, it can because I believe in the idea of prophetic double fulfillment, as you have already read in previous chapters. However, the question that should be asked and answered, regardless of your eschatological leanings, is what is most important: an isolated date in history or a soul in eternity? I believe we all know the answer to that one. At least, I hope we do.

An Inch Deep and a Mile Wide Will Still Cause Drowning (6:1-11)

There is so much that could be analyzed in minute detail in Hosea's prophecy; however, it is impossible in the space I have allotted. Yet, I must consider chapter six of Hosea because it is both beautiful and heartbreaking at the same time. We see the recognition by the Israelites of what they must do to have a restored covenant relationship with God (v. 1-3) and an acknowledgment by God that the so-called actions of the people are a surface-level response at best (v. 4-5). Surface-level at best because the actions are what the people believe is required of them and not what God truly wants from them (v. 6-7). Yet and, despite all the heartbreak God experiences in this relationship, they will one day be healed but there will be a lot of unnecessary self-induced pain along the way (v. 8-11).

---

[77] While the historical nature of the Palestinian Mandate and all that goes into the United Nations declaring Israel a

nation once again is not what is considered common knowledge anymore, I am going to ask the readers to do their own research on this issue for the sake of space and to not distract from the purpose of the book itself.

[78] Albert Barnes, *Isaiah* (vol. 11), Notes on the Old Testament: Explanatory and Practical, ed. Robert Frew (Grand Rapids: MI, 1950): 431-32.

[79] John Gill, "Isaiah 66," Exposition of the Entire Bible by John Gill [1746-63] Text Courtesy of Internet Sacred Texts Archive, https://biblehub.com/commentaries/gill/isaiah/66.htm; accessed 12 February 2024.

In my work among the Hasidic (ultra-Orthodox) Jewish people in Western New York, idioms and/or expressions are picked up almost without realizing it. I am also trying to become as fluent as possible in Yiddish, but that is a great deal harder – because it is a combination of Hebrew, German, Slavic slang, a touch of some Romance languages thrown in, and is written in Hebrew – because it is not my first or heart language and I am over fifty. Anyway, one of the expressions that I have picked up is *Ba'al Teshuvah,* which means "master of the return."

A *Ba'al Teshuvah* is a Jewish person who has "returned" to Orthodox Rabbinic Judaism after living a less observant Jewish lifestyle for a period of time.[80] The key word in this expression is *teshuvah,* for it has Hebraic/Biblical roots of *shub* ("return"). So ... when the people in 6:1-3 begin by saying, "Come, let us return to Jehovah…" it has the principle of returning back because they had left God: (1) He has torn/but he will heal; (2) He has caused us to be wounded/but he will bandage; (3) He will revive us after a period of time (two days); and (4) He will cause us to be raised up after three days so that we can live. The people were certain of God's forgiveness because they knew he had forgiven them before (v. 3)

These words sound wonderful and are truly examples of returning to God. Or do they? I feel the need to once again "channel" my mom is wonderfully wise West Texas words as we examine verses 4-5. In order to do so, I need to make a confession about myself: I hate dusting furniture with a passion, and growing up for a great deal of my life in West Texas only made that hatred of dusting grow exponentially worse with each passing day.

West Texas is known for mesquite trees, which enables Texas BBQ to be the best BBQ in the world, rattlesnakes if you live close to Sweetwater, cotton farms, and lots and lots of dust because there is nothing to stop the dust from blowing into your home. However, and being the youngest, dusting was the chore that had been handed down to me because my mom and my sister also hated to dust. Every week, I was expected to not only dust the furniture but to move all the knick-knacks (tchotchkes in Yiddish) and dust those as well. It was a hideous chore and I put it off as long as possible and almost every week I would end up apologizing to mama for not dusting on schedule or as I should have done it. Mama would also repeat almost word-for-word every week this same phrase – "Do not tell me you are sorry; show me you are sorry." In other words, do your chore like you are supposed to do it the first time.

---

[80] My Jewish Learning, "What Is a Ba'al Teshuvah?," available online at https://www.myjewishlearning.com/article/baalei-teshuvah/, accessed 23 April 2024.

We could summarize (not that we would) God's words to the Israelites in verses 4-7. He tells them that their loyalty is like a morning cloud and dew … that will disappear as soon as the sun starts shining. God knew the Jewish people were easily distracted by the next shiny bauble that might appeal to their eye, and what he truly wanted from them was genuine repentance.

The word that is used for that genuine repentance in verse 6 is often translated as "mercy" because the Hebrew word is *chesed* and that is an adequate translation. However, other options include loyalty or goodness, and those are the ones that I believe are better fits here. Mercy can so often be misunderstood today as someone who is compassionate or sympathetic, and those are wonderful attributes, but in this context, God is looking for a person who will be loyal and loyal to him alone.

Marriage requires loyalty, perhaps more than any other attribute, and I saw this with my parents. Mama followed daddy from pillar to post and to some of the most horrendous church parsonages and made them a home for all of us. Daddy protected mama at all costs and one of his last acts before he died from an undiagnosed aneurysm at the age of 66 was to ensure that she was guard her from the pain that her childhood could still inflict on her. They loved each other beyond a doubt, but their loyalty to each other defined their love – they could not be divided by anyone or in any situation.

This is the loyalty that God gives to us and the loyalty that God desired from Israel (and desires from us). It is not required because of the unconditional covenant, but it is ideal not for God's sake but for our own. If we teach anything less in our discipleship to believers in our churches and/or mission organizations, we are doing a disservice to them. They will be losing out on a greater relationship with God than they could ever grasp. And how dare we do that to anyone? God did not allow it with the Jewish people, and neither should we in our work with the people that God has placed in our care today.

This chapter on Hosea turned out to be much longer than I anticipated; however, I probably should have told you from the very beginning of this chapter that Hosea is my favorite "minor prophet." The angst and anguish we find throughout the chapter illustrate a God who loves his people, his bride. The heartache of a God who will not let go of his covenant marriage *no matter how many times the people commit adultery against him. To be honest with you, I do not understand those people who claim that the Hebrew Scriptures present a God that is full of wrath and judgment. They obviously have not read Hosea.

In these concluding paragraphs, I want you to consider briefly the words of chapter fourteen. God pleads with Israel to return and to confess, for he alone can heal them (v. 1-5). However, there is something startlingly beautiful in verse two that can be overlooked that I want to share with you. While God implores them to return to him in the plural form in Hebrew, the call to confession, "take away all iniquity and receive graciously," is in the singular in Hebrew. What does this mean? We should be asking, and I hope we are.

While Israel had to return corporately, the individual Jewish person had to ask God to forgive their sins personally. No family group, no nation, no tribe could ask God to forgive an individual's sin. That action had to be done personally and privately, even though the sacrifices were to be completed corporately. Think about the meaning and the application both for the people in Hosea's day, for modern-day applications, and for future events—especially as we consider Zechariah (see chapter 12).

Addendum Issue: Is Hosea 11:1 an Actual Messianic Prophecy?

WARNING ALERT!!! Another issue for which I am going to stir up some controversy. However, I must be honest with you on my understanding of Scripture. I do not believe that we should use Hosea 11:1 in our listings of Messianic prophecy. Please keep reading before you burn, throw away, or write to the good people of Illative House Press. Let me explain my perspective, and then if you still want to write to anyone … email me, and we can discuss it further (**downey@tzedakahministries.org**).

First, I have done my utmost, and I hope you can see that I am trying to do so as you have been reading to practice the hermeneutical rule of grammatical-historical method—which I personally define as understanding the historical background and the best exegetical or scriptural interpretation of the text. One also needs to understand the genre (i.e., prophetic, historical, poetic) and whether there are examples of metaphors and/or types that the writer is using in the text as well.

Additionally, and this is very important, any modern application of the text, whether one is reading the Hebrew Scriptures or the New Testament, must avoid the use of allegories or twisting the text to make it fit what I interpret it to mean. Let me give you an example of an allegory that we have all heard in a typical small group or Sunday School class sometime or somewhere. However, this example actually happened to me in my Bible Doctrine class in college.

The professor read to us John 14:6 – "(Jesus speaking) I am the way, the truth, and the life, and no one comes to the father except through me." The discussion that day was the exclusive nature of salvation (Jesus-Only) or universalism (many ways to Heaven). One of the students sitting close to me raised his hand and said, "I believe Jesus was meaning I am ONE of the ways, I am ONE of the truths, and I am ONE of the paths to the father." Many of the people in the class responded positively to the guy and I had to raise my hand and say, "If Jesus meant what you think … Jesus would have said it THAT WAY and not the way it is written."

The student was exercising a form of allegory in that he was seeking to interpret the Scripture in the way he wanted it to mean and not the way it clearly should be interpreted. Sadly, this does happen in small groups and Sunday School classes across America because the phrase "what it means to me" is allowed to go unchecked. We cannot engage in this practice any longer.

Second, we need to understand the biblical background and the passage context of not only Hosea 11:1 but also Matthew when he wrote these words (2:14-15) – *"When he [Joseph] arose, he took the young Child and His mother by night and departed for Egypt, and was there until the death of Herod, that it might be fulfilled which was spoken by the Lord through the prophet, saying, "Out of Egypt I called My Son."* We need to ask and understand whether the word "fulfilled" always necessitates the idea of prophecy or could mean something else in Matthew's first-century world. We also need to recognize that Matthew's gospel was writing to a Jewish audience of believers who perhaps knew the context of what Matthew's background in a way that we do not know in our 21st century world.[81]

Carr's usage of the word analogy (see fn. 15) is related to a Jewish approach to scriptural interpretation that was introduced during what is called the Intertestamental Period (Malachi to Matthew) and is still used today in Rabbinic Jewish circles – the Drash(a). A Drash is basically "an interpretation of something in scripture" (i.e., it could become something as formal as a sermon or a lesson).[82] This is my personal view of what Matthew was doing in 2:14-15. He was making an observation and/or an analogy to his audience, which was comprised mostly of Jewish believers. He was noting the connection between how God brought the Jewish people out of Egypt (which is the context of chapter 11) more than seeing a prophecy. However, there is another option that could prove me somewhat wrong.

---

[81] A. Carr, *The Gospel According to St. Matthew*, The Cambridge Bible for Schools and Colleges (Cambridge, U.K.: Cambridge University Press, 1916 rprt.): 37. I examined several of my commentaries and some utilized this verse as a rationale for Replacement Theology and some just noted the Hosea 11 usage by Matthew. However, Carr I believe phrased it best when he wrote, "Even particular incidents in the Gospel narrative have their counterpart in the O.T. history. Accordingly St. Matthew, who naturally reverts to this thought more constantly than the other Evangelists, from the very nature of his gospel, recognises in this incident an analogy to the call of Israel from Egypt" (emphasis added and British spelling and grammar rules were left as was).

[82] Rabbi Ruth Adar, "What's a D'var Torah?" The Coffee Shop Rabbi, available online at https://coffeeshoprabbi.com/2014/06/06/dvartorah/, accessed 24 April 2024. Garrett, *Hosea, Joel*, 220, also allows for what he calls a "Midrashic exegesis" when he considers Matthew's use of Hosea 11:1 yet does not come to a definitive conclusion as to whether Hosea was engaging in a form of *sensus plenior* (see Ch. 5 for a greater explanation of this term) or not. Garrett does, however, fall reluctantly into my perspective that this was probably a prophecy.

Third, Hank Hanegraaf wrote an article for the Christian Research Institute in 2015 that presents another possibility. Is it rife with problematic issues itself? Hanegraaf presents the likelihood that Hosea 11:1 and Matt. 2:14-15 is an example of typological prophecy.[83] Do not worry if you have not heard of this term … not many have.

Typological prophecy is the idea that something (person, place, or thing) can represent something greater spiritually (usually Jesus' first or second coming) at a future point in history. This is a very basic definition of the concept but I do not wish to get "into the weeds" defining the idea because it can and usually does get "into the weeds." And it should be noted that there are definitely TYPES in the Bible.

One such example is when Abraham and Isaac in Gen. 22 went to Mount Moriah because God told Abraham to sacrifice his one and only son. Just as God was to sacrifice Isaac, the Angel of the LORD (i.e., Jesus as a Theophany) stopped Abraham and showed him the ram that was in the thicket as a substitute for Isaac. The whole passage in Gen. 22 is full of typological examples from Isaac/Jesus to the ram/Jesus. Yet, those are obvious and clear types that are clear and discernible for the reader to see and understand.

Hanegraaf seeks to make such a typological example with Moses and Jesus and connect them to the "begats" in Matt. 1. And Hanegraaf does make somewhat of a point with his argument; however, I believe the better argument is the one that I make that Matthew was using a hermeneutic argument (the Drash) that he had been taught when he was young and in Hebrew school and learning about the Jewish teachers of his day – Hillel and Shammai.

Additionally, there are dangers with making the typological prophecy argument too freely. The primary danger with looking for types in scripture is that we can find types everywhere, but they simply are not there. The example I gave you of Abraham and Gen. 22 is quite obvious. However, seeking to find typology in every aspect of the Hebrew scriptures takes away from the message of the text that was meant for the Jewish people. There was a message for them that was **for them** and not simply predictive and future oriented.

---

[83] Hank Hanegraaf, "Typological Fulfillment: The Key to Messianic Fulfillment," Christian Research Institute (8 March 2015/updated 10 August 2023), available online at https://www.equip.org/articles/typological-fulfillment-key-messianic-prophecy/, accessed 24 April 2024. Please note -- this will be the only reference to this article but if I reference anything to typological prophecy, I am citing this article.

A perfect example of this is found in the concluding verses of Hosea 11. Verses 8-11 is a loving lament for the Jewish people as they are while also being prophetic and future oriented. The words "How can I give you up, hand you over, turn you into Admah, treat you like Zeboiim…" are the words of God who loves his covenant people" (v. 8). These words remind me of the scene in the film *Notting Hill* when the character played by Julia Roberts is pleading with the Hugh Grant character to love her. Yes, it is a pathetically poor example, but it was the one that played in my mind when I read this verse. God loves the Jewish people and wants a relationship with them – THEN and NOW. We must remember biblical background in our interpretation of scripture as we interpret and make application.

As I close this section and as you have found something in common with me, I must close with a personal story. When I lived in Dallas, I would often attend sessions that were directed by an acquaintance friend of mine who was also the pastor of a Disciples of Christ church. He was much more conservative than 98% of most Disciples of Christ ministers, and he had also developed a friendship with Rabbi Chaim (not his real name).

Pastor Dennis and Rabbi Chaim would often hold open house discussions on various bible passages and I would often attend – sometimes to listen and sometimes to be a thorn in Rabbi Chaim's side. One time the rabbi decided to chide Christians for taking Hebrew passages and make Messianic prophecies out of them and he particularly pointed out Hos. 11:1 as one of those passages. I raised my hand and said to the rabbi that I did not believe that Hos. 11:1 was a good choice for a Messianic prophecy but I personally saw it as a Matthew using the verse as a Drash comparing the life of Jesus to the Exodus. Rabbi Chaim was stunned by my answer, which then allowed me to mention my three favorite and very clear Messianic prophecies – Psalm 22, Daniel 9:24-27, and Isaiah 53.

These favorite prophecies, which are the three that I always go to in my discussions with Jewish people, are incidentally from passages that are never read in the synagogue and are avoided by the rabbis because they are obviously Messianic. As a missionary to the Jewish people, I prefer to begin and/or start with the undeniable options instead of going to those that are questionable. I also believe this is a better choice for anyone who is interested in the work of missions and evangelism and something that I used to teach my students when I taught college. It is not our task to "win the war" in a debate with a lost person but to engage them in a Gospel discussion that will provoke them to jealousy for Jesus. For sometimes we are the seed planters, someone else comes along to water for it is God alone who gains the increase (1 Cor. 3:6-9).

8. Malachi: The Hebrew Scriptures Version of a "Come to Jesus" Message (Not Just For Stewardship Month)

Introduction

When I was a professor at a small Baptist college, there were two particular students that I am particularly proud to call my former students. One is a retired basketball player and one will never play basketball until he reaches the gates of Heaven. Each of these former students experienced what they would call a Downey "come to Jesus" meeting. Both of these students knew before the meeting occurred that it would not be pleasant but they also knew that I conducted those meetings because I loved them and wanted them to be more than they were at the moment.

The basketball player was a bright young man who thought he could "skate by" on his charm and athletic ability until he could find a team in Europe to continue his basketball career. I called him into my office after yet another less than stellar test score and told him to cut if out or I would fail him (BTW, my language while not cursing was not near as kind as you are reading). He began to give me all sorts of excuses and told me that it did not matter if he failed because he could always play basketball in Europe if not perhaps the D-League in the NBA. I decided to be brutally honest with him and said that while he was talented (and he was) that he had something going against him that would prevent him from playing professional basketball – he was six inches too short to ever go beyond playing for a small Christian college. He looked at me in shock because no one had been that blunt with him before. We continued to talk and he decided to get serious about his education. He graduated the next year, and his mom hugged me when he graduated! Today, he is a teacher and a basketball coach (but teacher first) at a high school in Texas. And I am proud of the man, husband, father, teacher, and coach that he has become.

My other student never played basketball for the college because he has been in a wheelchair for most of his life. He was born with Duchenne's Muscular Dystrophy that will eventually end his life as well, but he has outlived his life expectancy by about fifteen years. When I first met this student, he expected a great deal out of me. He knew that he was allowed to have allowances for tests because he could only take his tests orally but he did not know that I would not give him hints as he took those tests from me.

During the first test and on the very first question, he waited to see if there would be any inflection on the first true/false question. He waited and waited and waited. There was no inflection whereby he could discern the answer and then told me, "So … you are not going to help me with the answer?" I told him, "You are physically challenged. You are not mentally challenged." He looked at me with shock and awe and knew that I was going to treat him just like any other student. Well … I actually did not treat him as any other student because I knew he was capable of actually more than other students for he had a bright mind that was trapped in a body that would just not cooperate.

So … every time this student began to whine (and that is the word for it when he reads this chapter, for he will buy the book), I began a "Come to Jesus" discussion with him. He ended up taking several classes from me and **earned** either an A or a B in every class – even Business Math, which he absolutely hated. One of my proudest moments as a professor was when this student rolled across the stage to receive his diploma with honors. He looked at me and said, "Thank you." And while one day, this student will die before the rest of the students I have taught, I will finally have the last word because he has already asked me to deliver his eulogy.

This brings us to the Jewish people as the words of Malachi were about to be delivered to them. They were in need of a "Come to God" moment as well. They were back from Babylon, and they had grown somewhat lazy, as we will discover shortly in the background section. However, we overlook those passages and settle for what we presume to be the stewardship passages. There is so much more to Malachi than simply passages on giving before the 400 hundred years of silence – including the last prophecy of the Old Testament!

Who Malachi Was and a Little Biblical Background

The name Malachi only occurs once in Scripture. No one else has this name, and perhaps it is because the name has a weighty meaning to it. Malachi means "my messenger." Can you imagine what a load it had to be for Malachi to know that his name stated his responsibility – to be an emissary for God to the people? A people who, by this time period (c. 500-450 BC/BCE), had been back in the land for about a hundred to 150 years. Just enough time to begin to become complacent once again … and complacent they were becoming.

We also know nothing about who was Malachi the man. The fact that we know nothing about the identity of Malachi has caused a great deal of speculation including the idea that Malachi is a pen name for Ezra.[84] Other Rabbinic sources have argued that Malachi had to have been Mordechai the uncle/cousin of Queen Esther (aka Hadassah) for after the death of Haman he was raised to be second to the king of Persia.[85] Ultimately, we have no idea of who Malachi might be. It could have been Ezra but that is doubtful for why would he have used a *non de plume* when he was known to be a scribe? It is unlikely that it was Mordechai for he stayed in Persia and the events in question occurred in Israel proper. And, ultimately, we only need to know that it was a man who fulfilled his role as a messenger of God and delivered a difficult and timely message to the people who were doubting in their complacency?

There have been questions about who Malachi is. There have also been questions about the timing of when Malachi was written. A general understanding and one that I confirm is the date that I have already stated above – c. 500-450 BC/BCE.[86] We also know that the Jewish people have a temple restored to them in Jerusalem, as can be seen in the text.[87] However, the question that is repeated over and over again to them to God via Malachi – where are you in your relationship with the Creator of the Universe?

---

[84] Rashi was one of the two great Jewish scholars of the Middle Ages – the other being Maimonides of whom I wrote about in *Maimonides's Yahweh* published by Wipf & Stock (2019). While Maimonides' was more interested in analyzing and interpreting the Talmud, Rashi devoted a great deal of time to being a commentator on the Hebrew Scriptures. Rashi notes in his commentator's note on Mal. 2:11 the following statement – "Our sages said that Malachi is Ezra." For many, even today, if Rashi said it Ezra that was sufficient to believe it. Available at https://www.chabad.org/library/bible_cdo/aid/16220/showrashi/true/jewish/Chapter-2.htm, accessed 18 April 2024. See also, "Targum of Jonathan on Malachi 1," available at https://www.sefaria.org/Targum_Jonathan_on_Malachi.1.1?ven=Sefaria_Community_Translation&lang=bi, accessed 18 April 2024.

[85] *Babylon Talmud Megillah 15a*, Available online at https://www.sefaria.org/Megillah.15a.4?lang=bi, accessed 18 April 2024.

[86] Eugene H. Merrill, *Haggai, Zechariah, Malachi: An Exegetical Commentary* (Biblical Studies Press, 2003): 323-29 and David W. Baker, *Joel, Obadiah, Malachi: The New Application Commentary – from biblical text … contemporary life*, gen. ed. Terry Muck (Grand Rapids: Zondervan, 2006): 207-10.

[87] Merrill, *Haggai, Zechariah, Malachi*, 321 and Baker, *Joel, Obadiah, Malachi*, 207.

Theme of Malachi – Do You Really Want to Doubt God
After All That He Has Done for You?

Do you not just love rhetorical questions? Yes, I know that was itself a rhetorical question. However, and let us be honest for a second, rhetorical questions are tough. Often, it is tough to recognize those questions for what they are … rhetorical and not meant to be answered. You are tempted to answer them, but then you realize they are rhetorical. Or … you choose not to answer a question because you think that perhaps it is rhetorical, and then someone becomes angry at you because you did not answer their question. A person sometimes just cannot win when another person asks a question. Right?

The oracle/burden/pronouncement of Malachi is chock-full of rhetorical questions. Some of them come from God to the people, and shockingly enough, there are times when people have the nerve or "a lot of gall" to ask God what appears to be a rhetorical question.

The focus of these questions, as I have written earlier, seems to indicate a lack of complacency, a lack of satisfaction, and a lack of gratification for what God has done for them. Both Ezra and Nehemiah as builders and Haggai as a fellow prophet will also speak to this lack of motivation amongst the people. However, Malachi, as the last of the prophets before the years of silence begin, has the responsibility to share the message from God that, in essence, tells them – "Shake it off!" or "Wake up!" or even "Get over yourselves!"

The British Old Testament evangelical scholar Joyce Baldwin says it better than I could when she wrote that God was seeking to "keep faith alive in Israel" and "[f]ar from being legalistic Malachi has penetrated to the core of both the law and the prophets. His one great plea is for a personal relationship with living God, who seeks men to 'walk with Him.'"[88] For doubt and complacency cannot co-exist when people are walking and living in a personal relationship with God.

---

[88] Joyce G. Baldwin, *Haggai, Zechariah, Malachi: An Introduction & Commentary*, The Tyndale Old Testament Commentaries 24, gen. ed., D. J. Wiseman (Downers Grove, IL: IVP Press, 1972): 217-18.

And while it is not wrong to ask God questions, and that is, in fact, a part of having a living personal relationship with God – and a mainstay of Jewish life both then and now. David, Jeremiah, and Ezekiel are just three examples of individuals who asked God extremely difficult questions that Jehovah had no qualms about answering. Faith exists when we live in the tension not of complacency (or self-satisfaction) but of the tension that we must be pushed to a greater or deeper relationship with God. The people of Malachi's day do not appear to want this tension and/or relationship and the apparent outcome was a silence that none of us desire. Consequently, let us examine what we can learn from them so that we will not make the same mistakes that they made all those years ago.

Do You Actually Doubt God's Love? (1:2-5)

I feel as if I need to begin this section with a giant siren that screams out – "WARNING! CONTROVERSIAL TOPIC AHEAD!" I actually thought about skipping these verses and going to the next section – especially since it covers a large swath of verses (1:6-2:9), and I just did not know why. I just had an uneasy rumble in my stomach as I read these verses as I considered how to cover these four verses in both an exegetical and applicational way. However, I cannot avoid these verses especially since playing on the TV behind me are Ivy League college students protesting **for** Hamas/Hezbollah and **for** the Iranian bombing of Israel just a few days ago from when I am writing this chapter. So … WARNING! CONTROVERSIAL TOPIC AHEAD!

I am going to make a confession to you as a missionary to the Jewish people – I sometimes get frustrated. One of the most frustrating aspects of being a Jewish missionary is that I often have to defend being a missionary to the Jewish people. Does that surprise you? Actually, I hope it does. However, one of the most often accusations I have received is that I somehow believe that Jewish people are the only people group that matter in the world as far as it relates to missions and evangelism.

Nothing could be further from the truth. I could defend myself by pointing out that for years, I personally supported friends who were missionaries to Muslims until they left the field. I have given to Wycliffe on a regular basis, and today, I give to a Christian food pantry in Western New York that feeds migrants from all over the world. It will not matter for some people because there is the perception among some people that missionaries to the Jewish people only care about Jewish people. And so before we go any further, I want you to know that while I do believe in "to the Jew first," I also believe just as strongly in "and also to the Greek" (Rom. 1:16).

Why is there this perception among some people? Why is there a subtle but dangerous jealousy among many Christians and churches regarding the Jewish people? Jealousy that is not limited to non-evangelical churches but can also be found in many Bible-thumping churches as well. The reason is passages such as Mal. 1:2-5 (cf. Rom. 9:13-18) and the confusion as to what it actually means when God tells the Jewish people that they are loved because of Jacob but the descendants of Esau are hated (v. 3) and cursed forever (v. 4).

The answer is emotional, the answer is familial, and the answer is ultimately covenantal. Everything returns to the question of the word covenant in not only the Hebrew Scriptures but also the entire Word of God. The creator of the Universe chose one man named Abram (later to be known as Abraham) from whom he was going to create a people that would bring the Messiah to the world.

This covenant between God and Abraham and his descendants would bring light, hope, and Messiah Jesus to the world. And while this is something we have discussed briefly in other chapters; it is not something that can be discussed enough. The Abrahamic Covenant is the heart of where so much begins. What began with Abraham continued with Isaac (but not Ishmael) and then on to Jacob (but not Esau). This is not about the "hate" of others as we understand it in our sense of the word but about choosing and, dare we use the word "election" of the Jewish people.[89]

We have to remember that the Jewish people are the ones through whom salvation comes (John 4:22). We need to remember this irrefutable truth … Jesus is Jewish. It is not about favoritism. It is not about love vs. hate from the view of humanity but about God's love for the whole world in that he did choose a people group – the Jewish people – and they are loved. They are loved. The Jewish people were chosen so that we could be chosen as well.[90]

---

[89] Bartholomew and Thomas, *The Minor Prophets*, 303-304; Merrill, *Haggai, Zechariah, Malachi*, 339-42; Baldwin, *Haggai, Zechariah, Malachi*, 221-23; Baker, *Joel, Obadiah, Malachi*, 218-24; and Bullock, *An Introduction to the Old Testament Prophetic Books*, 339.

[90] Obviously, I do not hold to a position that the church and/or Jesus himself has replaced the Jewish people as the True Israel. Replacement Theology and/or Supersessionism as it is also called creates exegetical and interpretational issues with Scripture that as are indefensible in my view.

So, as you can hopefully see ... I am not a missionary who believes that only Jewish missions matter. This goes contrary to the Word of God. I believe that another concept that goes contrary to the mission mandate of the Great Commission is to ignore the Jewish people in the 21st century. Missions to all people groups must work together – including missions to the Jewish people – if we hope to reach the globe. This is something I believe. This is something I follow. This is something that Malachi was seeking to convey so as to wake the Jewish people out of their complacency.[91]

Do You Think God Is Not Paying Attention? (1:6-2:17)

One of my favorite biblical characters is Leah. I realize that mentioning the wife of Jacob in this setting might seem like a huge diversion, but give me a moment to make my point. I believe Leah is my favorite because I could identify with her when I was younger. As I mentioned in chapter three (Amos), I was a nerd and went through a difficult, awkward period – especially for a young girl. Thick glasses, braces, too smart for my own good, and the goody-two-shoes pastor's kid are not a good combination for anyone trying to fit into high school life.

So ... Leah was someone I could identify with Scripture. She was not Jacob's choice for a bride but was used by her father (Gen. 29:15-25) to become his first wife over her sister Rachel, whom he really loved. However, she was also used by Jacob (and I will not go into the graphic detail as revealed in the Hebrew) to be a child-bearer for him simply (Gen. 29:26-35). However, and in the middle of this sad story of Leah's life, someone saw Leah and paid attention to her and that God himself (Gen. 29. 31). The verse says – "When Jehovah **saw** that Leah was unloved/hated, he opened her womb..." The word is better translated as "hated" than unloved, but even worse than how it reads is that it is a passive participle or an adjective. So ... we could also translate this verse as "When Jehovah saw that she was hated, **Leah**,..."

Wow, that is all I can say. But ... God saw her and gave her what she most needed in life to make her life, for lack of a better word – bearable or even endurable. And it is out of this same passage, even though Leah backslides in the next passage, that Leah begins to be able to praise Jehovah as she realizes that while Jacob may never love her, God does see her after she gives birth to Judah – through whom the Messiah will descend.

---

[91] Amy Karen Downey, "X + Gospel = World Evangelization," *Occasional Bulletin* (Spring 2009): 5-8, available online at https://www.emsweb.org/wp-content/uploads/2020/11/OB_Spring_2009.pdf, accessed 18 April 2024.

Now for my connecting point from Leah to Malachi (and even the one I have learned) – God always pays attention to those He loves and chooses as his people/his own. Leah was the mother of Judah, through whom Messiah would descend from many generations later. Malachi's burden/oracle was to inform the people that he was still paying attention to them and that he was not happy. And even for the teenage Amy Karen … life was going to get better one day as the braces would come off, nerdy people would one day be appreciated, and even if one is still called to be single, God is more than enough. Now … let us examine the passage in more detail.

Yes, these verses begin with God talking to the people (specifically the priestly class) about the idea of respect/honor and defiled sacrifices and the fact that the priests were just as guilty as the people. The verses are very straightforward and graphic in their description of how God feels about their lackluster obedience. If in doubt, the idea of fecal matter being spread all about one's face should grab the attention of the reader in 2:6. All I can write in that graphic visualization is … one simple word, and that is "ugh."

However, I would like for us to look at the essence of what God is asking with the questions about respect/honor and defiled sacrifices – the core being that God does pay attention to every aspect of the approaches that we take toward our relationship to him. He cares about our attitude of and reverence toward worship (1:6-14). He is especially concerned when those who have been given a special charge, such as the Levitical priests in Malachi, fail to lead the people towards godly living properly and instead direct them to things that God hates (2:1-17).

God Pays Attention to Our Worship Towards Him (1:6-14)

Do you remember the years known as the "Worship Wars"? This period in the late 1990s and early 2000s divided many people, churches, and even seminaries. In fact, I remember the worship group at my seminary (deep in the heart of Southern Baptist Texas) was disbanded after the president's wife at the time was offended by the idea of a worship song that we would one day "dance before Jesus" or even "in awe of him be still."[92] Our seminary's chapel returned to those good old Stamps-Baxter hymns – including some that I personally find doctrinally weak.

Even today, almost twenty years later after Worship Wars I ended, the battle is flaring up again as many leaders of a certain doctrinal stripe are stating emphatically that only songs written by Asaph and his sons, Solomon and David (i.e., Psalms) are biblical. Yet, I truly wonder whether the issue of electric guitars and drums or pianos and pipe organs is only of major concern to God as it relates to worship. In fact, and during the height of Worship Wars I, Barna conducted one of their research surveys and concluded something truly profound:

---

[92] Bart Millard, "I Can Only Imagine," *Almost There* Album (2003).

The major challenge ... is not about how to use music to facilitate worship as much as it is about helping people understand worship and have an intense passion for connecting with God. Citing various findings from three recent nationwide surveys he directed on the issue, Barna noted that relatively few churches have intense musical battles, but most churches have too few people who truly engage God in worship.[93]

I think this is also what God was saying through Malachi to the priests in 1:6-14. They were offering defiled food on the altar. They were offering blind and lame sacrifices to the King of the Universe. Food and sacrifices that they would not dare to offer to their leaders. Their worship was considered as nothing but despicable to God and they thought nothing of it.

God's priests were less passionate about him, and this trickled down to the people of God. The priests were living out an example that was saying "how tiresome it is" to worship God (v. 13), and so were the people in the offerings they were bringing to the Temple. And my question today is – are we doing any better, whether the churches are small or large? Are we engaging the people or entertaining them? Are we bringing them to the throne room to worship, whether we engage in three hymns and the offering on Sunday morning or blast their eardrums out with the volumes "set to eleven" (my ode to This Is Spinal Tap mention)? Do we have a Green Room for the worship band, or do we even care if the songs match the focus of the sermon?

I must tell you that the world cares about these minute issues when they put something together to reach the world with their message, whether it be millions of dollars or millions of minutes. They fine-tune to the smallest of details so that their false message reaches the maximum number of people. Do we?

I remember one of my favorite people and seminary professors, Calvin Miller, cared. From his profound works such as *The Singer Trilogy* to the time he spent with us in class and afterward, Calvin Miller emphasized that we should devote everything we have to make even the smallest act of worship to be one of the most profound moments of our lives.[94]

---

[93] Barna Group, "Focus on 'Worship Wars' Hides the Real Issues Regarding Connection to God," 19 November 2002, available online at https://www.barna.com/research/focus-on-worship-wars-hides-the-real-issues-regarding-connection-to-god/, accessed 21 April 2024.

[94] Calvin Miller, *Into the Depths of God: Where Eyes See the Invisible, Ears Hear the Inaudible, and Minds Conceive the Inconceivable* (Minneapolis: Bethany House Publishers, 2000): 40. Miller wrote this short statement that sees it best – "Bare faith treasures God, for all other values are to be seen only nakedness and poverty."

God himself said what he required for worship as well in Mal. 1:11 -- *For from the rising of the sun even to its setting my name great among the nations [Ani Shem Gadol b'ha goyim] and in every place incense is going to be offered to my name and a pure grain offering for my great name among the nations says Jehovah Sabaoth.* If we cannot lift up God's name among the nations – in whatever way we need – then we are not worshipping God. Regardless of how many hands are raised ... and God's approval is the only vote that matters.

God Pays Attention to the Leaders He Calls (2:1-17)

I mentioned in chapter one (Jonah) that Luke 9:62 is a verse that terrifies me. The idea of committing to Christian service and then breaking a promise to God was one of the reasons that I took so long to commit to my mission call. Those words – "putting my hand to the plow and then looking back" – fill me with fear every time I see those red letters, whether they are on my iPad or in my original KJV version that my parents gave me so many years ago.

And while we have a great migration of people leaving Christian service, as has already been discussed (again in chapter one), there is a greater problem that is threatening to overwhelm American churches and mission organizations. The crisis is one that parallels what is found in Malachi 2, and that is sin in the priesthood – and I am not talking solely about Roman Catholic priests.[95] The scandal is cross-denominational and cross-missional and includes my own Baptist denominations as well.[96] However, the reality of sin in the clergy is personal for me, and it involves one of my seminary friends Stan (not his real name).

---

[95] This link is a re-release of the *Boston Globe* article that launched the investigation into the Roman Catholic priesthood here in the United States. Please note that there could be a firewall issue -- https://www.boston.com/news/local-news/2015/11/03/read-the-first-globe-spotlight-article-that-helped-expose-the-catholic-church-scandal-in-2002/.

[96] Robert Downen and John Tedesco of the *Houston Chronicle* and the *San Antonio Express-News* engaged in several articles detailing the issue of clergy abuse in the Southern Abuse Convention. This link -- https://www.houstonchronicle.com/news/investigations/abuse-of-faith/ -- will take any reader to the whole series and additional articles as well. The Fort Worth Star-Telegram examined the Independent Fundamental Baptist world -- https://www.star-telegram.com/topics/fundamental-baptist-abuse. Julie Roys, former host on the Moody Network, examines evangelical abuse from an all-encompassing perspective – https://julieroys.com/about-the-roys-report/.

Everyone at Southwestern Baptist Theological Seminary knew Stan. He was, if it was possible, to have this moniker at a seminary, the unofficial Big Man on Campus (BMOC). He was single, and all the other single seminary guys flocked to him. He was a cowboy, and many of the single women on campus liked cowboys. Stan and I were just friends as I have never been into cowboys and C&W music, but I trusted him enough to even recommend him to my dad as a revival speaker at his church.

Eventually, Stan started a cowboy church and married another cowboy girl; however, that is when the trouble and rumors started. One of the youth in his church reported to the police that Stan touched him inappropriately and asked him to touch him as well. Then there was another report to the police, and soon Stan was in court when he pled guilty and is now on the Sex Offender Registry for life.

Everyone from our seminary days was stunned, offended, and horrified. How could Stan do this to us who could not imagine this was possible? How could he do this to the honor of Southwestern? But most of all … how could Stan do this as a pastor to God and to those young men who trusted, needed, and believed in him? Yet, every day there are reports of more and more men and women like Stan who disgrace the calling of God upon their lives and damage men, women, and children in ways – physical and spiritual – that will last for years, if not for eternity. And it is this damage that I believe that we need to consider in more detail, whether one is in full-time service or is an Awana leader or Sunday School teacher, as we look at Malachi 2:1-17.

We begin in verse 2 with the promise to the priests of Malachi day that there will be and there is already a curse from God awaiting them. A rebuke so disgusting (v. 3) that you can read it for yourself because Jehovah was wanting to grab their attention because they needed to revere his name (v. 5). The reason for this attention grabbing was because they belonged to a special covenant but not one that was unconditional and that should grab our attention as well.

For while the Abrahamic covenant is unconditional, the Levitical was not (v. 4). It depended upon him walking in peace and uprightness and encouraging many to turn back from iniquity (v. 6). Think about this idea for a moment and seek to make an application for us today. Do we employ that concept in our ministry (whether full-time or laity) – walking in peace, seeking uprightness/justice, and calling for repentance? It was/is a heavy burden, but Jam. 3:1 reminds us of what is expected of us (v. 7) – For the lips of a priest should preserve knowledge, *and they (the people) should seek Torah from his mouth for he is the messenger of Jehovah Sabaoth* (author's translation).

143

However, and in verse 8, the priests of Malachi's day have done the exact opposite of what verse 7 requires of them. There is a word in verse 8 that can be translated as path, way, journey, or road. It is the word *derekh* in Hebrew and it is the same idea of when Jesus said in John 14:6 that he was the WAY or when the first believers were called the followers of The WAY (Acts 9:1-2) that so infuriated a certain member of the Sanhedrin named Saul.

Derekh is a special word in Hebrew because it shows that people are focused on God alone, and these priests have actually abandoned (better translation in v. 8) the Jewish people from following the derekh and caused many to stumble away from the Torah (i.e., Word of God). The future Paul thought believers in Jesus were guilty of the same sin as the priests of Mal. 2:8, and that is why he attacked the believers until he became one himself later on in Acts 9. Then he became just as diligent of a guardian of the truth of Messiah Jesus and the true WAY, and that is what we must also do – whether we are laity or engaged in full-time Christian service.

However, we are also failing in another way, just as the priests of Malachi's day did. We are not guarding what should be the most cherished of our institutions: the home. Ezra discussed this sin of the priesthood, and so did Malachi (perhaps another reason some speculate for Ezra's authorship). Regardless of who the author of Malachi was, the sin of divorce in the priesthood was a prevalent sin in Malachi's day, and so it is in our days as well (v 15-17).[97] It is recognized that there are times when divorce is unavoidable and inevitable. However, and when divorce is because of sin on the part of the one in full-time service, the stain cannot be erased or ignored.[98]

Yes, Luke 9:62 still terrifies me, as does Mal. 3:1-7 and Jam. 3:1. I never want to be guilty of failing God in my mission calling. The idea of "FAILING GOD" makes me hold my breath at times. However, this does not mean that I do not experience anxiety or struggle with depression for I do. This section is not about a person who struggles or needs a Christian counselor (for I have one) or even a psychiatrist but about a person who flippantly disregards the calling that an almighty God places on their life. The priests of Malachi's days did not care that they were failing and we seemingly have members of the "clergy class" today who do not care as well.

---

[97] There are competing statistics on the issue of clergy divorce and so links for both views (10% -- Barna and 38% -- ChurchLeadership.Org) are being provided. However, and regardless of whether it is 10% or as high as 38% the number is too high. Both accessed on 22 April 2024 – https://www.barna.com/research/healthy-pastors-relationships/ and http://www.churchleadership.org/apps/articles/default.asp?articleid=42347&columnid=4545.

[98] David Wesley Reid, "Healing for the Divorced Pastor: How Can a Pastor Recover from the Impact of Divorce?," *Ministry: International Journal for Pastors* (November 1995), available online at https://www.ministrymagazine.org/archive/1995/11/healing-for-the-divorced-pastor, accessed 22 April 2024.

They are leading people astray spiritually. They are leading people astray emotionally with physical and sexual abuse. They are leading people astray via financial abuse as well, but that is a whole other chapter, book, and sermon. And this abuse must be confronted by those of us – including laity but especially by those of us who call it our profession. For if not, God will hold us accountable as well.

The Ultimate (and Final) "Come to Jesus" Message of the Hebrew Scriptures (3:1-4:6)

Before anyone gets far into this section and wonders – does the author believe in tithing? <u>I believe in tithing and I do so off the gross (not the net). I even round up!</u> My Scriptural basis for tithing is not because of Mal. 3:10 but because of Abram's gift to Melchizedek in Gen. 14:18-20. However, and since I believe Melchizedek is a type (or theophany) of Jesus, it fits into this passage as well. Please keep reading and it will all be explained to you shortly.

Perhaps you have heard that when the Scriptures say, "Therefore," stop and ask what it is there for. This is not a bad saying, and even though I ended a sentence with a dangling preposition, which I loathe doing, I will even say it is a good hermeneutical concept. There is another word that should grab our attention in Scripture and make us stop and wonder what is going on in the passage. The word is "Behold (*Hineni*)!" You can almost be assured that the word is an interjection and is meant to grab your attention.

The "Behold!" in Mal. 3:1 is definitely an attention-grabbing moment in scripture, and it carries us to the end of the prophecy. In fact, the Jewish Bible version does not have chapter four but continues on with chapter three, and 4:6 is 3:24 in their version. I actually believe they have a point with their numbering of the verses, and by the end of this section, perhaps you will agree with me.

The focus of 3:1 is the arrival of the coming of the messenger who will prepare the way for the arrival of Jehovah, who will suddenly come to the temple. The following verses (v. 2-7) relate to the arrival of God and the overwhelming power and refining glory of His coming, along with the judgment for those who have done evil. The judgment list in verse 5 includes the sorcerers, adulterers, liars, oppressors/exploiters of the wage earners and widows/orphans, abusers of the alien/stranger, and those who do not fear God.

Wow … verse 5 opens up a can of worms does it not? Perhaps most people would agree on judging the first three and taking care of widows/orphans, but the question of wage earners might cause some people to raise the question about the minimum wage. And today, whenever one sees the word "alien," then we have a whole boatload of opinions, and no one ends up happy. Yes, we could spill a great deal of ink regarding just who belongs to each category and we do need to debate this issue because God does care about each of these people groups – and not just in an election year. However, I am going to err on the side of caution and ask every one of you to read verses 6-7 and remind you that the Jewish people were deposed to Babylon not only because they worshipped false gods but also because they failed to do what verse 5 instructed.

Which brings us to the tithing verses (v. 8-12), or does it? The people are accused of robbing God because they have not brought all the tithes into the storehouse and then promised if they will only do what is commanded that, they will be blessed beyond measure. This is all about giving that 10% to the church every time you receive your paycheck … right? **Or is it?**

Let me write this again – I believe we should tithe. Let us give, at a very minimum, a tenth of what God has given to us, but not as a test of God and whether he will bless us. I believe we should tithe because we want to thank God for his bountiful gifts to us. He gave us the ability to have the job we have, and from my perspective, all that we have actually belongs to him. Our giving of a tenth (tithe) is simply a thank you for allowing us to have anything at all. Old Testament scholar Hassell Bullock saw the original command in this section as a way of repenting for being ungrateful in Malachi's time.[99] I believe that Bullock has a point in his perspective because we are so often ungrateful for the abilities that God has given us to have and keep the job. We too frequently believe that it is our talents that landed the position and not God who made it possible. This is why Paul told us to give with a grateful heart (2 Cor. 9:7).

Additionally, the whole context of the passage (3:1-4:6) deals with the coming of the messenger and Jehovah himself. To stop and deal in isolation with the subject of tithing outside of the context does not fit with the verses. Therefore, what do these verses mean in the entire flow of the passage – **Behold! The messenger is coming! Be prepared and get ready!**

---

[99] Bullock, *An Introduction to the Old Testament Prophetic Books*, 341.

This is obvious by what is found in 3:16 through the rest of the prophecy of Malachi. They are promised that they will belong to Jehovah Sabaoth (v. 17). Because and BEHOLD! (4:1), we have the announcement of the final prophecy of the Hebrew scriptures (4:5-6). Elijah will come to announce the coming of the great and terrible(?) day of Jehovah. Terrible? A better word than "terrible" for *yare* is "astonishing" or "awe-inspiring" or "reverent," and that is how we should see this day that John the Baptist described in John 1:29 when he looked up, saw Jesus walking towards him, and said the word of the day – "BEHOLD, the Lamb of God who comes to take away the sins of the world."

As I close this chapter, I remember one Christmas a few years ago when my sister, my niece, my mama, and I went to Branson, Missouri, to see "Miracle of Christmas" at Sight & Sound Theatre. The live animals were exciting. The actors were very good. The story was lovely. However, I began to simply weep at one particular song because it described the blindness of my people group not at Christmas but at Passover.

Every year at Passover, there will be a place setting for Elijah at the Passover meal because they know the last prophecy given in the Hebrew Scriptures was Mal. 4:5-6 (or 3:23-24 in their numbering). They set a place at the table for Elijah because they know that the Messiah is to come at Passover and the prophet (messenger) will come first to announce his coming. Right before the conclusion of the meal, the youngest child will go to the door to see if Elijah has come to announce that the Messiah has arrived this year, but every year ... no Elijah because they do not realize that John 1:29 was first for them and then for the rest of the world (Rom. 1:16).

And that is why the song "We Need a Savior" at Sight & Sound's Christmas performance will always make me weep. Here are a sampling of the words:

> *"How long, O Lord?...*
> *Does Yahweh hear me in my anguished prayer?...*
> *We need a Savior. We need a Savior. How we long for our Messiah...*
> *Heal our nation. Restore the wasted years."*

The Jewish people and the world need a Messiah because of how Malachi closes his prophecy (4:6): *He will cause the hearts of the fathers to be restored to (the) children and the hearts of the children to their fathers so that I come not (and) cause the land to be struck with a curse.* Indeed, the world needs the Messiah, and how will they hear unless we tell (Rom. 10)?

Section Five:
Before the Fall – Facing Ugly Truths
Micah and Habakkuk

It is never easy to be the bearer of bad news. I once had to tell a baseball coach that some of his best baseball players were not going to be playing for the rest of the season because they had been caught plagiarizing. I did not enjoy telling him this news. A few weeks later, the academic dean of the college informed me that my contract was not going to be renewed even though he had not been told why by the president. The dean did not enjoy telling me that news either – even though we both knew the reason.

Micah and Habakkuk were forced to share bad news as prophets of God that they did not enjoy sharing with the people. Yet, everyone knew the reason for the bad news that these two prophets had to share. The ugly truth was that both kingdoms – both the Southern Kingdom (Judah) and the Northern Kingdom (Samaria) had drifted far away from the covenant requirements that had been given to them by God through Moses and Joshua. They had drifted into idol worship, floated into biblical injustice towards the least of the citizens of the Chosen People, and their sacrifices wafted with aromas that stank in the nostrils of God.

Micah is divided in his prophetic book, and you can see it in his prophetic words. The chapters that we will be examining go back and forth between hope and despair. Micah knows the people of God deserve the punishment that is awaiting them, but he is also one of them, and he wants God to give them mercy despite what is coming. The greatest hope of all is found in Micah 5:2 but it cannot be read without the reality of all that is coming in the other seven chapters of the prophet as well.

Habakkuk is a frustrated prophet. He is angry at God for the evil that is coming at people that he does not even want to name, but he knows that he is allowed to voice this anger as well. We find the prophet struggling with why God would allow heathen countries to triumph over God's chosen people. We also find the prophet struggling with why he is being forced to share the vision with the people.

Micah and Habakkuk often represent us in this world today. God often asks us to do things that we do not want to do. God often asks us to share a message to people that they do not want to hear and that we do not want to pronounce – because it will make US the unpopular ones. Perhaps this is the reason why these two prophets are hardly ever read except for one Christmas prophecy and the final verse of Habakkuk. However, there is so much more to these two men than two verses if we are only brave enough to read them.

9. Micah: The Internal Struggle of the Prophet Micah

Introduction

I know for me the smell of Christmas cookies and my mama's cornbread dressing fresh out of the oven are the some of the things I miss most from the holidays of my childhood. I also remember a certain Christmas when the Salvation Army kettle and its bell represented the gift of Christmas love in ways more profound than anything else than I can ever describe aside from my own salvation. I also suspect that when many think of the prophetic book of Micah, thoughts most probably go to the smells and sounds of Christmas. Do they not?

People probably think of the little town called Bethlehem, which is mere miles from Jerusalem. I imagine that many people begin to think of "Silent Night, Holy Night" and all being calm and all being bright on that blessed Christmas morn. How could they not? Most sermons preached by Micah only occur during the Christmas season and only begin and end in the fifth chapter. The sermon speaking about this insignificant town and how Bethlehem will be the site of the most significant birth of a child in the history of the world stirs us all during those Advent mornings or during Christmas Eve services.

However, has anyone heard a sermon or had a small group Bible study devoted to Micah 3:2-3 with these words – ***You who hate good and love evil who tear off their skin from them and their flesh from their bones; who eat the flesh of my people, cause their skin to be stripped off them, break their bones, and chop (them) up as for the pot and as meat in a kettle.*** It is probably difficult to find songs for the worship time when Micah 3:2-3 is the passage. It is likely tough to find just the right backgrounds for those PowerPoints that we all love to use nowadays. What pastor wants to greet his parishioners after preaching a sermon that includes this passage? Yet these words are also found in Micah and they deserve our consideration and examination for they have a message we need to hear and apply in our lives.

Who Micah Was and a Little Biblical Background

So ... who was this Micah who could share with the people one of the most well-known Messianic prophecies in the Christian church but also write verses that are, to pardon the pun, so difficult to digest as Micah 3:2-3?[100] Again, like many of the so-called minor prophets, what is known is determined by what is not said as much as what is said in 1:1 of the book.

---

[100] I noted that Micah 5:2 (5:1 in the Hebrew numbering system) is well-known in the Christian church; however, it is not as well known in the Rabbinic Jewish world because it is not read in the synagogue during their Haftorah portion (scripture readings of the prophets) ever. The rationale for not including certain passages such as Micah 5:1, Psalm 22, Isaiah 53, the entire book of Daniel which has been redesignated as poetry, and other prophecy-rich passages is that it does not fit with the focus of the Torah portion of the week. However, I would argue that there is another purpose for avoiding such overt Messianic passages.

We can establish that Micah prophesied before the fall of the Northern Kingdom (Samaria) in 712 BC/BCE based on the naming of the kings in verse 1. Micah lists three kings of Judah – Jotham, Ahaz, and Hezekiah – and so his ministry spanned roughly a time period of 50 or so years (c. 742-687 BC/BCE). Jotham (2 Kgs. 15:32-38) was reported to be a godly king, but he did not remove the altars from the high places. His son Ahaz was evil (2 Kgs. 16:1-20), and even he sacrificed one of his sons to the false gods of the Canaanites. Ahaz's son Hezekiah is the most well-known of the three kings during Micah's prophetic phase, and he was one of Judah's most godly kings (2 Kgs. 18:1-20:21). However, his pride cost Judah (2 Kgs. 20:12-21; Isaiah 39:1-8) for as Isaiah prophesied the kingdom would fall to Babylon because of his desire to show off the wealth of Israel.

Micah's name means "who is like God," which, in its own way, is a burden to bear. However, and interestingly, the descriptor of his prophecy is not called an oracle or a burden but simply the "word of Jehovah" that "which he saw." The prophecy for the man from Moresheth was for both Samaria and Jerusalem, but what do we know about Micah's hometown of Moresheth, which lay in the Southern kingdom of Judah? The answer is very little, except that it was close to the larger village of Gath, where Goliath's most famous resident was. Moresheth was a tiny dot on a map from whom the prophet Micah was born. Today … you cannot locate Moresheth on a map even though archaeologists suspect they have found the ancient city or relative locale in the Valley of Elah.[101]

Theme of Micah – God Is Consistent Even Though Humanity Is Not

I have entitled this chapter, "The Internal Struggle of the Prophet Micah," and I believe the theme reflects this internal struggle as well. In the introduction to this work, I wrote that Micah is able to see both the immediate and the distant future – a future of horrendous difficulties brought about by their own actions and a miraculous and hopeful future because God will not forget his covenant people. While one might be tempted to quote that classic line from *A Tale of Two Cities* by Charles Dickens here, we should not because God is not Louis XVI, and the Jewish people are not the revolutionaries in this story.

---

[101] Nathan Steinmeyer, "Has the Home of the Prophet Micah Been Found: Study Identifies Azekah as the Mysterious Moresheth-Gath,?" *Biblical Archaeology Society* (9 October 2023), available online at https://www.biblicalarchaeology.org/daily/ancient-cultures/ancient-israel/home-of-the-prophet-micah/, accessed 24 April 2024.

Therefore, Micah's prophetic scroll of judgment and mercy, justice and grace, and sin and hope provides for all of us reading a rolling theme that despite humanity's actions, God is consistent in requiring obedience and, dare I write, holiness. The Jewish people had abandoned much of the pretense of following God's desire for justice and holiness in their daily work. Consequently, he had no choice but to extend the hand of judgment that they deserved as his covenant people.

Unjust Actions – Just Results (Specific Verses in Micah)

Aside from Micah 6:6-15 which will have its own section, this section will examine the issue of Micah's notations of injustice in one complete section (and this does include the stomach-churning verses of 3:2-3 which were mentioned in the introduction). The issue of biblical justice does matter greatly to God. And if I may use this term in reference to God, I would say that it is a personal affront when people are guilty of the sin of injustice. The people of Samaria (North Kingdom) and of Judah (Southern Kingdom) were guilty of treating the "lesser" in society badly, and God was about to bring what was due to them through Assyria and ultimately through Babylon.

Micah begins the declaration that God was not happy with their actions very early in his prophecy – 1:2. Micah begins with the word "Hear," which is a very important word in the Hebrew Scriptures. In fact, the most important prayer in Rabbinic Judaism today is the *Shema* from Dt. 6:4 and it begins with the word "Hear" as well. However, and what is missed in the uttering of the *Shema* and when we look at verse 2 today is that the word "Hear" is in its command form (Qal Imperative). God is commanding the people to **pay attention** to what he has to say to them in 1:2 and it does not get more pleasant from there.

Verse 2-4 goes on to tell the people that Jehovah Adonai (actually could be translated as "Jehovah Jehovah") is going to be the witness **against** them and the failures they have committed. Why is God going to come down and be the Star Witness against them? It is because of the rebellion of Samaria and the sins of Judah (v. 5). Many translations use the word transgressions instead of rebellion for the Hebrew word *pesha*; however, I believe the word "rebellion" hits closer to home for what the Northern Kingdom was doing.

For it is one issue to commit transgressions but the actions of Samaria had been rebellious for years. The best example that I can use to illustrate this further is when you see a child at Walmart who wants a candy bar. The parents say no. The child asks again. The parent says no. The child asks again and then we watch the back and forth again. The transgression began when the child asked the second time because the parent said … "No." Rebellion happens, and we have all been witness to such an event, usually because they are the ones in front of us in line when the child begins to throw a tantrum. After all, she believes that yelling, crying, and making everyone within a 50-foot radius uncomfortable by the scene. Samaria, or the Northern Kingdom, had long moved past the transgression stage with God and were living in Rebellion Town by the time Micah began his prophetic warnings to the people.

I will return to some key verses (v. 9, 16) in chapter one in the concluding thoughts on this section. However, let us begin to examine some of the crimes of injustice that the people of God were guilty of in the time of Micah. The first one that Micah mentions is found in 2:1-2, 9, and it begins with the interjection of Woe!

Micah, speaking on behalf of God, is appalled (Woe!) at the actions of verse two – coveting land, seizing property by violence, robbing a man of his home and inheritance, and oppressing (could also be translated as defrauding) people – because those actions were planned upon their beds. We also find in verse nine that defenseless women were being evicted from their homes, and their children were taken from them – presumably into servitude.[102]

This idea of planning such evil actions "upon their beds" gives one the sense that Martin Luther saw it as their fixation to make others destitute and miserable.[103] To add to Luther's thought, one could see it as something that they enjoyed doing – it was almost as if we could armchair diagnose them as a sociopathic desire to take something that belonged to someone else. If so, this is not just sinful but truly malevolent. This malicious behavior is why Micah wrote in verse six that when their judgment came (and it was coming), even if they wanted to speak up in their defense, the only ones who had the right were the ones who had been abused for "dishonor will not be turned back."

The second example of God responding to acts of injustice can be found in 3:1-7, and again, Micah begins with the command from God to "**Hear Now!**" However, he also includes a very important rhetorical question in verse 1 – "Is it not for you to know justice?" For if anyone in the Middle Eastern world of this time should understand the concept of justice, the Jewish people, whether they lived in Samaria or Judah, had been privy to God working out the scales of justice more times than anyone.

---

102 Luther, *Luther's Works*, 226.
103 Ibid., 222-23.

However, verses 2a tell us that they hate what is good and love what is evil (opposite of the command given to the churches in Rome – 12:9). We then are confronted with a descriptor that is obviously difficult to read, but why was it included in the introduction? If to be taken literally, the rulers of Samaria and Judah actually were cannibals. However, I was able to find a very old commentary by the founder of my seminary, B. H. Carroll, who dared to deal specifically with these verses, and he, ironically enough, an account from the French Revolution (i.e., *A Tale of Two Cities* setting) to argue that it was more of a comparative illustration of how the Jewish poor were made to feel as if they were nothing but food to their leaders.[104] Carroll's position can be further justified when one could perceive that they are more interested in war than peace. A point justified by Scripture itself when one reads the accounts of the kings of Samaria and Judah, who often went to war unnecessarily and heedlessly, and the poor were often the first casualties of those wars.

This is why God refuses to answer the cries of the leaders (v. 4, 6-7), even though Micah has been commissioned (v. 8) to call out the sins of these nations. A call that has been invigorated because Micah has been filled with the power and the spirit of God and with justice and courage. A call that we should also petition to God to have the honor of bearing as well. For we live in a society that hates what is good and loves what is evil and I do not have to provide a litany of examples for you to see the truth of this statement. We live in a society in which the physical needs of the poor are ignored so that a few can become richer than they were yesterday. We live in a world that cries out for peace but seemingly looks for excuses to destroy the weak around the world if it means more oil, more diamonds, or more sneakers on our feet. The only question is whether we have the courage to cry out against these injustices so that we have the credibility to cry out with the truth of the Gospel of Messiah Jesus.

However, and tragically, Micah repeats the mantra or refrain that these injustices do not only occur at the governmental or power-hungry level. They also happen within the houses of worship (3:11). Priests and prophets who will say whatever the people want to hear if the money keeps coming into the coffers, and this is an evil that has continued on through to the 21st century (Tit. 1: 10, 11; 2 Pet. 2:1-3, 14-15). We also need to speak against those individuals as well – whether they be our pastor or the one who spouts drivel from the TV screen. For we must not allow the mournful verse of 7:2 to be truth in today's world – "The godly person has perished from the land, ***and there is no one upright among them (for) all of them lie in wait for bloodshed (and) each of them hunts the other with a net.***"

---

104 B. H. Carroll, *The Prophets of the Assyrian Period* (vol. 7), An Interpretation of the English Bible, comp. and ed. J. W. Crowder (Nashville, TN: Broadman Press, 1948): 289.

The final example begins in 7:3 with almost a repeat of 3:11, but then Micah adds the ominous phrase – "so they weave/scheme it together." The verb is in the Piel form, which gives us a sense of intentionality and evil machinations or purpose. The evil of Micah's grew only worse in verses 5-6 because there can be no trust among friends, neighbors, and/or family members – "a man's enemies are the men of his own household." A warning that Jesus himself gave to us in his discipleship chapter in Matt. 10 (v. 21, 35, 36). Micah was telling the people of his time, and we can make an application for today as well, that people will hate not only what is good but also the truth, for you are to "guard your lips" against such people.

This was why judgment awaited Samaria and Judah. They had lost their sense of truth, of goodness, of a love for justice and compassion, and for what is right. This is why Micah was instructed to tell them that destruction awaited them (1:6, 9) and that they should prepare for the ritual act of mourning because their children would be exiled from them (1:16). And we, as believers in Jesus and churches are not exempt from this same condemnation for we as well have lost our sense of truth and goodness. We often look to politicians to answer our problems rather than seek a love for what is right so that we may engage in justice and compassion for those less fortunate than ourselves. We donate to political campaigns rather than mission funds and then wonder why the world continues to grow more evil with each passing day. Are we not guilty of the same sins as the people of Micah's days? If so, should we not prepare ourselves for the same judgment? However, please keep reading to the end of the chapter because there is hope for those who choose a different path than the one we are currently walking…

Only One God Can Truly Administer Justice (4:1-5:1)

In today's world, justice is a tough word for many people to define. Asking three people will result in a multitude of definitions. People want justice to be fair if it relates to them but not if it relates to someone they disagree with on an issue. People want justice to be impartial, but is that even possible with very flawed humans seeking to administer the word justice? People want justice to be honest, and so should we; however, modern American justice can be skewed so easily depending on who can afford the best attorneys or how the evidence is presented or not presented at all.[105] Yet, we find in Micah 4:1-5:1 the essence of truth, justice, and God's way because God himself is the one administering the justice.

Isaiah 2:2-4 and Micah 4:1-3 share a biblical passage in common. In today's world, such obvious commonalities would result in questions of plagiarism and wondering who wrote which passage first – especially since they prophesied at the same time. However, we cannot ask them since they are not here ... but it does not prevent some from asking the question. However, I believe John Goldingay said it best when he wrote that since it was written down twice in scripture, it must be important.[106]

It will come about in the last days that the mountain of the house of Jehovah will be established as/on the chief of the mountains; it will be raised above the hills, and the people will stream to it. Many nations will come and say, "Come and let us go up to the mountain of Jehovah and to the house of Elohim of Jacob that he may have cause to teach us (Hiphil Imperfect) *about his ways/path and that we may walk in his ways. For from Zion will go forth the Torah – even the word of Jehovah from Jerusalem – and he will administer justice between many peoples and have to cause to decide on the mighty distant nations* (Hiphil Imperfect). *Then they will break into pieces their swords into plowshares and their spears into pruning*

---

[105] Since 1961, 182 death row prisoners were exonerated or ultimately acquitted from the crime that placed them on death row in America – 94 were African-American and 69 of the 182 were white. Additionally, according to a report by the U.S. Department of Justice in 2021 (https://bjs.ojp.gov/content/pub/pdf/cp20st.pdf), African Americans make up 41% of all individuals on death row even though they only comprise 13.5% of the U.S. population. See also, Phillip Morris, "Sentenced to Death, but Innocent: These Are Stories of Justice Gone Wrong," *National Geographic* (18 February 2021), available online at https://www.nationalgeographic.com/history/article/sentenced-to-death-but-innocent-these-are-stories-of-justice-gone-wrong, accessed 26 April 2024.

[106] Goldingay, *The Lost Letters to the Twelve Prophets*, 128; Gaebelein, *Daniel to Malachi* (vol. 5), 182; Carroll, *The Prophets of the Assyrian Period* (vol. 7), 292-93; and Rick Byargeon, "The Relationship of Micah 4:1-3 and Isaiah 2:2-4: Implications for Understanding the Prophetic Message," *Southwestern Journal of Theology* vol. 46, no. 1 (Fall 2003): 23-25.

hooks; nations will not lift up sword against nation and never again will they train for war. (Micah 2:1-3; author's translation)[107]

It is important and it is also prophetic of a future time when not only have the Jewish people returned to the land but also the nations as a whole seek out the lessons which God wants to teach the world. Obviously, this has not happened in a holistic or complete manner. The Jewish people returned to the land in 586 BC/BCE and then were expelled again twice in AD/CE 70 and 135 before returning again in 1948. When Jesus walked the earth, many Gentiles (i.e., people from other nations) came and believed, but not the Jewish people as a whole. Most of the world today has heard or is in the process of hearing the Gospel, but again, all components of verse 2 have not yet been fulfilled. This must be a future-oriented prophecy that is still to come.

Incidentally, this is why many Jewish people decline to believe in Jesus as Messiah. It is because they cannot separate first coming prophecies from second coming ones. Or and this has been more likely the case over the centuries, they have chosen to ignore the prophecies which relate to the fact that the Messiah must come first as a Suffering Servant. However, and the missing prophecies in the Jewish liturgy is perhaps a subject for another book, the reality is that one day God will come and bring the people together to worship him alone and that is the point of Micah's (and Isaiah's) prophecy.[108] The next verses of this passage (v. 4-8) relate how everyone – Jew, Gentile, disabled, and the outcasts – will join together in this kingdom, which shall never end. They will learn the Word of God (specifically mentioned here as the Torah) from God himself. This was to offer hope to a people who were afraid because of their present circumstances (v. 9-10a) because the Messiah is coming (v. 10b-5:1). However, his coming will be quite unexpected and in any way that they were (and still are) expecting.

The Bethlehem Prophecy (5:2-5a)

If you have been to Israel today, whether it be on a tour or on your own, you know that one of the places many desire to visit is Bethlehem – the birthplace of Messiah Jesus. I have been to Israel four times in the last fourteen years, but I have only been to Bethlehem once, and that was my first time when I was on a tour with about 50 other people from churches in my community. Bethlehem today is in the Palestinian Authority/West Bank, and it is very difficult to get into Bethlehem and out of the city because of the necessary checkpoints.

---

[107] Go to the Addendum Section of Ch. 12 to see the explanation as to why the author noted the Hiphil imperfect in these verses.

[108] Byargeon, "The Relationship of Micah 4:1-3 and Isaiah 2:2-4," 23-25.

158

It is not that I am reluctant to go into the West Bank as I have a dear friend who lives in the West Bank and I celebrated my birthday there on the eve of Rosh Hashanah in 2013. There is a Palestinian man named George (not his real name) who I would trust with my life if I needed a ride to the airport from Jerusalem to Tel Aviv. George is a Palestinian Christian, and his heart for Jesus is as great as that of anyone you might know. I have friendships with many Arab people, and I know the situation there is exceptionally complicated, even if I believe Israel has a right to their homeland.

I honestly just do not enjoy going to Bethlehem because of the spiritual darkness I believe you could find within the Church of the Nativity. This is my opinion only, and many might have a different perspective, but I did not enjoy my visit. During my visit, I would have rather gone out into the hillside near Bethlehem and imagined what it must have been like to be a shepherd who was blessed and startled to hear that amazing news.

Perhaps this is because I enjoy viewing historical landmarks in their basic and most intense forms. I love to walk the grounds of a historical site and imagine who also walked and perhaps who was born and/or died there. So … as I merge my experience in modern Bethlehem and the Micah 5:2-5a passage, I must imagine what it was like then as an insignificant village and not the centerpiece of political and emotional trauma that it has become.

For Bethlehem in the days of silence since Malachi was a dirt spot in the road on the way to Jerusalem. The phrase, "if you blinked twice, you would have missed it," would have perfectly described Bethlehem in Micah's day and the days of the birth of Jesus. Bethlehem Ephrathah ("House of Fruitful Bread"), which was once the birthplace of King David, will be home to a greater king whose historical roots are not historical at all … but eternal.

For it is time to go deeper into the Micah 5:2 prophecy than just Messiah's birthplace that is found in the first part of verse two. Let us continue to look at the whole context of this prophecy, which tells us so much more. The phrase in 5:2b is often translated as "his goings forth are from long ago," which simply does not tell the whole story even though it is a perfectly good translation. A more Hebraic understanding would be to say, "his going forth are from before time" for the word that is translated as *qedem,* which is also the Hebrew word for east.

We can see then that the Messiah's "goings forth" are from the East, which has a much deeper meaning in the Middle East than it does here. The east is, for lack of a better way of expressing it, where time began because that is the direction from which the sun appears. This idea is validated by the next clause, which affirms that the Messiah is from the days of eternity. The Messiah is before time and beyond time itself.

This is key because, within Judaism today, the Messiah is seen as a man who will be born, live, and die.[109] But ... Micah 5:2 tells us that he is so much more. Additionally, in verses 3-5a, we see that the actions of the Messiah are not a once-for-all event but a progression. We have his birth, and then "the remainder of his brethren will return to the sons of Israel," or after the Messiah's birth, the entire family of Messiah (i.e., the Jewish people) will return to the land. In verse 4, we see another **then** "**he will arise and shepherd in the strength of Jehovah**," so we can **follow the progression ultimately to** the moment in which the Messiah sits down with Jehovah Elohim because **now** is the time for the Messiah to be magnified (Phil. 2:5-11). For the Messiah is the epitome of peace (v. 5a).

This story of Messiah's birth, which is humble but ends glorious, can be no one else based solely on the biblical evidence alone but Jesus of Nazareth. The sequence, the Hebraic evidence of his deity and divinity, and the role Messiah plays with God the Father indicates no one else but Jesus. The odds alone are astronomical. It could be anyone else, especially considering the reactions of the priests in Jerusalem (Matt. 2:5-6) as well as Herod.[110]

However, this wonderful prophecy should not be taken in isolation from the whole message of Micah. The promise of Messiah is that the people were incapable of doing what was necessary to satisfy God's requirement of perfection. The truth of the Messiah is that we cannot save ourselves, but Jesus did. The hope of Messiah is that we were and are in a hopeless condition without him.

What Does God Want from His People? (6:6-8)

As I was sitting down to write this chapter, I had a completely different outline charted out on my notes. I was going to write a whole section on the "Case Against the Chosen People of God" (5:10-6:5). It was going to be an overview of these verses, which are a recitation of how God protected them in Egypt and throughout the wilderness period – including the whole Balaam and Balak scenario. It was going to include the litany of punishments that they were going to experience and deserve because God is, after all, a just God. The litany of punishments that would include both the first deportation to Babylon and the deportation they did not know yet was to come – the Roman deportation in AD/CE 70 and 135.

---

[109] This is a common knowledge idea within Judaism itself. However, and as I have already cited, my dissertation was on the life of Maimonides who devoted to demoting the true essence of the Messiah.

[110] Bullock, *An Introduction to the Old Testament Prophetic Books*, 120-21.

However, I decided to go straight to the core of what was missing in the core of the Jewish people during God's time, and that is a kernel of compassion towards those who need to know from his chosen ones what compassion meant in a compassionless time. Therefore, we are headed straight to one of those favorite verses that people pull out of Micah but do not quite understand, which is Micah 6:8. However before we can examine verse 8, we must consider the admonition of verses 6-7.

One of the first things we must ask is who is talking in verses 6-7. Is it God through Micah being sarcastic? No. Is it Micah asking God what he wants of the people? No. The most probable answer is that the people have decided to answer God with what can only be called sarcasm… something I would not dare to do.[111] In these two verses, we see an elevation from simple to extreme of proposed offerings to God – from bowing down to God to offering thousands of rams to sacrificing their firstborn in order to satisfy God.

Obviously, this is not what God desires. However, before we examine what he does want, perhaps we should consider whether we are not guilty of this same effort (whether engaging in sarcasm or not) of trying to elevate our giving but not elevating our hearts. The best way I can illustrate what I am trying to ask you to consider is to use my own church as an example.

I love my church here in Western New York. We have moved from one location to another, and I joined the church when we were meeting in a storefront property that had Alcoholics Anonymous that would often meet on the floor above us and a Polish grocery store next door to us. Finally, the doors were open to allow us to begin leasing a church building because the previous church that had met there decided it was time to merge with another church because they had declined so much in attendance. My church now has space for a fellowship hall and Sunday School classes when we grow to that point. We were even able to have our first VBS last summer because of the new space God had opened up to us.

The building where we are now meeting has a wonderful history that dates back to approximately the Civil War, and there is a cemetery behind the church with tombstones dating back to the 1840s. The worship center has stained glass windows with the names of individuals who lived and died more than 150 years ago. And while there is nothing wrong with putting one's name on a stained-glass window that one donates, I cannot help but think, however, about who were they honoring with their names on the glass – God or themselves? Only God knows, and perhaps I am being judgmental for even asking the question, but it is one I still ask.

---

[111] Carroll, *Prophets of the Assyrian Period* (vol. 7), 298 and Bartholomew and Thomas, *The Minor Prophets*, 192.

161

God tells them he does not want sacrifices or (especially child) but requires of them three simple things – to do justice, to love loyalty, mercy, and/or kindness; and to walk humbly with your God. They sound simple, right … but are they? **First**, how do we "do justice" when we do not even really understand what justice is in our fallen state? The idea of the word in Hebrew finds its definition in its root word of *shaphat* – to judge or govern. God was asking them and we should take this to heart as well as whether we are we judging and/or governing well?

Maybe I do not want to ask this question right now, for as I am typing, the United States is in the heart of Election 2024. Democrats are against Republicans and Republicans are against Democrats. Everyone is suspicious of Robert Kennedy, Jr., and his independent run for the presidency and absolutely no one is approving of the Congress right now. However, we still need to ask the question – are we governing or judging well?

Are we holding everyone to the same standard regardless of their wealth or social status? Do we care for those who cannot care for themselves? Do we hurt when the widows and orphans hurt? Do we love the unlovable? Do we share the Gospel with those who are homeless, those who are drug addicts, and those who are prostitutes as quickly as we would those who comfortably middle or upper middle-class? These, I believe, are the heart of God's command to do justice. If you cannot say that you do, are you doing justice as God would require of us?

Another requirement is **secondly** to love loyalty, kindness and/or mercy? How is that shown to satisfy God's conditions? One could argue that if you are seeking to "do justice," then the second requirement is much easier than one might realize. For if you choose to treat others as yourself (i.e., judge/govern), then loving others is easy as well.

My mama has Matt. 5:8 etched on her side of the tombstone that she shares with daddy (Pro. 29:18 on his side). My sister and I chose this verse because mama who was not perfect truly was one person who was pure in heart. She loved to be kind. She extended mercy even when I thought it was unnecessary and she was the most loyal person you could ever imagine. However, the greatest gift she ever gave to me was the one she gave two days before she died in June 2020.

Mama knew she was dying. We all knew she was dying. She did not have COVID, but her diverticulitis had finally become something that was outside of human control. Two surgeries in six weeks had not helped the situation but only left her weak and ready to go home to Heaven. When she began to bleed internally and the third surgery that was proposed was nothing something that any of us wanted for mama to have to face. She chose to forgo the surgery and prepare herself and her daughters for what would happen when she was not here.

We had almost a week to hold her hand and to bring her home so she could die in the bed that was hers and not a hospital bed. Hospice was amazing and one nurse even came to mama's service but mama wanted "her girls" beside her. The last night that she was fully conscious, she took separate time with my sister and me to tell us how proud she was to be our mother and that she hoped she had been as good of a mother as we had been daughters. In our special time with mama, she hugged us both, told us how much she loved us, and did what she could to get us ready for life without her. I remember holding her hand for what seemed like forever and just leaning my head on her shoulder like I had always done when I was tired, sick, or just hurting.

I tell this story because to me this is the perfect illustration of seeking "to love loyalty and kindness and mercy." She was not my grandmother, her mother. She was the woman who never knew unconditional love until she married my dad and lived out unconditional love to her very last breath.

Consequently, when you seek to do those first two steps, you are able to walk humbly with God because it is as easy as breathing. Barbara Downey loved many (or lived out "to do justice") who might be considered "the unlovable" from the first time she and my dad worked in the worst part of Louisville, Kentucky, in 1973 on church bus routes. Loving and hugging and sharing Jesus to the children of prostitutes and gang members because they did not know what a mother's hug was before my mama gave them one. Loving her daughters so much that she put aside her pain two nights before she died to make sure that our pain of losing her was lessened – even though her entire life as a mom was devoted to unconditional love. She walked with God and now is walking with him face-to-face.

Final Promise of Hope (7:7, 18-20)

At the United Nations, there is a powerful statue of a man beating his swords into plowshare as is mentioned in Isaiah 2 but also as we know the words of the prophet Micah. Ironically, and something I only found out as I decided to use this illustration in this final section, the UN statue was a gift from the Soviet Union in 1959.[112] The Communist sculptor Evgeniy Vuchetich created an austere but beautiful piece of work that is supposed to symbolize the words of Isaiah/Micah but means nothing in today's world. No swords have been beaten into plowshares. Peace is not breaking out in the world but the globe is falling into pieces because they are looking to each other and not the Sar Shalom, the prince of peace, Messiah Jesus.

---

[112] Description and illustration of the sculpture are available online at https://www.un.org/ungifts/let-us-beat-swords-ploughshares. Accessed 26 April 2024.

Yet, Micah closes his prophetic scroll with the promise and hope of true peace. We need only to watch and wait for God (v. 7). For as verse 18 reminds us, there is no one who is like God (Mi KaMocha) who is able to pardon our sins and move on past the rebellion/transgressions of his covenant heritage. Who is like God, who can choose to let go of his anger because he delights in and truly defines what mercy and loyalty are (v. 18)?

The final two verses of chapter seven relate directly to the Jewish people, the covenant people of God (v. 20b). The promise of sins being forgiven because (and this is key) truth will be given to Jacob (v. 20a). As will be brought to fuller light in the Zechariah chapter, the Jewish people will be given truth, but it is still up to them to accept it. There is no special dispensation (pardon the loaded theological word) that allows for any person or people to gain approval from God unless they hear and receive the truth of Messiah Jesus.

I know that these verses could be read in a universalistic bent if one chooses to read them that way. Certain pseudo-theological conservative groups hold more to Dual Covenantalism (two covenants that allow for the Jewish people to avoid acknowledging Jesus as Messiah) than to concrete Biblical truths. This would certainly make the work of missionaries much easier – would it not? However, it is one thing to "give truth" and another thing to receive truth. It is for those who receive the gift of truth that have the promise of all that is offered in verses 19-20. And so whether you are a professional or laity but you are engaged daily in the work of evangelism, you still have a job to do. Yes, there is hope, but that eternal hope for any of us is only possible because of the child who was born in Bethlehem Ephrathah.

10. Habakkuk: The Prophet Who Struggled with God's Plan and Dared to Tell Him About It

Introduction

When I was a professor at the small Baptist college in Texas, my view on education that it was my responsibility to teach my students how to think and not what to think. Yes, I provided them with the indisputable facts that they needed to be informed citizens of the world. However, I also sought to give them the analytical tools they needed to know what to do with those facts. For example, it is one thing to know from history that "In 1492, Columbus sailed the ocean blue" as the old rhyme goes.

This is an indisputable fact but they also needed to know that Columbus was not the first to discover the "New World" but that the Vikings were a century or two earlier and that the world Columbus discovered was one by accident. They also then need to know why Columbus set sail. Columbus was attempting to find a shorter route to India and no one knew there was an entire continent (or two) in the way – which is the only ONE of the reasons for the WHY he was on the journey.

However, the students also need to be able to analyze WHAT are the long-term results of Columbus' journey from an economic, social, and religious perspective. Yes, the danger of analyzing facts is that we can get bogged down into a quagmire – especially if the professor has an agenda of any perspective – but we are doing students a disfavor if they are not taken to that next level. Today's students can be taught how to think if we trust them enough with real truth. I actually do believe that to be true.

All of that background to tell you a story of something that I challenged my Speech students with every semester. For I was a renaissance teacher for the college in that I was known to teach English I, Speech Communications, American History, American/State Government and Business Math all in the same semester! At a certain point in the semester, I would insert a section on Christian apologetics because I really wanted to teach apologetics and not business math(!). During this section on defending the Christian faith in our public speaking, I would ask the students a rhetorical question – "Have you ever been angry at God?"

The students were always stunned by the question because they were not supposed to raise their hands to the question – but I could tell by their faces who would have raised their hands if they had been allowed. I then told them the story of when I had been incredibly angry at God – angry to the point that I yelled and screamed at him in frustration. I then told the students that it was allowed to be honest about this emotion because God is God enough to handle our feelings and reactions but ... we then have to allow him to respond to us. I also told the students that we must avoid the temptation to stay in our anger or it will consume us.

The faces of the students when I finished with my account of being angry at God were one of relief because I had given voice to their emotions and their fear that they had done something wrong and set them free. For God is "big enough" to handle our anger at him. In fact, God allowed Habakkuk not just one time to voice his frustration at the situation he saw around him but two moments and they are recorded in the Word of God. Is not God amazing that not only did he allow Habakkuk to question him but also told the prophet to write it down for the ages?

Who Habakkuk Was and a Little Biblical Background

How can one not feel sorry for Habakkuk? Most people do not realize that his prophecy is in the Bible. Many might confuse him with King Hezekiah and begin looking for Hezekiah instead of his book in scripture. Finally, there is the issue of how does one pronounce his name?

I have heard people pronounce it so that the final syllable sounds like "uh." I have others pronounce his name so that one wonders if someone is about to "cook" something for dinner. It is probably the latter pronunciation, but I do not know if it really matters at this point as long as you read this important prophecy. What I do believe is important is that you know the meaning of his name which goes back to the Hebrew root word of *chabaq* that gives us the idea of embracing, hugging or to clasp. Therefore, Habakkuk was the prophet who embraced, which, as we go along in this chapter, takes on greater meaning than it might now.

Habakkuk was a prophet in the Southern Kingdom (Judah). We do not know where he came from, who his father was, what he might have done for a living except be a prophet, as Amos provided for us, or who the kings were during his prophetic period. It is also difficult to know with any sense of certainty the time period that Habakkuk prophesied.

We can only have a general sense of the time – before Judah fell to Babylon in 586 BC/BCE – as Habakkuk laments the coming of the Babylonians and not their arrival.[113] We can perhaps narrow it down slightly as 586 BC/BCE was their final attack on the land as they took a large group (including Daniel and his friends) to Babylon around 606 BC/BCE, so we can assume Habakkuk wrote his prophecy before then as well.[114] Therefore, dating Habakkuk is anyone's guess, but I would say it was before the expulsion group that included Daniel in c. 606 BC/BCE.

---

[113] Bartholomew and Thomas, *The Minor Prophets*, 224. This book gives a range of 620 to 587; however, I believe the final date is too late based on what we find in the words of Habakkuk.

[114] Gaebelein, *Daniel to Malachi* (vol. 5), 10.

Theme of Habakkuk – The Hebrew Scriptures "Answers" the Question of Why Is There Evil in the World?

How many have you heard this from someone who claims to be an atheist and/or an agnostic – "If there is a God, why is there evil in the world?" First, I think this is a cheesy question. Yes, I just wrote the phrase "cheesy question" because they are wanting to blame the God who they are denying or questioning if he exists for evil in the world. Second, by putting all the blame on a God who they claim does not exist, they are refusing to acknowledge any of the responsibility for the existence of evil in the world.

A much better and more accurate question is simply, "Why is there evil in the world?" This is, in essence, theodicy. Theodicy can be defined as understanding God in the face of evil, and I have attempted to answer this question since my first master's thesis in 1996.

I will not bore anyone with the long title of the thesis, but it basically sought to examine how the Jewish people viewed God in light of the Holocaust through the writings of that period and slightly after. I looked at poems, songs, diaries, biographies, and almost anything that one can imagine and tried to answer the question that is so difficult to answer. I do know that for many months after I graduated with my MAComm from Southwestern Seminary, I was haunted by the questions and the words that I had read from predominantly Jewish people who never had their questions answered in this world.

I could not sleep, and if I did, my dreams were filled with Holocaust imagery. My mama (yes, another mama story) knew I was struggling, and even though I was 26 years old at the time, it grounded me from reading or watching anything to do with the Holocaust for six months. My mama was very wise, and this gave me time to heal from the words I had absorbed and the questions that filled my mind.

Yet, Habakkuk was not as lucky as I was. He saw what was coming. He knew the evil that awaited Judah and perhaps even awaited him when the Babylonians arrived. This led to one of the overarching questions of his prophecy – do the good have to suffer as well as the evil? And is this not one of our questions today? When COVID was attacking millions around the world, was that not a secret thought that many of us had? When we see someone we love stricken with cancer, do we not have the question of why he and/or her? Yet … evil in all its forms attacks the good and the bad among us. And we are left just as Habakkuk was with the question of why?

How Long Is This Going to Last? (1:2-4)

Do any of you remember when COVID first hit the United States and we were told to isolate and the phrase was "two weeks to curb the spread." We know that it was far, far longer than two weeks. It felt like it was never going to end but it did and we now are many months away from the lack of toilet paper, the lack of being able to connect with each other, and entirely too many Zoom meetings.

I would never mock those months in 2020 and 2021 as I lost friends to COVID. I had one of my best friends from college almost die from COVID-19 and is still suffering from the effects of it. I also question whether any of us will ever recover from the loneliness that we all experienced. Yet, despite all that the world has experienced, I would imagine that Habakkuk would look at us and say you have no understanding of what it is to suffer from the devastating impact of evil. And honestly … he would not be wrong.

Habakkuk begins his oracle (1:2) with a profoundly simple question – *"How long, Jehovah, will I call for and you do not hear?"* We have all been there, and if we are honest, we have all asked that question. How long and do you hear us? This is a gut-wrenching question that describes for many of us where we are personally and as the world seemingly is falling apart around us.

As I am writing this chapter, the war between Israel and Hamas has exceeded six months, and college campuses in America are exploding with protests that defy explanation, and I want to ask "how long" as well. Habakkuk describes a world in which he is surrounded by violence, iniquity, and wickedness, just for starters (v. 2b-3). However, the prophet devotes his greatest concern (v. 4) to the fact that the Torah (often translated as "law") is ignored and no one is concerned about the issue of justice.

And this leads me to remind all of us about how many times the issue of justice has been an issue for discussion in the minor prophets. Obviously, it is true by now that God cares about being just and caring about being right before him. For when the love of the Torah (i.e., Scripture) grows weak, justice for all grows cold and perverse. And the righteous will feel as if they are surrounded. This is the substance of Habakkuk's first complaint, and we have all been there. We have all uttered some version of **"It's not fair, God!"** My only question is, have we listened when God responded?

God's First Response – Watch and Be Amazed! (1:5-11)

God's first response to Habakkuk basically was not something that he wanted to hear or anything we would want to hear either. The exact statement in v. 5b is *"Indeed, I am preparing to do something in your days—(that) believe or not (even) if it was made known (to you)."* The believe it or not moment is that the Babylonians are coming and it is going to get worse.

Talk about a punch to the stomach moment. The air must have been sucked out of Habakkuk's lungs at that moment. However, God continued by listing all the strengths of the Babylonians – fast horses, warped view of justice, love violence, collect hostages for fun, and laugh about the pain of others (v. 6-11). Just when it could not get worse … it went from bad to horrible in a nanosecond. And I do not know about you but if I were Habakkuk, I would have had my mouth open and looking up at Heaven going, "WHAT? WHY? HUH?," all the same time. For just in reading the words of God, much less hearing the words directly – does it feel as if God did not listen to what Habakkuk was saying?

But … he did even if we or Habakkuk did not realize it at that particular moment. And that is the hardest thing about being at the bottom of the valley and feeling as if God has forgotten or perhaps even enjoying our pain – because let's admit it to ourselves if no one else. Have we not wondered if God is punishing us for something that we did not realize that we had done? Have we not asked ourselves if God is unfair while not realizing that our pain was for a greater purpose that might be decades away from even the possibility of understanding it?

My dad died on July 4th 2000 at the age of 66. He had been through a very difficult pastorate in Texas and had moved to a new church in Oklahoma where he truly hoped that he could find some peace. Mama and daddy both needed some time together to just heal from the East Texas church that had just battered them needlessly after they had stood up to sins in the church and had been asked to leave because of it.

However, and unbeknownst to all of us, there was a slow-leaking aneurysm in my dad's lower intestines and the stress of the last year had only made it worse. Daddy's final Sunday morning sermon on July 2nd of that year was about the ultimate Independence Day that believers would one day experience in Heaven – but only for those who had a relationship with Messiah Jesus. His final sermon was from Jeremiah about the potter and how we need to be willing to be molded into the image that God knows is best for us. Talk about foreshadowing…

At 3:48 a.m. on July 4th, I received the call that told me my daddy was gone. He had been struggling all day with pains but thought it was just a stomachache and had fallen asleep in his recliner. He woke up and made it to the bedroom before he fell and died beside the woman he had loved for 39 years.

My grief for the next year was almost overwhelming. I struggled to watch my mama lose her "knight in shining armor." Mama had to build a life without Daddy for herself and start over again. I had lost my best friend in all the world when that phone rang and I could not understand WHY God would take someone as good as daddy from this world when the world needed him so much. By the way, I had just begun my work as a missionary in New York City to the Jewish people and I had to carry on even while in the midst of my overwhelming grief and worry about my mama. Luke 9:62 and my promise to God was at the forefront of my mind even while I cried almost every night for my daddy, my best friend, my spiritual rock in this life.

It took me almost a year to realize that my grief was allowed. Grief is a part of the process of saying goodbye to those we love. Grief is not allowed, and there is no timetable for how long we hurt for those we have lost. And while I will never get over missing daddy (and mama), I have been able to help people in their grieving process. I have been able to be "that person" who helps people when they first experience such a profound loss. This was my purpose and I believe we all have our own purpose that we can find if only we will try to find it. Habakkuk was not there in chapter one but by the time we get to chapter three … we will discover that Habakkuk learns to find the "silver lining perhaps not" but the lining of hope.

But God … Why Do the "Good" Suffer? (1:12-2:1)

I have to admit that I have never read the book that I am going to mention in this introduction but I do know the motivation behind its writer so I feel comfortable discussing it. In 1981, Rabbi Harold Kushner wrote *When Bad Things Happen to Good People* in response to his son Aaron's diagnosis with progeria – the genetic condition that causes children to age rapidly and often die before they are two (per Mayo Clinic). In this book, Rabbi Kushner concluded that God is limited in his ability to stop tragedies from happening to humanity.[115]

One can only grieve deeply with and for the rabbi and even to an extent understand why he wanted to come to this conclusion. Watching a child die is something I cannot fathom and would never wish upon anyone. It should be noted that I affirm the rabbi's right to ask the questions he asked in the morass of his grief. However, the rabbi was wrong in the conclusion that God cannot control the tragedies that happen. God's omnipotence is a cornerstone reality of who he was and is. This is why Habakkuk's questions are very understandable and appropriate as we shall see…

---

[115] Ben Harris and Philissa Kramer, "Rabbi Harold Kushner, Who Wrote Bestselling Works of Practical Theology, Dies at 88," *Religion News Service/Jewish Telegraph Agency* (29 April 2023), available online at https://religionnews.com/2023/04/29/rabbi-harold-kushner-whose-works-of-practical-theology-were-best-sellers-dies-at-88/, accessed 28 April 2024.

Habakkuk acknowledges God's omnipotence and eternality (v. 12) while also bringing up the covenant promise that the Jewish people had with him – but here are "the Babylonians" who are being allowed to judge "us." Additionally, have you noticed how Habakkuk will not even name the Babylonians but instead uses the pronoun "they" throughout this section?[116] It is like, and this is my own understanding of the section, that the prophet cannot even force himself to name them because he does not understand why God is allowing this to happen.[117]

Habakkuk knows God's character but he still wants to ask the questions that we often all want to ask – WHY? and ARE YOU SURE? This is why in 2:1 we see this confused man of God basically saying that I am not moving from where I am and I am going make my stand until I hear from you.[118] And there is nothing wrong with this attitude. In fact, perhaps our prayer lives should be more like this with God – especially as Habakkuk states that he knows that God will speak to him and that he will be reprimanded and/or reproached and/or punished for these questions. But he wants or needs these answers and God understood. Rabbi Kushner might have found more healing answers – and perhaps even Messiah Jesus – if only he had followed Habakkuk's path as well.

But God ... Who Can Hit Softest? (2:2-20)

Did you ever play this game with your brothers and/or sisters when you were young – "Who Could Hit Softest?" If not, you did not grow up in the 1970s and suffer through endless car trips to West Texas, where there was nothing to do except worry that your sister was stealing your oxygen if she got too close to your side of the backseat. Anyway, the goal of "Who Could Hit Softest" was basically a game of chicken as each person would try to "hit softer" on the other's arm than the other person until someone decided to break down and wallop your sister and then shout out, "You win!" while the other person rubs the bruise. Everyone knows how the game is going to win but no one knows who is going to do it first so everyone flinches every single time. By the way, I never lost this game.

Can you not imagine Habakkuk basically flinching after he calls out to God in 2:1 that he was not moving until he heard from him? I can just see the prophet flinching and waiting for God to "wallop" him big time but ... the hit never came. Instead, Habakkuk received the answers that he needed to hear even if they were not the answers he wanted to hear.

---

[116] Perhaps your Bible translation, such as the NASB or the CSB, has *The Chaldeans* in italics. It is in italics because it is not in the original text and was added to make for a smoother translation.

[117] Bartholomew and Thomas, *The Minor Prophets*, 226.

[118] Ibid., 227.

God begins in 2:2 with two command (imperative) verbs – Record (the vision) and inscribe/write (on tablets) so that anyone who reads it "may run." In other words, spread the news because while it may take a while (v. 3), what I have prophesied will indeed happen. And, yes, God is aware of the sinful nature of those people, but "the righteous will live by his faith." This does not mean that bad things will not happen but it does mean that they can be assured in the sole trustworthiness of God. This is why Paul mentioned Hab. 2:4 in Rom. 1:17. This is what led Martin Luther to discover the true meaning of faith and ultimately to nail those 95 Theses to the door of the Wittenburg Church in 1517. The sole trustworthiness of God (i.e., absolute faith) will see us through regardless of our visible circumstances.

Yes, God knew how evil the Babylonians were and he was merely using them as a tool to get the Jewish people's attention – something he often does to us as well today. He begins verse 4 by telling Habakkuk that the coming invaders have a soul that is just not right and then spends several verses pronouncing WOE(s) upon the Babylonians.

- Woe – for their thievery
- Woe – for their covetousness
- Woe – for their malicious violence
- Woe – for their sexual sinfulness
- Woe – for their worship of idols[119]

The WOE(s) that God pronounces against Babylon will be their death knell eventually and even though Habakkuk will never see that moment. God wants the prophet to know that sinfulness will never go unpunished – especially when it is committed against his covenant people. This is the power of verse 20 and how God rests his case against Habakkuk and ultimately against those who claim that God is too small for the evil that is in the world today.

I admit that I need to read Rabbi Kushner's book. However, I have read Corrie ten Boom's *The Hiding Place*, which tells the story of Corrie and her Dutch Reformed Christian family who, at great risk to themselves, protected and hid Dutch Jews during the Holocaust. Her family was arrested in February 1944 for this heroic action that many European Christians refused to undertake. By the end of the war, Corrie lost her father, sister, and brother in the camps and she herself spent several months at Ravensbrück and was only released due to a clerical error on 28 December 1944.

---

[119] Bullock, *An Introduction to the Old Testament Prophetic Books*, 180-81.

The Hiding Place tells the story of both the efforts to protect Dutch Jews as well as the time that she and her sister Betsie spent under arrest and at Ravensbrück. Upon their arrival at the notorious camp, they sought to smuggle a Bible into the camp but were unsure how that could be done. They were able to sneak the Bible past the initial inspection, and upon their arrival at their barracks, they found it overcome with fleas. The fleas were so numerous that the camp guards would not even go past the doors into the barracks.

Consequently, the Bible was never taken away and was used by Betsie (who died 16 December 1944) and Corrie as an evangelistic tool in the middle of what could only be described as hellish. No, God never did take away the fleas from the barracks, and the sisters struggled against the flea bites constantly, but they had the word of God with them every day. The women who were with them in the barracks – many of whom were political prisoners and criminals – were able to hear the Gospel that they never would have heard without those fleas and without that Bible. After Corrie was released due to a clerical error, those same women in the flea-ridden barracks were gassed sometime in January 1945.[120] The ten Boom sisters along with their father Casper (1859-1944) were named as Righteous among the Nations by the Holocaust Museum in Israel, Yad Vashem (https://collections.yadvashem.org/en/righteous/4014036).

The story of the ten Boom family reminds me of Habakkuk. If you have read her autobiography, you will agree with me that Betsie was the more spiritual of the two sisters. Corrie was the one with the questions for God. She could not understand why this was all happening to them – especially once they arrived at Ravensbrück. Corrie, like Habakkuk, wanted answers and needed them at times. It was Betsie, as we read in the book, who told her that "there is no pit so deep that God is not deeper still." And yet, it was Corrie who survived and not Betsie. Perhaps it was because God knew that it was he needed the sister who struggled with faith and belief to tell his story … just like he needed Habakkuk. And perhaps why God needs you.

Habakkuk's Response of Prayer and Praise (3:1-16)

There are two musical terms in Habakkuk that are often overlooked when we read Habakkuk's response to God's answer and they should not be ignored. These terms are the words – *Shigionoth* (v. 1) and *Selah* (v. 2, 9, and 13). The word *Shigionoth* in Hebrew technically means an aberration, a rambling poem, or a dithyramb. And since probably all of us know what a dithyramb is except for me, according to Vocabulary.com, a dithyramb is "a speech or piece of writing that bursts with enthusiasm." This means that basically, Habakkuk was so filled with emotion by God's answer to him that his emotions and feelings were all over the place.

---

[120] Corrie ten Boom, *The Hiding Place* (New York: Bantam Books, 1974).

The word *Selah* is the idea of a pause and/or a rest when singing. However, it is more than just a rest like you often hear in music. It is the idea of taking a breath before a giant moment of exultation or interjection. The only way I can illustrate this is to mention the final moments of Handel's *Messiah* – and the moment right before the final Hallelujah is sung there is that large moment of pause to fill the audience with anticipation – that is *Selah.*

Habakkuk knows the Babylonians are still coming (v.16) and it will be a horrific day, but … he can still plead for revival (v. 2). The prophet can do so because God's glory covers the heavens, and his power can devastate the earth (v. 3b-15). Habakkuk goes into amazing details of God's omnipotence, omniscience, and omnipresence because while verse 16 is an inevitability, God is still God.

Interestingly, and as I was writing this paragraph, the story of Job came to mind because he also struggled with the question of suffering, evil, and the nature of why with God. Job never received an answer to his questions. Habakkuk did. Job's fortunes were restored, but Judah was decimated by the Babylonians. Yet, God will always be the King of the Universe, and this is the focus of verses 17-19 as the prophet closes his prophetic message.

Hinds Feet on High Places … the Real Story (3:17-19)

Many have heard about or read *Hinds Feet on High Places*, written by Hannah Hurnard and based on Habakkuk 3:19, which was first published by Tyndale House in 1955. The book, which was an allegory much in the vein of *Pilgrim's Progress* by John Bunyan, tells the story of Much Afraid's effort to find faith despite her disabilities. The allegorical story has a great deal in common with Hurnard's own life of growing up in a Quaker family and of struggling with self-doubt, a stutter, and thoughts of suicide.[121]

The book has inspired many people in their own Christian journey; however, I do not know if many people know, as the old radio voice Paul Harvey used to say, "the rest of the story" of Hannah Hurnard's life. Hurnard became a missionary to the Jewish people in what was then called Jaffa, Palestine (prior to 1948) – even though she had not liked Jewish people before she went to Israel. She became the author of several books beyond *Hinds Feet on High Places,* and that is where the story takes a detour.

---

[121] The biographical information of Hannah Hurnard's life was gleaned from the following: Dan Graves, "Miserable Hannah R. Hurnard Was Converted," Christianity.Com, (28 April 2010), available online at https://www.christianity.com/church/church-history/timeline/1901-2000/miserable-hannah-r-hurnard-was-converted-11630738.html, accessed 28 April 2024.

For in her later books, one can find Hurnard taking an alternative route from her Christian roots. Her final book of the trilogy *Eagles' Wings to the Higher Places* (1981) opens the door to universalism and pantheism. In fact, one positive review on Amazon states – "*I like her ideas very much; and so would Buddhists, many Hindus, Pagans, and anyone else who understands we are all one.*"

How could Hurnard take such a wrong direction in the latter years of her life? I could point out that this is one of the dangers of using only one verse as a starting point, but I believe I have made that point already. Instead, I will go back to the whole issue that has been the crux of this chapter – questions to God are allowed, but becoming trapped in the morass and marsh of our pain is not. For it is when we become overwhelmed by our pain that we become deaf to God's answers and to God's hope that he is the overcomer.

This is the point of the **context** of Habakkuk 3:17-19. Everything can fall apart, as we find in verse 17. However, we can still find a reason to rejoice in the God of our salvation (cf. Ps. 51:12). I mentioned the verse in Psalm as this was something that David also found as he sought forgiveness for his sins after the whole horrific episode with Bathsheba, Uriah, and himself. It should also be noted that life for David after this section of his life was never smooth and simple again, but David could rejoice in God's salvation and not his own. For God is own strength and only he can make our feet straight on the rocky places of our life.

I cannot close this chapter without admitting that evil is real, just as suffering is in this world. Evil seems to grow exponentially greater every day that we live on this planet. Famine exists around the world. Children suffer and are trafficked in untold numbers. Women are abused in ways that seem to make the mind shudder at the evil of it. Diseases beyond COVID and Ebola seem only to be waiting to ravage the world. Dictators have their fingers on buttons – both nuclear and biological – only waiting to destroy their neighbors and their own people.

So how can we honestly say that God is good and wants to save people through the gift of Messiah Jesus? Christians and churches must say this because it is the only hope for the world. **Evil exists today because there is a vacuum in the world of the Gospel being shared.** Christians and churches have abandoned the world and have retreated to our safe zones because we are afraid, because we are appalled, and because we are unsure of what to say in the face of such evil abounding across the face of the globe.

What we must say is that the only hope for the world is the truth of Messiah Jesus. What we must say is that Jesus lived, died, and resurrected for the sins of the world. Habakkuk was not yet aware of the end of the story when he prophesied to the people of Judah that evil was coming, but he knew that the righteous can only live by HIS trustworthiness/faith (2:4). And let me repeat once again … **Evil exists today because there is a vacuum in the world of the Gospel being shared.**

Section Six:
After the Return – Does Anything Really Change?
Haggai and Zechariah

How many of us have heard the old adage, "Fool me once, shame on you. Fool me twice; shame on me." Or how about this one: "Trust but … verify." When I searched the internet for the history of the origin of the trust/verify the quote, I found that while Ronald Reagan made it famous during the height of the Cold War and Nuclear Treaty discussions with Mikhael Gorbachev in the 1980s, it actually has its roots in Russia itself.[122]

It turns out that President Reagan was seeking to make the point with the USSR that while the USA was signing treaties with the Soviet Union, we did not necessarily trust them to honor them and was using a Russian proverb to do so. In many ways, Haggai and Zechariah were prophets used by God in their post-exile (coming back from Babylon days) to make the point – "I am keeping an eye on you because I know the bad habit of my people to slide back into their old ways."

Haggai was used to reprimand the Jewish people who had returned from Babylon to build their own homes but then allowed the Temple not to finish being rebuilt the moment they ran into some outside opposition (cf. Ezra 4 for the details on the opposition). Haggai was also calling them to task for choosing selfishness over proper worship of God. He also chose to remind them that they cannot be blessed if they choose their own comfort over the purposes of God. Yet, and even today, we continue to operate in this mentality and wonder why God's spiritual blessings are denied from us.

While many tend to turn Zechariah into a book on prophecy, and there is a great deal of prophetic hope in this book, the crux of Zechariah's message begins in 1:3 – "Return to me, says Jehovah Elohim, and I will return to you, says Jehovah Elohim." This is the message of Zechariah, and it is encircled by the prophetic messages one finds in the "minor" book that provides so much hope to all of us.

Returning to God, following God, doing God's will, sharing God's message, and living out God's hope will bring out God's purposes for not only the people of God but also the whole world. Yes, there are a plethora of prophetic signals in Zechariah, but it is not a wholly prophetic message, and it should not be considered one. We should not be fooled into thinking it is and ignore the other messages of Zechariah.

---

[122] Nikolay Shevchenko, "Did Reagan Really Coin the Term 'Trust but Verify,' A Proverb Revived by HBO's *Chernobyl*?" Russia Beyond (17 June 2019); available online at https://www.rbth.com/lifestyle/330521-reagan-trust-but-verify-chernobyl, accessed 29 April 2024.

And while I had as interesting of a story for the first adage I shared into this introduction – "Fool me once…" – I could not find anything except to tell you that it first appeared in a book entitled *The Court and Character of King James* allegedly written by Anthony Weldon (1651). And unless you are able to decipher Middle English easily, it is not an easy read. However, I can tell you that God will never be fooled by any words that we utter or any promises we make. So … I would suggest that we dare not try.

11. Haggai: God's House Is More Important than Any Other House on the Market

Introduction

When I lived in Texas, I was about 1.5 hours from Waco. Many Southern Baptists know Waco for Baylor University. However, many women (and some men) know the city of Waco because of two people – Chip and Joanna Gaines. Chip and Joanna, as they are known by fans of their TV show Fixer Upper and their Magnolia TV Network, have put the city of Waco on the map because they brought another word into the modern home remodeling vernacular – "shiplap."

Chip and Joanna Gaines became famous on HGTV for the catchphrase – "turning the worst house in the neighborhood and turning into our client's dream home." They turned a simple remodeling company into a multi-million-dollar enterprise and have been able to maintain their Christian testimony at the same time. Their life story is quite remarkable, even if you are not interested in home remodeling shows or HGTV.[123]

However, the first home remodeling success story is not Chip and Joanna Gaines but Haggai's prophecy to the people who had returned to Judah and had rebuilt their homes but had not finished the Temple in Jerusalem. Therefore, and in many ways, Haggai becomes not only a prophet for God but also his real estate agent when he instructs the Jewish people to get busy finishing the House of God. For while nothing was going to be "For Sale" when the remodeling was done, the people were going to be instructed by God via Haggai that it was beyond time to get their priorities and their properties in order. God's House must always be first – whether it was a physical Temple in the Hebrew Scriptures or it is our spiritual temple today.

Who Haggai Was and a Little Biblical Background to God's Real Estate Prophet/Agent

Compared to some of the prophets who are called "minor prophets," Haggai has a veritable abundance of information. We know not only the year in which the prophet conveyed his message to the people but we also know the month and date along with who was king of the Persians. We also know who was serving as the governor of Judah (Zerubbabel) and who was the High Priest (Joshua).

---

[123] Testimony of the Gaines' Christian faith is available online at https://www.crosswalk.com/video/how-god-brought-chip-and-joanna-gaines-together.html. Accessed 29 April 2024.

Haggai, whose name means festive (or festival), was a prophet during the reign of King Darius I of Persia in the year 520 BC/BCE from the first day of the sixth month on the Hebrew calendar – Elul (1:1) to the 24th day of the ninth month of Kislev on the Hebrew calendar of that same year.[124] Many commentators will provide exact corresponding dates, like September 1st to December 15th or something similar; however, I am going to avoid that specificity and just provide you with what we know from Scripture. Haggai's prophetic work covers around 120 days in actual time, but it has a message that is far more expansive in its purpose and power. It was a message to the returnees from Babylon about priorities, and it could be a message for those of us today about putting our house in order if only we sought to find it in those final pages of the Hebrew Scriptures.

Theme of Habakkuk – Location, Location, Location!

We have all heard it said that in the real estate game, the key issue besides good bathrooms and living rooms is "location, location, location." The same could be said for the theme of Haggai. The people of Israel had returned from Babylon after seventy years in exile. Under the leadership of Nehemiah and Ezra they had begun to rebuild the walls and the Temple as was the plan. However, Ezra 4:1-24 shares the story of how the people who will come to be known as Samaritans disrupted the building when they, for lack of a better word, complained and/or whined about it to King Artaxerxes.

Eugene Merrill holds to the position that their lack of building was more of an excuse to build their own homes than anything else, and perhaps he has a point.[125] For the location of the Temple was not going anywhere (and still has not from my perspective), and the people only needed the faith to build at the location upon which God had given the land to David and the Jewish people hundreds of years before (2 Sam. 24:18-25). Location was not in doubt but the people were doubting God and only needed the God's prophet and real estate agent to move them along to what they needed to do.

---

[124] It should be noted that today the Jewish people have two calendars – a civil calendar that begins with Rosh Hashanah and a religious calendar that begins with Passover. Prior to the destruction of the Temple in AD/CE 70, the Jewish people only had one calendar and that was the religious calendar.

[125] Merrill, *Haggai, Zechariah, Malachi*, 25.

It Is Not Time, but It Is past Time: Challenge & Response (1:2-15)

There is a phrase that is repeated twice in this section of Haggai – "Consider Your Ways!" The first time it is used is because Haggai asks the question why are you living in paneled houses why God's house is in disrepair? The second time it is used is when Haggai asks the people to think about why it might be that crops are failing and the people are lacking for what they need. Could it be because they have forgotten the priority of God's house being in disrepair? In other ways … CONSIDER YOUR WAYS and do something to fix the problem in your house and God's House.

Haggai then gives the people specific instructions in verses 8 and 9b on what he wants done. God wants the people to go up into the mountains and bring lumber down to build the Temple. The word in Hebrew is *ha bayit*, which literally means "the house" because it is God's house. He wants his people to build it for him so that (1) God will be glorified (v. 8) and (2) I admit this is implied, but I believe the argument is still obvious – so that God's anger would be lifted against them for focusing on their needs over worship to him (v. 9b).

There is a lesson for us as well today in these two verses as I take a small rabbit trail moment here. There is nothing wrong with enjoying "things" in life, but dare we take such a privilege when our personal Christian life is in shambles? There is nothing wrong with central air and heat, and this is especially so if you live in the southern area of the United States, but dare we take privileges in life when the world is starving while we throw so much away in life? There is nothing wrong with padded pews or even a cappuccino coffee bar in the lobby of our churches but what about our brothers and sisters in Iran and North Korea who are starving for even one page of God's word that can be shared among their members. Could this not be the modern-day equivalent of what God was saying to the people of Haggai's day? Is this perhaps why God is not blessing us because we actually are blessed but perceive that we are hurting?

Okay … enough of the rabbit trail for the moment because it is time for us to examine how the leaders and the people of Haggai's day responded to the prophet's word. The first action was the word *Shema ("heard")*, which is often translated as "obeyed" as it relates to Zerubbabel and Joshua. They heard/obeyed Haggai's message, and they feared and/or showed reverence for what was told to them (v. 12). Both of these verbs are important to the action of obedience in verse 14. For it is one thing to hear, but it is another to show reverence and/or be fearful of the message.

The evidence of this reality can be found in one word … teenagers. Teenagers will do what is told of them to do – sometimes eventually. However, the angst that defines teenage life often means that doing so out of respect is another action altogether. However, Joshua and Zerubbabel heard and showed reverence in their obedience, and that was what was needed by the leadership so that the people would do so as well. We see this obedience in verse 15, in which the people worked on God's house beginning on the 24th day of Elul (September).

Solomon's vs. Zerubbabel's Temple (2:1-5)

Perhaps one might wonder why Haggai was so specific about marking the dates on the Hebrew calendar in his prophecy. There is a reason aside from his work as God's real estate agent, and it is all related to Leviticus 23. Yes – I suggest we take a quick look at what many consider (sarcasm alert) the most exciting book in the whole scripture.

Leviticus 23 gives a general overview of the Hebrew year, from the weekly observance of the Sabbath to every biblically required Jewish holiday from Passover in the Hebrew month of Nissan to Sukkot (aka Festival of Booths) in Tishrei. This is important as we consider the dates that Haggai gives to us and, especially, as we look at chapter two. For without understanding the Hebrew calendar and the Jewish festivals, we will miss the nuances that are subtly mentioned by Haggai and the message that God is sending to the people.

The second chapter begins with the date – the 21st of the seventh month (520 BC/BCE). This often does not mean anything to a typical Christian and/or church; however, for the people of Haggai's time, it was the seventh day of Sukkot (aka Festival of Booths). Leviticus 23:33-44 provided the instructions for what was to be done and the why for the people.

This festival is an eight-day festival in which the Jewish people are to build tents/booths and to live in those outside tents for as a reminder of how God protected them during the forty years of the wilderness (v. 43). Additionally, the seventh day (or the 21st day of the seventh month) is to be a holy Sabbath for them **unto** God.[126] This was the setting for when Joshua, the High Priest, and Zerubbabel, the governor of Judah, began to speak to the people with the message that God had given to them through Haggai the prophet:

---

[126] Much of this information was provided by my own common knowledge. However, you can also find a reference to this information in Bullock, *An Introduction to the Old Testament Prophetic Books*, 306.

The message from God is very similar to the one that he gave to the successor of Moses in Joshua 1. We find the phrases "take courage" and/or "be strong" (v. 4) as well as "have no fear" (v. 5), for God is still with them as he has always been with them since they left Egypt. The Joshua from the time they entered the Promised Land to this Joshua who returned from Babylon can rest assured that God will hold true to the covenant he had made with Abraham, Isaac, and Jacob. He was with them in the wilderness (hence the reason the message was given on Sukkot), and he will be with them now and in the future.

This might have been hard for the people to grasp because the Temple that they were seeing at the moment was not as glorious as Solomon's by any stretch of the imagination. In fact, Joshua and Zerubbabel admitted this reality, as did some of the older people who were there and been alive to see Solomon's Temple before it was destroyed (v. 3). However, the people were not to look with human eyes at what God was doing because there was something greater in store for them that was going to simply blow their minds…

A modern-day example of such boldness and perseverance is when Jerry Falwell decided to build what is now Liberty University on "that mountain." I know the name Jerry Falwell today can be a divisive name in the Evangelical world but if you are as old as me then you might remember watching "The Old-Time Gospel Hour" on Sunday mornings and hearing Robbie Hiner singing "I Want That Mountain." Dr. Falwell used the song and Robbie Hiner's singing to raise funds to build the college that even today is on a mountain in Lynchburg, Virginia.[127] Between this song and those "Jesus First" pins, Jerry Falwell built the largest Christian university in the world because he believed in location, location, location.

Prophecy of the Future Temple (2:6-9)

When one considers the description of the building of Solomon's Temple in 2 Chron. 2:1-5:14, it is no wonder that the people who were alive when it was destroyed feel humiliated as they examine what they were able to build under the direction of Joshua and Zerubbabel. The remnant builders could never equal the thousands upon thousands of workers who crafted such a magnificent structure as was formulated under the architectural design of Solomon. Who could? Yet … the prophecy of Haggai promises them that a temple even greater than Solomon's Temple will come to the people.

---

[127] Robbie Hiner returned to Liberty University in 2018 and sang the song for the college chapel. Available online at https://watch.liberty.edu/media/t/1_ii3giuh1 (song begins around the 37 minute mark). Accessed 29 April 2024.

In verses 6-7a, Jehovah Sabaoth proclaims that in a little while he will shake it all up (heaven, earth, dry land, the sea, and the nations) and everyone shall come to what can only be described as a unique phrase "Desire of All Nations." Is it simply only about other nations bringing sacrifices to the Temple because they are now included as some commentators have speculated?[128] I do not think so. I believe there is a great deal more of a Messianic hope and expectation than even Eugene Merrill realizes.[129] For who is the Desire of All Nations and what could cause God to say that everything (gold and silver) is his and that the latter temple will be greater than the first if it is not eschatological and Messianic in nature (v. 8-9)? And who alone, other than Messiah Jesus, the Sar Shalom (prince of peace), can bring peace (v. 9b)?

However, we are allowed to ask if this is not a prophecy that has a multiple and/or double fulfillment in mind, as was discussed in an earlier chapter. Jesus' first coming did shake up the place, did it not? He is the "Desire of All Nations" as the Great Commission was to be first to the Jews and also to the Gentiles (Matt. 28:18-20; Acts 1:8; Rom. 1:16). We bodies are called the temple of God (1 Cor. 6:19-20). Therefore, and in many ways, this prophecy has the "already, but not yet" nature of being fulfilled that can be seen in so many double fulfillment prophecies. Obviously, there is so much to Haggai's prophetic role that needs to be considered in our own role as missionaries and evangelists that still needs to be considered and yet we are not even to the end of the short book.

Meaning of the Ruling on Holiness vs. Unholiness (2:10-19)

In the midst of the discussion about the rebuilding of God's House (i.e., the Temple) in Haggai's Day and the building of the future temple, we have this most interesting discussion about holiness and unholiness. Taken in isolation, it might appear that it is, in biblical terms, an interpolation (an interruption of the text and it does not belong there). However, this argument can be disputed by the text itself – Haggai gives a date for when this question or request for a ruling on holiness is given.

It is the 24th of the ninth month of Kislev (December), and Haggai asks a two-fold question of the priests. The first part of the question involves "holy meat" that is protected by a prayer shawl (i.e., garment) and the garment touches bread that is not holy – does the bread suddenly become holy? The priests answer correctly ... no. The second part of the question is whether something that is unclean touches the "holy meat" and whether the meat becomes unholy. The priests then again answer correctly ... yes.

---

[128] Baldwin, *Haggai, Zechariah, Malachi*, 48.
[129] Merrill, *Haggai, Zechariah, Malachi*, 41.

Haggai then communicates the message that God wants him to deliver that the people are unclean because they have been behaving as dead people because they still need to repent of their thievery towards God (v. 15-19 and see chapter 1).[130] However, and do we not love God's "buts" and "howevers," with the rebuilding of the temple and "from this day forward," they can do what is necessary to make things right with God. Additionally, the inference and/or implication given in verse 19 is that God will be counting!

It is not that God needs the offerings from the people (or from us). He wanted their obedience just as he wants our obedience and gratitude for what God has given to the people who proclaim his name. It is a simple thing in all respects, but yet it was then, as it is now, such a difficult thing for people to do apparently. Giving back to God seems impossible for so many people to do.

In one of my dad's churches when I was about 12 years old, there was a man who was the owner of the only grocery store in the small town. Mr. Thompson was a tight-fisted, angry old man, and for years, he was proud of the fact that he gave one dollar a week to the church … and only one dollar. When my dad became pastor of the church, which also happened to be the church that he and mama were married in many years before and the church that daddy swore he would never pastor, Mr. Thompson walked up to daddy and announced before everyone that he had decided that he was going to double his weekly offering (i.e., two dollars a week). He also told my dad that he better be happy about this weekly increase, and he never wanted to hear a sermon about stewardship or tithing, or he would walk out.

As you can imagine, everyone also felt sorry for Mrs. Thompson in the church, in the town, and in the grocery store. And no one was surprised when the rumors began that Mrs. Thompson was seeing someone on the side. The response in the community was – "who could blame her after being married to him for all those years." Now, my dad had to deal with the situation and brought them both in for counseling and to find out if the rumors were true. Mrs. Thompson denied it and there was no obvious proof of the affair … but everyone "knew" it was true because he treated her like he treated the church and his grocery store – angry and mean. By the way, my dad also tried to talk to him about how he treated his wife, but he would not listen.

Today, if you drive through the small town, the building where the grocery store once stood is an empty shell. The Thompsons have long since died, as has the church, which never called either of the Thompsons to account for their sins—her affair or his meanness. Indeed, robbing God, whether it is by our offerings or by our lives, will truly result in God taking what belongs to him back in one way or another.

---

[130] Baldwin, *Haggai, Zechariah, Malachi*, 50-51.

Promise of David Restored (2:20-23)

As is common to almost all of the prophetic books of the Hebrew Scriptures, God offers hope. Indeed, Jehovah Sabaoth is good that way. God promises to the descendants of Zerubbabel a signet ring. This signet ring is to be worn only by the king, and Zerubbabel is only the governor of Judah, and Judah is still under the authority of Persia and King Darius. In fact, Judah/Israel has never had a true king since the last king of Judah fell to Nebuchadnezzar. What could this prophecy mean that was given by God to Haggai on the 24th of Kislev in the year 520 BC/BCE?

Only the most important prophecy that could ever be imagined – the restoration of the Davidic Covenant! But wait … Zerubbabel is a descendant of Coniah or Jeconiah, and Jer. 22:24 tells us that a descendant of his will never again sit on the throne. How can this be? But wait … Jeremiah also gave us the promise and prophecy of 23:5-6 which tells us that a "branch of righteousness" from the line of David will sit on the throne once again. And this time, this king shall be called "LORD our Righteousness (*Jehovah Tzidkenu*).

How can all the prophecies (the one from Haggai and the two from Jeremiah) be true? God does not contradict himself, and he has resolved them all in the lineages of Jesus, as found in Matt. 1 and Luke 3. Joseph is a descendant of David, Zerubbabel, and Jeconiah (Matt. 1:11-12) through Solomon, which provides Jesus a lineage connection through his adopted father. Mary is a descendant of David through Solomon's brother Nathan, who provides Jesus with a second royal and most important blood lineage (Luke 3:31) to the Davidic Covenant. The Davidic Covenant is restored through Zerubbabel's obedience. The Davidic Covenant is preserved through Nathan AND Solomon to Jesus. However, and most importantly, the Davidic Covenant is unconditional based not on the obedience of the people but on the promises of God alone. This is how we knot that God has all things planned before the foundation of the world to save the world through Messiah Jesus.

And this is why we must pay attention to such a small but impactful book like Haggai as we consider those "minor prophets" that are located towards the end of the Hebrew Scriptures. They are small but they are powerful with their not-so-hidden messages if we only pay attention to the details like a good real estate agent does. We cannot fail to give God what is due to him, not because he needs anything but because we need to give him our praise out of gratitude for what he has given to us.

We also need to give him our all as we share the Gospel around the world. We do not need to bring sacrifices to a centralized temple as there is not one. However, we can show our sacrifices to him by giving our lives in holy service to him as Rom. 12:1-2 encourages. This can be locally or evangelistically in a missional setting.

However, and as Haggai reminded the remnant people of his time, our focus must be fixed on the main thing and not on other issues such as what we might desire. This includes the work of sharing the Gospel around the world. The great Southern Baptist missionary Lottie Moon once wrote in one of her mission letters – *"Why this strange indifferences to missions? Why these scant contributions? Why does money fail to be forthcoming when approved men and women are asking to be sent to proclaim the 'unsearchable riches of Christ' to the heathen?"* Lottie Moon was being truthful when she wrote these words over a century ago, and she would be truthful if she were alive to write them today. More money will be donated to political campaigns for president than given to missions in any given election year, and I cannot help but wonder why people ask – why are we suffering? Perhaps they should read Haggai again or maybe they need to realize it is even in the Hebrew Scriptures. I wish I had the courage to write a ministry newsletter with half the chutzpah (courage) as Lottie Moon!

Addendum Issue:
Significance of "Lord of Hosts" (Jehovah Sabaoth)

Repeatedly throughout the "minor prophets," the phrase "LORD of Hosts," which has been translated as Jehovah Sabaoth in this book, was used by the prophets to describe the power and authority of God the Almighty. Joyce Baldwin notes that in total it is used nearly 300 times in the Hebrew Scriptures because God is the commander of the armies that can and will defeat any army that seeks to overcome the Jewish people.[131] This was the message that God knew he needed to share with the Jewish people, especially during the days of Haggai and Zechariah, because while they were no longer exiles, they were not yet a nation like they had once been – but they had a commander of armies that could not ever be defeated.[132]

Jehovah Sabaoth is a powerful name of God that is often forgotten in the pantheon of names for God. We have Jehovah Shalom (God of Peace). We have Jehovah Rapha (The God Who Heals). We have Jehovah Nissi (God Who Is Our Banner). Indeed, these are all wonderful names for God, but without the truth that God is our Jehovah Sabaoth … our commander and LORD of the Host of the Armies … where would we be?

---

[131] Baldwin, *Haggai, Zechariah, Malachi*, 44-45.
[132] Merrill, *Haggai, Zechariah, Malachi*, 27. See also, Goldingay, *The Lost Letters to the Twelve Prophets*, 163.

12. Zechariah: The Message of Zechariah (and All the Prophets) – Return to God Already

Introduction

As I am writing the introduction to this chapter, I am "smack in the middle" of my personal sad period. It begins around the first of May and ends on July 7th. I know that sounds like a rather long period but let me explain the sad anniversaries of this time period for my family. Anniversaries that revolve around the deaths of both my mom and my dad.

Mama began the final illness which ended her life around the first of May. The first surgery on her intestines was on 4 May 2020. She came home for a few weeks for round the clock care from my sister and I (along with health care nurses) until June 3rd when we tried a second surgery as the first surgery did not clear out all the infection and her colon was completely impacted and she needed an ostomy inserted. This surgery which was supposed to last only three hours ended up lasting lasted 7.5 hours and she ended up in ICU for two days and rehab for a few more days. She began to bleed internally on 15 June and this is when mama decided to forgo a third surgery and prepare all of us who loved her dearly for her heavenly homegoing. I signed the papers and brought her home for hospice care until she passed away on June 20th at 8:29 a.m.

Daddy as far as we knew was in good health but he was exceptionally tired – emotionally and spiritually – from a church pastorate that had been beyond difficult. The first few months of 2000 were something that no pastor should ever have to experience as he was dismissed from a church because the youth pastor had an affair and my dad would not cover it up for him or for the church. Yes, you read the sentence correctly. The pastor was fired in May 2000 because the youth pastor committed a sexual indiscretion and the pastor wanted to be transparent about sin in the church ... how times have changed in the last quarter of a century.

Anyway, my dad had begun a new pastorate in June 2000, but he was still a tired man who probably should have taken a sabbatical, but he believed in serving and ministry. On July 3rd, he took his car in to have the front wheels aligned even though he said he was not feeling well as his stomach was bothering him. He told mama that he would go to the doctor after the church's 4th of July picnic if he were not feeling any better. At about 2:15 a.m. or so on July 4th, mama heard him stirring around in the bedroom, and then she heard him fall onto the bed. Mama jumped out of bed and turned on the light but daddy was already gone – from what was diagnosed as an abdominal aneurysm. The death certificate shows that Jack Henry Downey died on his ultimate Independence Day at 2:48 a.m. after the EMTs stopped trying to revive him. Daddy's funeral was on a dusty, hot hill in the middle of West Texas on 7 July 2000. And that is why the beginning of May to the early days of July every year are difficult days for me as they are filled with tough reminders of sadness and signposts of when I lost the two most important people in my life. And did I mention that my parents were married on 20 May 1961!

This brings me to my point that even today, Jewish people observe significant moments of sadness similar to what I describe to you. Perhaps you have heard of Tish B'Av or seen it on your calendars and wondered what does this mean? This is a significant fast day in Judaism, but it is not commanded as an ordinance in Scripture, but it is noted in Zechariah 7:1-7. Tish B'Av (usually in July or August) is the date believed not only for the destruction of Solomon's Temple in 586 BC/BCE but also believed to be the date for the destruction of the Second (Herod's) Temple in 70 AD/CE.[133] Additionally, it is believed that the Jewish people were expelled from Spain and England during the Middle Ages on Tish B'Av.[134] The 9th of Av (actual date on the calendar) is not a good date for the Jewish people as other events have happened throughout history since the destruction of Solomon's Temple. However, as we will see as quickly cover that section in Zechariah (for it would be impossible to cover this minor prophet in any in-depth manner), God asks through Zechariah are you really fasting for me or to be seen by each other? That is a rather awkward question to be asked by God, is it not?

---

[133] Bullock, *An Introduction to the Old Testament Prophetic Books*, 320 and Bartholomew and Thomas, *The Minor Prophets*, 267-68.

[134] "Tish B'Av 101," My Jewish Learning, available online at https://www.myjewishlearning.com/article/tisha-bav-101/, accessed 19 May 2024.

This is something I also have to ask myself as I still mourn for my folks. They are in a much better place than I am and they are together – for mama never stopped missing my dad. What is accomplished by my "dark period" anymore? I can only look forward to the day that I can "return to them" and be with them before the throne of Father God. Being joyful for what they are experiencing at this moment is a much better use of my time and something I believe Zechariah would approve of us as well. It is easy to type but much harder to experience…

And I can only wish this message could be conveyed to my mission people as well. Focus on the good God and not on the bad that has happened in the past. Focus on the truth of who Jesus is and not on what they have been told to expect of the Messiah. Focus on what Zechariah reports and not on what their rabbis have gotten wrong…

Who Zechariah Was and the Biblical Background to the Prophet

You might have wondered why I grouped Haggai and Zechariah together when you saw the Table of Contents. Haggai wrote one of the smallest of these prophets, and Zechariah wrote one of the longest. One reason was that Haggai and Zechariah fall into the group of prophets who are considered as post-exilic – they wrote to a group of people who were returnees (yes – you will see that word a lot in this chapter) from Babylon. Another reason is that they wrote at the exact same time – 520 BC/BCE. For while Haggai wrote about rebuilding the Temple, Zechariah began writing in the eighth month (Heshvan) about rebuilding and preparing the people of the Temple for the hope that was waiting for them. Joyce Baldwin phrases it so eloquently that I cannot help but include what she wrote in her commentary – "If Haggai was the builder, responsible for the solid structure of the new Temple, Zechariah was more like the artist, adding colourful windows with their symbolism, gaiety and light."[135]

---

[135] Baldwin, *Haggai, Zechariah, Malachi*, 59.

Zechariah, whose name means "Jehovah has remembered," was the son of Berechiah ("the blessing of Jehovah") and was the grandson of Iddo – "timely." This lineage is important on several different levels as it provides a connection to his priestly qualifications (cf. Neh. 12:4,16).[136] Arno Gaebelein, who was one of the earliest of what could be described as proto-Zionists among twentieth century evangelicals, also provided these interesting nuggets that one should take with three grains of salt as they are difficult to verify – (1) he was buried alongside his compatriot Haggai and (2) he worked in the compilation of the liturgical order for worship services in the Temple.[137]

What should be noted, and something that I brought out in the chapter on Joel (see Ch. 6), is that the word prophet and/or prophecy does not necessarily mean foretelling a future event. Prophecy is most often about sharing or forth telling a message from God. Zechariah is a prophetic book in that he shares the specific message he is given from God. However, it is also an apocalyptic book – much like Ezekiel, Daniel, and Revelation – in that it shares specific messages about future events.

A simple explanation of apocalyptic, even while I am uncomfortable with the word "alleged" in the middle of the definition, is provided by George Eldon Ladd – "… those writings because they contain *alleged* revelations of the secret purposes of God, the end of the world, and the establishment of God's Kingdom on earth (emphasis added)."[138] The visions found in the first sections of Zechariah and the obvious prophecies of the future in the second section, it could be argued, place this prophet's message in a situation where it falls into a both/and situation, as C. Hassell Bullock determines.[139] Zechariah is not entirely a book of prophecy or apocalypse. In my humble opinion, it is an entirely new book given by God as a message for the people then and for the people in the future—much like Revelation.

---

[136] F. B. Meyer, *The Prophet of Hope: Studies in Zechariah* (Grand Rapids: Zondervan Publishing House, 1952), 11; Bullock, *An Introduction to the Old Testament Prophetic Books*, 310; and Bartholomew and Thomas, *The Minor Prophets*, 249.

[137] Gaebelein, *Daniel to Malachi* (vol. 5), 263. I find both of these "nuggets" highly doubtful not only due to the fact that they are unverifiable but also due to the fact that Talmudic sources are limited in their mention of the prophet at all. Additionally, Gaebelein who was a fairly reputable commentator was in my opinion prone to be hyperbole in his Zionistic days.

[138] George Eldon Ladd, "Apocalyptic Literature," *Zondervan's Pictorial Bible Dictionary*, ed. Merrill C. Tenney (Grand Rapids: Zondervan Publishing House, 1963), 49-50.

[139] Bullock, *An Introduction to the Old Testament Prophetic Books*, 312.

Theme of Zechariah – Return to God Already

I personally am not a big fan of Western movies. I do not stop and watch old John Wayne movies when they come on TCM or other channels like some people do. However, there are two classic Westerns that I will stop and watch because they are just classics. One is *High Noon* with Gary Cooper and Grace Kelly. The other is *Shane* with Alan Ladd and Jean Arthur. Both films end with the major character(s) leaving in the final scene, but only *Shane* has the classic line – "Shane, come back."

I sometimes feel as if God has the same feeling about us but somewhat in reverse. For while the Alan Ladd character needed to leave for some obvious reasons, if you have seen the movie, the people of God (and I do allow this to include us today) do not. Yet … we often do and for the most foolish of reasons, much like the Prodigal Son did in Jesus' parable (Luke 15:11-31).

We leave because we are tempted by the allure of fame and glory that falls apart as quickly as it appears because Andy Warhol was right in that fame only lasts about fifteen minutes. We abandon the security of God's protection because we are charmed by the desire for someone who promises us a carnal love that is nothing but a second-hand emotion, as Tina Turner once sang so honestly. And since I am giving away that I am a teenager of the 1980s, we run away from what God knows is best for us and believe the lies that we "do not need no education" from God and end up hitting "The Wall."[140]

In Zechariah, you will find the constant idea of "Return to me" phrased in many different ways throughout the book. And it is this idea of returning that I see as the theme of Zechariah; I know that many commentaries will choose the idea of hope as the primary theme of the book, and that is a good thematic argument as well. However, I believe God's call to return is optimal in this setting because true hope only exists if they do return. However, if either view is correct, you can decide for yourself which one best fits the text.

Return to Me … "Jehovah Was Very Angry with Your Fathers" (1:1-6)

Imagine being Zechariah, the prophet and most likely a priest (since his grandfather was a priest according to Nehemiah), and the first words he receives from God were something that he already knew, but … to be reminded of this fact right off the bat. Indeed, Zechariah knew that Jehovah had been angry (could also be translated as "wrathful") with his forefathers.

---

[140] I was never a fan of Pink Floyd but the lyrics of this song just popped into my mind when I was typing and I could not resist using it. However, I was a fan of Tina Turner during the 1980s and her recent death was heartbreaking as she became a Buddhist in her later years and one cannot help but wonder if she ever had a personal relationship with Messiah Jesus.

It is probable, and some have speculated, that Zechariah was born in Babylon.[141] He had heard the lament for Zion as sung in Psalm 137. He had walked back with the returning refugees to the homeland and saw what was left of Solomon's Temple. He had seen Jehovah's anger firsthand, and now God is telling him this truth that he already knew. One could only imagine what Zechariah must have thought and felt, but then we have Jehovah's next words...

"Return to me ... so that I may return to you." Again, I can only imagine Zechariah thinking to himself, "We have returned from Babylon ... what do you mean?" In verses 4-6, God explains that God wants not only a physical change of location but also a heart change as well. For there is an interesting expression in verse 4 – they are "Be not like your fathers" who did not listen to the prophets but to "Return now (or to turn) from their evil ways **and** evil deeds." There is the implication that the people of God could **and** can **and** even will backslide if they are not cautious of the evil ways **and** evil deeds that led their ancestors into captivity in the first place.

However, what does this expression mean by "evil ways **and** evil deeds"? Eugene Merrill describes it basically as not just as accidental sins but intentional and a "whole pattern of rebellion and disloyalty."[142] I grew up with the words – omission and commission – to describe this concept. Sins of omission (accidental) were sins that we committed without even realizing or recognizing that they were sins, such as bumping into someone and not apologizing to someone. Sins of commission (intentional or purposeful) are such sins as having a "lead foot" while driving (i.e., an unrepentant speeder) to the act of being the next Jeffrey Dahmer. The Scottish theologian Sinclair Ferguson described it wonderfully in this saying, "Evil deeds are the fruit of an evil heart. They are not an aberration from our true self but a revelation of it."

Jeremiah had spoken this phrase to the people before the captivity (7:3; 18:11; 26:13), but they had not listened as God reminded Zechariah (v. 4). Ezekiel had used this phrase (36:31), and finally, the people listened. Still, it was a costly lesson (v. 5-6) to learn. Therefore, Zechariah was given this phrase to share with the people to remind them not to go down this path again, or the results would be the same.

---

141 Meyers, *The Prophet of Hope*, 11.
142 Merrill, *Haggai, Zechariah, Malachi*, 89.

This is a lesson that we would be well advised to listen to today as well. For while, we love to point out the sins of "them" with a disgusted sneer and scowl on our face, the evil ways **and** evil deeds exist within our houses and churches as well. As I am writing this chapter, a former seminary professor from my own beloved Southwestern has been indicted for falsifying and destroying records related to a sexual abuse (rape) claim against one of the seminary students. In South Carolina, a pastor is being investigated for possibly being involved in the suicide of his estranged wife.[143] The examples that could be listed here could fill an entire old-fashioned twenty-six volume encyclopedia set that salesmen would try to sell to homes in the 1970s. The evil deeds **and** evil ways do exist today, and it could be stated that Jehovah is very angry with us today as well. The only question that must be asked before we move on to the next sections ... will we repent as Zechariah's forefathers did after they were led off to captivity (v. 6), or will we learn from previous mistakes and repent before judgment comes to our house?

Return to Me ... the Visions of Zechariah (1:7-6:15)

While it might be tempting to devote an individual section to each vision, this would be self-defeating in many ways. The first reason is that the purpose of this entire book, of giving people a missional perspective of the sometimes-neglected prophets, would be overwhelmed by the sheer size of the chapter for Zechariah. The second and most important reason is that Zechariah's visions, in so many ways, are a panorama of one giant picture. To separate each vision into its own separate section would be like not seeing the forest for the trees to borrow from the old cliché. And while this section will only be able to glance at each vision, the goal is to see the forest and the trees at the same time so that the whole picture of God's plan will be seen.

Now that this introductory paragraph is out of the way, did you realize that Zechariah experienced all eight of these visions in one night? Talk about an overwhelming experience! Yet it is true, as we read in 1:7, that it was on the 24th day of the eleventh month (Shevat/February) around 520 BC/BCE, as it was in the second year of King Darius of Persia's reign. Now, it should be noted that February/Shevat is a colder month in Israel (as I have been to Israel in December/January). It is possible for light snow to fall in Jerusalem during February and, so Zechariah's vision(s) happened on a night when a fire would have likely been lit. A blanket would have been in ready reach for the prophet/priest to tuck around his shoulders for a night that was different from one the prophet would ever experience again.

---

[143] I have chosen not to cite the sources for these examples as they involve spousal and/or sexual abuse.

Vision One: The Man on the Red Horse (1:7-17)

Zechariah encounters a man on a red horse in a group of myrtle trees surrounded by more red, sorrel, and white horses. And while it is almost natural to wonder what the meaning of these horses is (especially if our mind wanders to those horses in Revelation), the point is not the color of the horses but the man himself and the message he has come to share.

And I will be the first to admit that there can be some confusion in this section as to who is "the man" to whom Zechariah is talking to at times. I had to go back and forth in my own study to decipher carefully who was doing the talking, who was reporting to whom, and what is the message that was given to Zechariah and who was giving it to the prophet.[144] However, once this was deciphered to the best of my ability … it was a little mind blowing!

Others (the "These are those" in v. 10) were coming to report to the man engaged with Zechariah in conversation about what is going on in the earth – "all is peaceful and quiet" (v. 11). The identity of the man with the red horse is revealed in v. 12 as the Angel of the Lord who then begins to engage with Jehovah Sabaoth and asks how much longer will he be angry with Jerusalem as he has been for seventy years? This is perhaps one of the most intriguing conversations ever observed until we are allowed to read of Jesus' prayer in the Garden of Gethsemane the night before he is crucified.

Why did I write this last sentence above? Eugene Merrill struggles with this potential thought as well because the possibility that the pre-incarnate Jesus, as the Angel of the Lord, having a discussion with God the Father in front of Zechariah seems impossible to him.[145] However, I have no choice in my understanding of Scripture but to ask what else or who else this could be. For if we interpret the Angel of the Lord[146] as a Christophany in all other places … why not here? And while this is not the full complement of the person of the Trinity in action, these are two members and this is simply mind blowing is it not?

---

[144] Merrill, *Haggai, Zechariah, Malachi*, 94. I am glad to report that someone as distinguished as Eugene Merrill also had to study these verses seriously as well to decipher the who was speaking to whom as well.

[145] Ibid.

[146] I could reference other commentaries to validate my position, and I mean, I have absolutely no disrespect for Eugene Merrill. Therefore, I am going to take the shortcut route and simply direct individuals such as yourself to Bible Hub -- https://biblehub.com/commentaries/zechariah/1-12.htm.

However, and as wow-inducing as verses 12-13 are, we must not stop there in our glance at the first vision. Jehovah's message to Zechariah from the Angel of the Lord is a lovely and terrifying message all at once. Zechariah is to proclaim to the people – "*Qinne tiqanah gedolah…*" (v. 14). In English … "I am greatly zealous/jealous" for Jerusalem and Zion. God is passionate about his covenant people, and he does remember them. What a lovely message to hear after seventy years of being a refugee people.

However, there is also verse 15 for those who enslaved his people. He is very angry (in Hebrew, the idea is exceedingly wrathful) with the nations who might be at ease at the moment but who contributed to the burden of the Jewish people with whom he was only a little angry. Jerusalem will prosper once again because God has again chosen his people and his city (v. 16-17) to blossom and prosper.

Before we go on to the second vision, I need to take a quick moment to caution all of us about something that we all tend to do when we read apocalyptic or vision portions of scripture. We all want to read some sort of code or hidden meaning into the text that is probably not there, such as trying to discern if the white or sorrel or red horses of Zechariah's vision have a deeper meaning. They do not, in my opinion. They are just the colors of horses. We do know what the horse colors mean in Revelation because John tells us that we should not seek to find deeper meaning when there is no deeper meaning there. Sometimes, a horse is just a horse unless it is the fabulous Mr. Ed saying, "Hello, Wilbur."

Vision Two: Four Horns and Four Craftsmen (1:18-21)

The paragraph I wrote above fits in perfectly with this vision because one's automatic response is to go … who are the four horns, and who are the four craftsmen? Believe me, I understand because I did it myself! Zechariah did it as well, and he was given the answer that they (the horns) represented those who have winnowed and/or scattered Judah, Israel, and Jerusalem, and the four craftsmen will cause those same horns to be terrified and want to return the people to the land.

Of course, everyone wants specific answers as to what exactly the horns mean and who the craftsmen are. I will be honest: I wrote down in my own notes a guesstimate for the horns—Assyria, Babylon, Greece, and Rome—but that was only a guess.[147] Why do I say that is a guess because? I also wrote down that those four horns could be the four directions on a map or those who were in complete opposition to the God of Israel. In other words, I am just guessing, and I do not wish to lead anyone astray with my "best guess." Eugene Merrill took the same approach in his commentary, while F. B. Meyer mentioned the compass points but also listed a plethora of national possibilities, including the choices I mentioned above.[148]

Many within the premillennial Dispensational camp will provide a quick answer as to whom the four horns represent, and while I hold to a great many of their beliefs, I choose not to be concrete in stating categorically that I know for certain as the identity of anything or any time.[149] In fact, I believe Meyer explains it best when he mentions that in his timeframe of the 1950s, the four horns could be categorized as priestcraft (a tactful way of saying the Roman Catholic Church), worldliness, Christian Science, and spiritualism.[150] Meyer's point was that the four horns change over time for every generation and that we should not label either one of what Zechariah saw but recognize that they represent something timeless and perhaps even seek to be oppositional to God's purpose but never successful to what to God's plans. For nothing can defeat God's plans in the end.[151]

Vision Three: Man with the Measuring Line (2:1-13)

There is so much depth and meat to this chapter that I believe a whole book could be written on just these thirteen verses alone. However, we only have a couple of pages, and so we will only be able to skim the surface of all that God showed Zechariah in this vision. And, no, we will not try to uncover the identity of the man with the measuring line in his hand, regardless of how tempting it might be.

---

[147] I did not even attempt to guesstimate as to who could be the four craftsmen.

[148] Merrill, *Haggai, Zechariah, Malachi*, 101 and Meyer, *The Prophet of Hope*, 25.

[149] If you have noticed in this work, I have determined to not label myself as this or that eschatologically. This will be the closest you will find my position. For ultimately, I believe God finds our best efforts to know the end of all things woefully inadequate.

[150] Meyer, 26-27.

[151] Ibid., 28-29. Meyer wrote – "The Lord knows where to find his servants, and when the predestined hour strikes, there will stand the workmen ready."

By all accounts, the man appears simply to be a surveyor seeking to mark the boundaries of where the future city walls of Jerusalem should be built.[152] He is doing his job and, a job that will eventually be completed by Nehemiah in c.445 BC/BCE. Yet, we find a most unique moment in verses 3-5 that indicates that this surveyor exists not in Nehemiah's time in a spiritual and physical sense.

Zechariah is commanded (in both the imperative and intensive verbal tenses) to tell the surveyor to stop what he is doing because Jerusalem will be a city without walls as Jehovah will be a "wall of fire encircling her" and "the glory in the middle (of her) (v. 5)." Jerusalem will be not an "international city" as some say but simply and only God's city and populated by his people who are comprised by the Jewish people as well as the Gentiles who have been engrafted into the covenant as well … but more on that later.[153]

One of the words that I love in verse 5, and that can be found throughout these overlooked prophets, is the word "declared." I want to spend a precious paragraph or three on this Hebrew word, and now is the right time. For when I first saw the word, I imagined God DECLARING himself but actually the word is more like Jehovah declaring himself. The word in Hebrew is ne-um, which in its most sense is "to whisper." In other words, God does not need to shout to make his point but only needs to whisper when he makes an announcement. The prime example to illustrate this concept from 1 Kgs 19 when Elijah fled from Jezebel.

Elijah ran to the cave at Horeb. He was exhausted and afraid and longed to hear from God after his battle with Ahab and Jezebel, for he felt all alone. However, Jehovah was not in the strong wind(s) nor the earthquake or even the fire. Jehovah's voice was in the sound of a gentle blowing (wind). Elijah needed this whisper. The prophets heard the whisper. And the question I have for all of us today (including myself) is do we overlook the whisper of Jehovah because we are listening to the earthquake and the fire and the false winds around us?

---

[152] Merrill, *Haggai, Zechariah, Malachi*, 103.

[153] Bartholomew and Thomas, *The Minor Prophets*, 257. I believe that the authors used the term "international city" innocently, but the connotation today implies something political that we need to avoid.

Now as we return to the rest of the third vision, let us consider what is being said about this ultimate City of God known as Jerusalem. First, he commands those who stayed in Babylon to come home (verses 6-7). And given that this is a future-oriented prophecy, and not simply one in the immediate sense of Zechariah's time, there is a tendency to overanalyze just who and what and when the Babylon of this prophecy might be.[154] However, I want to focus on the urgency of the command – come home from wherever you might be because God scattered them to "the four winds of the heavens" (v. 6) and given that I have shared the Gospel with a Jewish man in Leedey, Oklahoma, I can say for certain that the Jewish were indeed scattered everywhere!

Verses 8 and 9 also portend that they will be returning after a time of difficulty and oppression. The apple of God's eye is an expression found first in Dt. 32:10 and then again in Psalm 17:8 in which David asks to be vindicated against those who persecute him. This promise of deliverance in this unwalled city in which Jehovah God lives in the midst (v. 10) is one that has never yet been fulfilled but is yet to come, and will have some most unique and new citizens.[155]

For many nations will join themselves to the city as the new people of God. This is the ultimate fulfillment of the Abrahamic Covenant found in Gen. 12 and Rom. 11. However, this can only happen when his people – both Jew and Gentile – share the message of his kingdom to the people of the world first. Indeed, did I not tell you an entire book could and perhaps should be written on the third vision alone?!

Vision Four: Joshua the High Priest v. The Adversary of the Ages (3:1-10)

How many trials of "The Century" have we had over the recent years? O. J. Simpson, Casey Anthony, Alex Murdaugh, Gore v. Bush, Donald Trump v. Seemingly Everyone to name just a few. However, the fourth vision is a humdinger as they used to say of a trial. It is the trial of a high priest of Israel versus Satan himself.

---

154 Merrill, *Haggai, Zechariah, Malachi*, 109.
155 Baldwin, *Haggai, Zechariah, Malachi*, 111-12.

Joshua is standing in filthy clothes in verse 3, and the filth described here can be understood as human dung.[156] Yes, we can all affirm that there is nothing filthier to be covered in than excrement. However, instead of being repulsed by Joshua, Jehovah rebukes the Adversary (*HaSatan* in Hebrew) instead. The accusations of Satan, which were deserved, fell by the wayside as God himself commanded that Joshua who represented not only himself but all the Jewish people, according to Joyce Baldwin,[157] to be clothed in what should be translated as the high priest's garments or festal robes and not simply as rich robes.

Jehovah also causes Joshua's sins/iniquities to be removed from him (example of the Hiphil verb as explained earlier). This changing of garments and removal of sins was necessary so that he could begin his role as the High Priest of Israel – a role that had not been filled since the scattering to Babylon. However, without being cleansed both inwardly and outwardly, Joshua could not be the man the people needed him to be.[158]

Today, we who are called to ministry in whatever way it may be (full-time missions, full-time church service, and also in the work of the laity) also can make this same application. I am reminded of the warning(s) that Jesus gave to the people at the Temple in Matthew 23 when he compared the Pharisees to white-washed tombs in 23:27. The tombs looked beautiful on the outside but were filled with dead men's bones on the inside. Having a nice, shiny exterior is nothing if our inward souls are filthy before God who knows who we are in public and in private. We must not and cannot be hypocrites and not simply because social media will reveal our secrets. We must not and cannot be frauds because we represent the King and Creator of the Universe. To fail him is infinitely worse than ever being doxxed by anyone on Facebook or Instagram.

This is why Jehovah gives the conditions and the promises in verse 7. The If/Then component of verse 7 is something that the people of God have long been aware of since the days of Deuteronomy. And while the conditions and promises of verse 7 are significant, they hold but a flicker to the flame of verses 8-9. For while the installation of Joshua as High Priest is a great day, the coming of The Branch is THE DAY that everyone will long to see (HINT!).

---

156 Bartholomew and Thomas, *The Minor Prophets*, 259.
157 Baldwin, *Haggai, Zechariah, Malachi*, 113.
158 Merrill, *Haggai, Zechariah, Malachi*, 121-23.

However, and this is significant, the Jewish people have nothing to do with bringing in the BRANCH. They are merely a symbol because Jehovah himself will cause (Hiphil verb again) the servant, who is the branch, to appear. And if you are not thinking of Isaiah 53 (and all of the Servant Songs at this moment, I hope you are beginning to consider these verses right now for even the British theologian Joyce Baldwin mentions them.[159] And what happens when the BRANCH appears, iniquity is removed in one day. Indeed, Jehovah wins this court case!

Vision Five: Lampstand/Menorah (4:1-14)

How does one even begin to describe the menorah, the lampstand, that Zechariah was privy to see in this fifth vision? A golden lampstand that I cannot seek to visualize even with my imagination that was described by my parents as wild when I was a child, for I was known to try to give CPR to my teddy bear wearing a red raincoat and using a toy ironing board as a stretcher.[160] The seven lamps, the seven spouts, and the corresponding bowls, all in gold (v. 2-3) and flanked by two olive trees, create a visual that outdoes anything I can fathom.

Therefore, I can understand Zechariah's question in verse 4 which basically was … "what?" And even after Zechariah is asked again if he does not understand the meaning of all this visionary splendor, he answers plainly in verse 5 – "No, my lord." It is then we have a simply wonderful and plain answer that we all need to be reminded of quite often – because it is not by might or by power but by the Spirit of Jehovah Sabaoth (v. 6).

Perhaps it is only me that needs to be reminded of v. 6 quite often as I am one of those people who tries to fix things myself instead of allowing God to do it for me … BIG MISTAKE. However, this was the message that Jehovah Sabaoth was sending to the people of Israel – Zerubbabel and Joshua, and Zechariah and all the others who are building the Temple can do what they can do, but it is ultimately God who finishes it all – a very similar idea to what Paul wrote in 1 Cor. 3:5-8.

We are not to think that our "small efforts" are small when they are done for the work of God. Nothing is ever small or insignificant in the household of Jehovah. This is the beauty of the phrase in v. 10 – "for who has despised the day of small things." The 19th century Christian poet Christina Rosetti (1830-1894) saw the beauty of this line as well and wrote a poem to describe the idea:

As violets so be I recluse and sweet,
Cheerful as daisies unaccounted rare,

---

[159] Baldwin, *Haggai, Zechariah, Malachi*, 116.

[160] The teddy bear, which I still possess, suffered internal injuries from the CPR but was brought back to health by the surgical hands of Dr. Mama who repaired the wounds with a needle and a thread.

Still sunward-gazing from a lowly seat,
Still sweetening wintry air.

While half-awakened Spring lags incomplete,
While lofty forest trees tower bleak and bare,
Daisies and violets own remotest heat
And bloom and make them fair.[161]

I must be honest: My mama could make anything grow, and I can kill a cactus. However, I love daisies in all their simple beauty. When I first lived in New York, I worked in the city and would often stop at a flower stand every Monday morning to buy daisies for my office, bringing a small quantity of color and life to my surroundings.

Therefore, I understand the beauty of this poem and the idea of simple actions making a profound difference in someone's life. Over the weekend, I was able to rectify the categorization of someone in the Yad Vashem database from "Unknown" to "Survived." Her family did not know that my friend who died in 2017 had been labeled in such a way and when I let them know of the switch for their mother (all it took was an email and some verification), they were so relieved to know that the situation had been reversed. No big deal, but it allowed me to continue to find small connection points to share the Gospel with my friend's daughter and sons. Indeed, there are no small things in the work of Jehovah.

This is why that while it is tempting to focus on the identity of the two sons of fresh oil – whether it be Zerubbabel or Joshua or Moses and Elijah or the two witnesses in Revelation 11 – in this vision (v. 11-14), the purpose of this vision is that God controls it all and nothing is left outside of his purpose and plan. God is present in his Temple which is the point of the whole vision and he is present everywhere because he is God over all the earth. And all we do for him is not small because it serves his purpose and plans.

Vision Six: The Flying Scroll (5:1-4)

A few years ago, there was a Burnett Family Reunion held in Albuquerque, New Mexico. The Burnetts in my family tree belong to my mama's mother. Yes, I have written previously and several times that my mama's mother was not a kind woman but I like the Burnett branch of my family tree. My cousins and great-aunts are and were amazing people. Many of them have died since this reunion, but we all had an amazing time together, and I finally had a chance to really get to know my great aunt Opal, who named my mama (as to why my grandmother did not is a long story).

---

[161] Christina Georgina Rosetti, *Who Hath Despised the Day of Small Things?*

My Aunt Opal was a stunningly beautiful woman and was as kind as she was lovely. My cousin Melody is one of my favorite people, and spending this time with them was highlighted by the International Hot Air Balloon Festival, which is held every October. Watching hundreds of hot air balloons rising up in the sky was breathtaking that brisk October morning surrounded by family and I can only imagine that must have been how Zechariah felt as he saw this gigantic flying scroll above him in this sixth vision (5:1-4).

The scroll was approximately 30-34 feet long and 15-17.5 feet wide. One could say it was definitely an Unidentified Flying Object if there ever was one. However, what must have terrified Zechariah was not the scroll but what was told to him about the scroll, for it represented a curse for everyone who steals and for everyone who breaks an oath (to God) – they will be purged/expelled/cut off (v. 3). Now did you notice what I just wrote in parentheses ... to God? These offenses are not simply about stealing and lying. These offenses are about stealing and breaking one's promise and/or oath to God. They will be purged and/or cut off from the covenant promises that were given to the people.[162]

However, and again as a word of caution, I think we must be to specify exactly what type of covenant we are speaking of at this moment lest we create biblical confusion. There are certain covenants that are unconditional, and a person cannot be cut off as God alone made and/or "signed" the covenant with the people – Abrahamic, Davidic, and the New Covenant mentioned in Jeremiah. This one is specifically related to the Mosaic Covenant, which was not unconditional, and we can see the obvious allusions to the Torah scroll that is flying above Zechariah's head.[163]

Now that we have made that important distinction let us look at the frightening nature of verse 4. For not only does the flying scroll soar above Zechariah's head in the vision, but he is told that thieves and those who swear false oaths will have it visit their homes, where it will set up residence and destroy it in one night. For one who has lived several years in the tornado zone, the visual image that this verse creates in one's mind can be summarized by one word ... chaos.

---

[162] Merrill, *Haggai, Zechariah, Malachi*, 149-151 and Bartholomew and Thomas, *The Minor Prophets*, 262-63.

[163] Eugene Merrill does not necessarily make the connection that I make but he does note the Deuteronomy references in much more detailed form that Bartholomew and Thomas.

For when one's home or community is destroyed by a tornado, people are often left desolate. They are empty emotionally, physically, and often spiritually. They are left stranded and looking for something or someone to reconnect to in their lives. If you have never been through such an experience, watch the faces of individuals on television as they go through what remains of their homes. They are lost and I believe this is what God wanted to communicate to the prophet Zechariah in this vision – God takes the sins of theft and bearing false witness very seriously even if it appears that his people do not as seriously as he does.

Therefore, and obviously, there is a lesson for us today as well. Stealing from God – and this does not relate to the offering plate – is a grievous action against him, and it is something that we are all guilty of today. We rob God by denying him of our time that belongs to him. We rob God by keeping back a part of ourselves because we do not want to give all of ourselves to him even though he gave his life for us. Additionally, and we have all been guilty of this one when we promise to pray for someone and then somehow never get around to doing it. Is this not swearing an oath and not keeping our word, or what? These are just some final thoughts before moving on to the seventh vision.

Vision Seven: The Wicked Woman in the Basket/Ephah (5:5-11)

Visions seven and eight are perhaps the most fantastic of all the visions for me personally. And for me, the seventh vision brought to my mind when I first read it was the evil and/or harlot woman of Revelation 17. However, is this an appropriate interpretation or just my immediate reaction based upon growing up in churches that often had evangelists coming with flannelgraph versions of their Clarence Larkin charts so that we would all be ready for the end-times?[164] Or could it be an example of a warning for Zechariah's day that also had a prophetic meaning for future times?

The commentaries that I have utilized in this chapter have taken the approach to explain simply the passage as it is read in the text – albeit some of them did take a lot of ink to explain why the word appearance could be translated as the eye in verse 6, but I will not go there. The woman is the personification of wickedness. She is contained in the basket/ephah by a lead weight. The basket is being escorted to Shinar (Babylon) by two angels, who are building a temple for her and where she can be worshiped. This is what is known of the vision and this is what Zechariah is told.

---

[164] Clarence Larkin (1850-1924) was an American Baptist pastor who, along with C. I. Scofield and J. N. Darby, influenced many in Evangelicalism toward the eschatological view of Premillennialism Dispensationalism beginning in the early days of the twentieth century. For more information on Larkin, go to https://www.larkinestate.com/about/rev-clarence-larkin.html.

However, I completely understand if you want something more as you are reading the text. And regardless of whether you see the vision as solely future-oriented or you see it as having a both/and orientation, there is a real and practical application that can be taken away from the text – **stay away from evil or it will destroy you.** Now it is time to look at the text in more detail…

Shinar was an ancient name for Babylon, and the city's name, regardless of what it was called, has always represented power and wickedness. As much as it pains me, being a woman, to write this fact, the female goddess in this time period and even into Greek/Roman idol worship in the latter centuries served as the seductress. Therefore, it is not enough that Wickedness is in a basket/ephah, but she must be covered in lead apparently so that she cannot escape or that her evil will not become pervasive among the people … again.

I have to admit that I thought of Kryptonite and Superman when I saw that the basket/ephah was covered with lead. For even though Batman is the greatest of all the superheroes in my humble opinion, we should all remember that Superman's weakness is any type of rock from his home planet of Krypton. However, placing a piece of kryptonite in a lead box will protect Superman from the effects of the rock. The same imagery is true here – placing wickedness inside the basket/ephah with a lead over it will protect the people from the impact of Wickedness. However, and you knew there had to be a however, the people must stay away from both Shinar/Babylon and from the temptation to remove the lead from the basket/ephah, and this is where Israel failed, and we today also often fail as well.

Israel in Zechariah's day was drawn by the allure of Wickedness and what Babylon sought to offer. Today, we are tempted by the temptation of, dare I say it … Washington, D.C., or any halls of power that one might name. Christians (and churches) want to have power and to be influential but what does it gain us in the end? Perhaps we should put a lead weight back on whatever might be the basket/ephah that is drawing us to the desire to be in control or to be in political power and to return to the idea of serving God instead. For Wickedness destroyed in Zechariah's day and it will destroy us today.

Vision Eight: Return of the Horses and Return of the Branch (6:1-15)

The first of the visions began with horses. The fourth vision mentioned the trial of Joshua and the arrival of the BRANCH. This final vision encompasses the horses (and chariots), Joshua, and the return of BRANCH. The horses are sent from heaven to go out to all the earth – from the north to the south. And it is with vision that we have a culmination or completion feature that can be seen as a prophetic image that links the beginning words of Zechariah to the rest of the apocalyptic imagery of Zechariah's prophecy. This imagery begins in verse 9 and goes to the end of our chapter.

Joshua, who was the high priest in Zechariah's day, is, in essence, a representative of the BRANCH that is to come. He will be the one who completes the ultimate Temple of Jehovah (v. 15). He will also fulfill the role of the High Priest and King of Israel (v. 13) and the nations, as we shall see in chapter fourteen.[165] Eugene Merrill makes an important point in his commentary. However, he fails to provide additional explanation as to why this was important to the confusion over Jesus' truthful claim of Messiahship – the Interbiblical period (the years between Malachi and Matthew) understanding of two Messiahs coming.[166]

I know that the idea of two Messiahs in Judaism is one that most people have never heard of, whether one is Jewish or Christian. Therefore, I am going to try to briefly explain it here in the following one or three paragraphs. During the period that I personally believe is mislabeled as Interbiblical, there was a thought that can be found in Talmudic and other Jewish sources that there would be two Messiahs – one to suffer and die for the people (Messiah ben Joseph) and one to come triumphantly claim victory for the people over their opponents (Messiah ben David).

After the Maccabean Revolt in c. 165/165 BC/BCE, the idea of Messiah ben Joseph began to lose its appeal, and the people only wanted a Messiah ben David figure. This is why in John 10:22-31 (during Hanukkah), the people asked Jesus if he was the Messiah. Jesus stated that not only was he the Messiah but also "I and my Father are One." In other words, Jesus is also God. They wanted a Messiah to expel the Romans but not a Messiah who was also God himself. The confusion created by the period between Malachi and Matthew had clouded the minds of the people as to who and what the Messiah would be, and so when Paul wrote that their minds/hearts were blinded (Romans 10:1-4) – he was absolutely right.

The Jewish people missed the first coming of Messiah Jesus and this allowed the rest of the world to be included in what was first offered to the Jewish people – the time of the Gentiles (Lk. 21:24; Rom. 11:25). The Jewish people are not excluded as there will always be a remnant and it is the responsibility of the Gentiles to make the Jewish people jealous for what they have given away for a time (Rom. 11:11) because they did not completely obey Jehovah Elohim (v. 15). Yet, and this is my personal mission burden, the Jewish people have for too long and for too many unforgivable reasons been overlooked by missions and Christians. The time for this "overlooking" needs to end today – as it is time already.

---

[165] Baldwin, *Haggai, Zechariah, Malachi*, 137 and Merrill, *Haggai, Zechariah, Malachi*, 175 and 177.

[166] Merrill, *Haggai, Zechariah, Malachi*, 177.

Be Restored to Me … the "Warnings" of Zechariah (7:1-8:23)

<u>Restoration Is Not About Fasting – It is About Obedience (7:1-14)</u>

Whew … we made it through the visions! Honestly, it took longer than I expected to cover adequately the visions in just a glance – and it was just a glance. And based on the dating of verse 1, one can only imagine that the people were a bit stunned by what Zechariah shared with them.[167] In fact, we next hear from Zechariah in the fourth year of King Darius, which is approximately 518 BC/BCE, in the month of Chislev/Kislev, which usually falls around November or December. Men from Bethel to ask the prophet about how to best respond to questions regarding fasting in the fifth and seventh months of the year.

These first seven verses of chapter 7 were already discussed in the introduction of the chapter and so I will not repeat it again. Instead, we will jump ahead to Zechariah's message, which covers verses 8-14. It should be noted that the verbs in verse 9, which are from Jehovah via Zechariah, are all in the imperative/command tense. God is giving orders not about fasting but about how they are to treat each other and the stranger/alien.

One never wishes to read intent in God's reaction (and one never should). However, it is almost as if Zechariah is communicating to the men of Bethel that fasting is a minor issue now that they are home from Babylon. They should be focusing on avoiding on what sent them to Babylon in the first place, such as the following:

- Executing true justice
- Practicing kindness/loyalty/goodness and compassion to their fellow countryman
- NOT oppressing the orphan/widow OR the sojourner/stranger/foreigner[168] OR the poor
- NOT devising evil in your hearts towards one another

Zechariah points out that they refused to pay attention to the more important things of the Torah, and this was what caused their captivity.

---

[167] Bartholomew and Thomas, *The Minor Prophets*, 267. The authors of this commentary provide an interesting line that is worth sharing – "Good preaching always calls forth questions, which in turn reveal a lot about those who ask them." In other words, did the men of Bethel really understand what Zechariah was sharing or did they focus on the minutiae and not the message?

[168] The word *ger* in Hebrew has a multitude of meanings. It can range from alien, foreigner, sojourner, immigrant, and/or stranger. The word is often used in the Torah as referring to the Israelites as they traveled in the wilderness or even when Abraham described himself on his travels. Obviously, the word opens up Pandora's Box for many in today's world as we consider our own immigration issues here in America and this is something that each individual reader will have to consider as they read this passage for themselves.

In fact, Zechariah pointed out in verse 12 that they made their hearts "like flint" so that "they could not hear." Another word for *samir* which is often translated as "flint" is the word diamond – which is the hardest naturally occurring substance on earth.[169] The people before they were taken captive to Babylon were immovable and beyond stubborn in opposition to God. In other words, they loved the trappings of being the people of God more than being God's people.[170] Zechariah is telling them in this section not to make the same mistake again.[171] It is a good reminder for anyone at any time and in any place where they might find themselves.

Restoration Will Happen to the Remnant (8:1-23)

In this chapter, Zechariah offers several promises of hope and several affirmations from Jehovah Sabaoth to his people. He tells them he is exceedingly jealous for Zion – twice in verse 2. He promises them that not only will he return to Jerusalem but also that he will dwell in their midst (v. 3) and then will the city be a city of truth and the mountain upon which the city sits will be truly holy.

This promise in verse 3 is interesting because it raises a question—why and how will he return? Has Jehovah Sabaoth been to the city? Yes, in the sense that the Shekinah dwelt in the Temple, but should that be the literal interpretation, or is Eugene Merrill correct when he writes that this must have a dual fulfillment prophetic interpretation attached to it?[172] I believe the answer should be and could be evident, but let us look at the next few verses as well.

Verses 4-15 provide two recurrent themes – (1) the idea of the remnant and (2) the phrase "in these/those days." Both of those themes have a future-oriented focus to their meaning in the sense that there will be in the land because the old and the young will be able to move about freely and in peace (v. 4-5, 10). They will also be returning from what appears to be a second dispersion that takes them not from the north and the south as it was with Babylon but from the east and the west (or as it should be understood – everywhere on the globe).[173] This return from being scattered will result in their becoming a blessing to the world and if we watch the news we recognize that this has not yet happened.

---

[169] Yes, I actually checked myself on this issue. It earns a ten on the Mohs Hardness Scale due to the fact that it is made up of five carbon atoms. For more information, see Hussain Kanchwala, "What Is the Hardest Material on Earth?," ScienceABC, 19 October 2023, available online at https://www.scienceabc.com/pure-sciences/what-is-the-hardest-material-on-earth.html; accessed 29 May 2024.

[170] Merrill, *Haggai, Zechariah, Malachi*, 188 and Baldwin, *Haggai, Zechariah, and Malachi*, 147-148.

[171] Meyer, *The Prophet of Hope*, 70.

[172] Merrill, *Haggai, Zechariah, Malachi*, 194-95.

[173] Ibid., 196.

How then can I say this with such certainty – the rest of the passage (v. 16-23). For while Israel today is the only democracy in the Middle East, they do not yet truly represent God's desire in verses 16-17 – (1) speaking truth to one another; (2) judging with truth; (3) having peace within their gates; (4) devising evil against anyone; and (5) hating perjury. Yes, they are a good nation but definitely not a perfect nation – neither internally nor externally – and I have been to the land four times and have many friends who are citizens of the nation. Additionally, Israel today is not yet a nation that believes in Jesus as Messiah because they have not reached Zech. 12:10 yet.

For in those days after 12:10 (and we are fast approaching this section), we will find the fulfillment verses 18-23 when the fast days turn to feast days and when people from all nations come to Jerusalem to seek the face of Jehovah. And when finally, the world ceases to hate and despise the Jewish people and grabs hold of them and begs to go with them to Jerusalem because they know that God is with them (v. 23). Indeed, this is a prophetic message and a promise of a restoration but sadly not for all the Jewish people but only for the remnant. So ... who will be a part of this remnant? The final pages of this chapter will answer this question.

Eternity with Me ... the Prophecies of Zechariah (9:1-14:21)

As we begin this final section, there are two issues that quickly need to be addressed. The first is that you will find some people who do not believe that the prophet Zechariah actually wrote the final five chapters of the book.[174] The rationale for this argument is based on the same arguments that some mistakenly make for not believing that Isaiah wrote all of Isaiah – a change of focus from historical to prophetic and/or a shift in writing style. This can be easily answered and is by Eugene Merrill when he writes – "to deny that a single author could change his compositional techniques ... is to place restraints on ancient writers that modern critics would not tolerate if placed on themselves by others."[175] In other words, and this must be remembered, Zechariah wrote this prophecy over a period of time (at least four to six years) for different reasons and to different people at times. He would not have written in the same way and style in each situation, and neither would any of us.

---

[174] Baldwin, *Haggai, Zechariah, Malachi*, 62-70. It should be noted that Baldwin leans towards single authorship, but she provides a detailed explanation for those who do not. Much of the same arguments are repeated by Merrill, *Haggai, Zechariah, Malachi*, 71-75, but he is in stronger in his defense of single authorship.

[175] Merrill, *Haggai, Zechariah, Malachi*, 211.

The second issue is that this final section will focus primarily and perhaps even solely on the prophecies that Zechariah writes about in these verses that relate to the first and second coming of Messiah Jesus. The reason for this decision is because of the focus of this book – what the minor prophets can teach us as it relates to Christians and churches being a missional people today. Yes, it might be fascinating to uncover the meaning of 9:1-8 but will that help us today be a better missional people? Perhaps not, but the prophecies of this final section will help us in our missional efforts.

The 10th of Nissan (aka Palm Sunday) Prophecy (9:9-10)[176]

Perhaps you are wondering why I entitled this section. For we all know what Palm Sunday is on the Christian calendar—the day that Jesus rode through the streets of Jerusalem on a donkey, and the people laid down palm branches and proclaimed, "Hosanna, Hosanna." However, what is the 10th of Nissan, and why should this date be so important?

Nissan is the first month of the Jewish religious calendar (March/April), and we can find this first mentioned in Exodus 12. In Exod. 12:3-5, we see that the Passover Lamb is selected for the family or families and kept until the fourteenth. Now if you are curious as to why the people selected the lamb on the 10th but did not sacrifice until the 14th, you should be. It was so that the people would bring the lamb into the home and inspect it closely for faults and defects. On the fourteenth, the lamb then is sacrificed and the blood of the lamb was to be put on the doorposts and over the top of the door so that God himself would pass over the home that first Passover (Pesach) night in Egypt.[177]

Now … let us jump to approximately 29 AD/CE, and we see Jesus instructing his disciples in Matt. 21:1-11 to go and secure for him a colt, the foal of a donkey, so that he could ride through Jerusalem and to fulfill Zech. 9:9. However, I want to propose to you that not only was Jesus fulfilling 9:9 but also asking the people to select him and inspect him closely to see if he was the Messiah and their Passover Lamb as it was the 10th of Nissan.

The people from all over Judah and all Jewish people from all over the world were in Jerusalem for Passover as it was commanded. However, they were also in Jerusalem because they were bringing their lambs to be inspected by the priests in the Temple. Hence, the reason why Jesus went to the Temple after the procession in Jerusalem and overturned the moneychanger's tables – not only because they were robbing the people but also because Jesus was/is the Passover Lamb for the people.

---

[176] Nissan is also known as Abib/Aviv in Scripture.

[177] Two quick notes – (1) it was not a Death Angel but God alone who went through Egypt. This is a common mistake, probably due to the Charlton Heston movie and (2) Moses's provision of further Passover instructions later on in the Torah. I am simply providing the introductory story for Passover here.

Now that you can deduce that Jesus was crucified on the 14th of Nissan which is the beginning date of Passover as he is our Passover Lamb. Messiah Jesus fulfilled Zech. 9:9 easily but what do we do about verse 10 which speaks of "peace to the nations" and a "dominion from sea to sea and from the river to the ends of the earth." Has this happened? Is this an example of the phrase "already but not yet" that was often used? Joyce Baldwin refers to these verses as a partial fulfillment.[178] Merrill, who falls much more into the classic American Evangelical camp than Baldwin, who is a British evangelical, acknowledges the same problem and calls on Christians and churches to face the issue as well.[179] They are both right that we cannot ignore what seems to be a disconnect because I face the issue as a missionary to Jewish people, and anyone who points out this prophecy will need to be honest about verse 10 if they show verse 9. So how should we answer it honestly and apologetically and in a way that does not create the confusion that often follows the "already but not yet" response?

I will walk you through some approaches that I took in the process, as it was not easy for me. I went first to my favorite systematic theologian, James Leo Garrett, as I worked for him when I was in seminary, but I also went to several other systematic theologies. Interestingly, Dr. Garrett's two-volume work was the only one that mentioned verse Zech. 9:10. I went to several of my books that deal with the "life of Christ," and none spoke to the verse. Therefore, I can share with you, before going into what Garrett's theology tome mentioned, that most of the verbs from verse 10 to the end of the chapter are in the perfect tense indicating that the action most often has been completed. What does this tell us … it lends credence to the idea of "already but not yet," but how does one explain that to the general public?

---

[178] Baldwin, *Haggai, Zechariah, Malachi*, 164.
[179] Merrill, *Haggai, Zechariah, Malachi*, 220-21.

Dr. Garrett cites a man with a troublesome past, Joachim Jeremias, who believes that Zech. 9:10 is primarily for the mission to the nations. This could satisfy some; however, we must acknowledge that Jeremias has not only some problematic theological issues but some "German" (i.e., Fascistic) connections that are unsavory. And even Garrett is not entirely satisfied with Jeremias' answer.[180] Instead, I would recommend following my favorite systematic theologian's model in which he shows that Paul, the missionary to the Gentiles, went first to the Jew and then to the Gentiles. It was not that he sought to "Judaize" the Gentiles but that he understood the ongoing mission/work of the Gospel – "speaking peace to the nations" and "having [Jesus'] dominion from seas to sea and from the river to the end of the earth" includes both groups of people.[181]

Missions are a whole-wide concept for Christians and churches. No group of people can or should be excluded from the work of the Gospel, and I would argue that verse 10 is a continuation of this idea. Yes, its ultimate fulfillment will be realized in the second coming but its ongoing realization is found in what we do in the here and now. Do we share the Gospel as we should? Do we continue the work of "Hosanna, Hosanna," from sea to sea? Or are we waiting for someone else to do it for us?

<u>Good/Bad Shepherds, 30 Pieces of Silver, Broken Staffs (11:1-17)</u>

If anyone tells you that Zech 11 is easily understood, I honestly will ask them to put their hand on a Bible and repeat that again. It is not an easy chapter, and that is even true with us not including chapter 10 in the mix. Both of the primary commentaries that I utilized to help me in my understanding of Zechariah (Baldwin and Merrill) admitted that it was not easy to understand this chapter.[182]

The question(s) of who the bad shepherds are, why the good shepherd breaks the staffs, what do the staffs mean, and what is the meaning of the thirty pieces of silver all create a jumble of confusion for anyone who is honest enough to admit it. Therefore, and for the sake of space and time, this section will focus on the final five verses of the chapter (12-17) as these verses summarize the chapter as well as bring the focus onto the final three chapters of the book, which relate to the second coming of Messiah Jesus. And can we admit those are the chapters that we have all been looking forward to reading about anyway...?

[180] James Leo Garrett, *Systematic Theology: Biblical, Historical, & Evangelical*, vol. 2 (Grand Rapids: William B. Eerdmans, 1996): 489.
[181] Ibid., 494-95. On a side note, I worked for Dr. Garrett as a typist/editor for this particular volume before I committed my life to Jewish missions.
[182] Baldwin, *Haggai, Zechariah, Malachi*, 179 and Merrill, *Haggai, Zechariah, Malachi*, 249.

The prophecy of verse 12 begins with Jehovah speaking in verse 6 when he declares that he will no longer have pity on the land, in verse 8 when he destroyed the three evil shepherds, and in verse 9 when he broke the staff called Favor and broke (suspended) the covenant with the people.[183] This is the background to the passage, and it is important to understand the prophecy itself and its fulfillment in the lives of Judas and Jesus. For as hardly been explained in this chapter, and due to the confusion over the two Messiah concepts from the time of Malachi to Matthew, the people were wanting and longing for a Messiah when they saw Jesus riding through the streets of Jerusalem on the 10th of Nissan. However, they did not recognize nor want the Messiah Jesus they needed when he was standing before them on the 14th of Nissan.[184]

In verses 12-13, we see that Jehovah (who is still talking, if you will notice from verse 6) tells the people to give **him** his wages as a good shepherd. The people dispense a wage of thirty shekels, which is the price of a slave (cf. Ex. 21:32; Hos. 3:1-5 [see Ch. 7]) as they see this as the value of the **Shepherd Jehovah**. Jehovah then tells Zechariah to throw the "magnificent" wages back "at which I was valued by them."

As I consider these two verses, I sense a small amount of angry sarcasm in this reaction by God, but again, this is just me. In fact, I wrote the word "sarcasm" in my notes beside the word "magnificent" because I could not imagine how much chutzpah it must have taken the people to value God himself at only thirty pieces of silver. But … then we must turn to Matt. 26:15-16; 27:9 and realize that God the Son was betrayed for and/or valued at thirty pieces of silver in fulfillment of Hos. 3:1-5 and Zech. 11:12-13 (see chapter 7 again for additional consideration of this prophecy).

We can speculate as to why Judas chose this path of betrayal, and we will never understand it. Yet, we do know Jesus' reaction to it in the Gospels. He forgave the people, including Peter, on multiple occasions—Matt. 26:51-55; Lk. 23:34; John 21:15-18. How dare we not forgive those who were there that day as we were and are just as guilty as they were for the death of Jesus as anyone who has ever lived.

---

[183] Merrill, *Haggai, Zechariah, Malachi*, 259. Merrill points out several Biblical passages that point out that a broken covenant does not mean that it is irreparable – Ps. 89.34; Is. 54:9-10; Jer. 31:35-37; 33:19-26.

[184] Baldwin, *Haggai, Zechariah, Malachi*, 179. Baldwin did not phrase it as I did above, which was from my own thoughts, but she wrote an interesting sentence that deserves to be expressed as well – "One insight of this prophet is that such a ruler would not only be not welcomed, but he would be positively hated and rejected." I take a little issue with the idea of "hated" but sadly Jesus was rejected by many of his own people.

Yes, I am speaking of the Jewish people with that last sentence. For we all know the Jewish people have been cast with spurious and unfair accusations regarding the death of Jesus. In fact, it was not until 1964 that the Roman Catholic Church renounced their charges of deicide (Death of God) charges against the Jewish people.[185] The Jewish people have suffered for nearly 2,000 years by people, whether it be Crusades, Inquisitions, or Pogroms, who propose to be Christians but exemplify nothing of the characteristics of the name. I have friends who suffered in the Holocaust and lost all or nearly all of their family in the Holocaust by people who told them they deserved what was being done to them because "they killed Christ." It is important to remember that no one killed Jesus but he allowed himself to be killed for the salvation of us all – John 10:18. Therefore, if anyone attempts to take verses 14-17 and justify their hatred towards the Jewish people, I will point them towards the Tribulation period and the word anti-Christ for that is who the worthless of this passage is describing and I will discuss it more detail as we consider 13:7-9.

Prophecies of the Second Coming (12:10-14; 13:7-9; 14:1-21)

I do not argue about people's positions on eschatology (end times). I do not share much of my personal position on eschatology. As I have stated in an earlier chapter, I think when history completes itself, we will discover that we have all missed/erred on some aspect of how the Second Coming will turn out. I will admit that I am a premillennialist and I do believe in a Rapture but I will not share my view on the timing (pre-, mid-, post-) of when Christians will be removed from the world. Why … because I do not want to influence towards my view in case I am wrong. I do not want to be responsible for leading someone astray on something that cannot be categorically proven in Scripture.

However, these three prophecies do not depend upon my view of the Rapture or even my view of the Millennium necessarily (except perhaps 13:7-9). These three prophecies relate first to the Jewish people but also to the rest of the world missionally and eternally. This is why we will consider them as carefully as we can but also as succinctly as we can.

---

[185] "Declaration on the Relation of the Church to Non-Christian Religions," *Nostra Aetate*, Proclaimed by His Holiness Pope Paul VI, 28 October 1965. This is a quote from the statement – "True, the Jewish authorities and those who followed their lead pressed for the death of Christ;(13) still, what happened in His passion cannot be charged against all the Jews, without distinction, then alive, nor against the Jews of today."

Look on Me Whom They Pierced (12:10-14)

> I will pour on the house of David and on the inhabitants of Jerusalem the spirit of grace and supplication so that they will have cause to look on me (Hiphil Perfect) that they have **pierced,** and they will **mourn** for him as one mourns for an only son (YACHID), and they will be **desperate to weep** over him like the desperate weeping over a first born/first fruit. (Emphasis Added and Author's Translation)

Many times, verse 10 is used as a rationale to justify a national salvation for Israel upon the return of Messiah based upon six words in one verse – Rom. 11:26. Here is the verse in question and 11:25-27 is included for context:

> For I do not desire, brethren, that you should be ignorant of this mystery, lest you should be wise in your own opinion, that blindness in part has happened to Israel until the fullness of the Gentiles has come in. *And so all Israel will be saved*, as it is written: 'The Deliverer will come out of Zion, And He will turn away ungodliness from Jacob; For this is My covenant with them, When I take away their sins.'"

However, is that what verse 10 or even the context of the prophecy says? Does Rom. 11:25-27 promise a blanket salvation for Israel in the future in light of what Paul wrote in Rom. 9:1-3 that he was willing to give up his own salvation if it was only possible?

Ultimately, this is why a proper understanding of scripture is so important and why it is so vital that we never take a portion of God's Word out of its context for our own purposes. An excellent quote that has been attributed to the father of evangelical scholar D. A. Carson (Tom) says it best – "Any text without a context is a pretext for a prooftext." Now … let us consider what the Zechariah prophecy really says and we will also quickly consider Rom. 11:26 says as well.

The verse is spelled out in the beginning of the section. However, there are a few words that need to be considered in more detail for a more thorough understanding of the verse, along with verses 11-14, as this is critically important to an overall understanding of the prophecy. The first word is pierced (*daqar*), and this is not the word connected to Psalm 22 regarding the nails that pierced the hands/feet, but more along the idea of the spear that pierced Jesus' heart. The second word is the twice used word for mourn(s) which is *saphad*. This word is the idea of lamenting/wailing. The final word is translated as weep(ing) and/or grieve(ing), and it is *marar* – which should be seen as bitter weeping.

It is important to go into this detail because I want you to see that there is lament and there is grief … but where is there repentance? We must be careful not to see and hope for national repentance where it is not absolutely evident and obvious. The only hope for repentance that can be found is in the words of the spirit of grace and supplication being poured out upon the people, but even then, we cannot and must not attach national repentance (i.e., an inaccurate interpretation of Rom. 11:26a) to this prophecy. Repentance must be found in the individual hearts of the people, and this is found in verses 11-14 as it is found in the hearts of all those who live today.

F. B. Meyers says it so beautifully when he writes – "We repent when we turn from sin to Christ; we are penitent when we meet his eyes, as Peter did, and go out to weep bitterly. To repent is the definite act of the moment, but penitence will accompany us to the very gates of heaven, only to flee away before the light of eternal blessedness."[186] Repentance for any person, Jewish or Gentile, is an individual act, and Zechariah points this out when he notes the comparison to the day that Josiah died on the plains of Megiddo in 609 BC/BCE (v. 11).

Zechariah uses this example to show that repentance, while beginning in the house of David, cannot be done corporately or by the community. It has to be done by the husband alone. It has to be completed by the wife alone. Every individual, from the highest to the lowest, from the house of Levi to the house of the nobodies, has to be completed alone. Repentance for sins is a lonely act, for "excessive grief seeks seclusion."[187]

So how will all Israel be saved, and who is all Israel? The people who repent and believe in Messiah Jesus are the remnant and are "all Israel," and that is constantly mentioned throughout the Hebrew Scriptures (especially Isaiah) – 4:2-4; 6:13; 10:20-21; and 60:21. Paul also uses the language in Romans 9:24-27. God keeps his promises, and now we have to answer the question – who is the remnant that will repent and believe?

The Final Remnant (13:7-9)

I mentioned their names in the preface, and I will mention their names again here – Josef, Vera, William, Rosalie, Agnes, Suzanne, and Jack. These are seven individuals who profoundly changed my life as they shared their lives with me and their stories of surviving the most horrible tragedy that any human can even imagine – the Holocaust. All seven are gone now, but I continue to count each of them in varying degrees of closeness to my friends. I cried with them, and I apologized to each of them as they shared with me how they lost family members – including Agnes, who lost every member of her family in Auschwitz (June 1944) when she was thirteen years old.

---

[186] Meyers, *The Prophet of Hope*, 107-108.
[187] Ibid., 106. See also, Merrill, *Haggai, Zechariah, Malachi*, 284.

Yet, we see in 13:7-9 that there is a greater horror awaiting many Jewish people in the future as the anti-Christ of Zechariah. For it is in Zech. 11:14-17 that the anti-Christ rears his ugly head to take his vengeance upon the people of God for the final time, and the reality is seen in the passage we see now. The sheep are scattered in verse 7 because they are without the true shepherd (Jesus), and we find them desolate and at the mercy of the false shepherd of Zech. 11. This interchange between the chapters, I admit, is confusing, but it is key to understanding verses 8-9 as well as the promise of chapter 12.

However, and before the hope and promise of chapter 14, comes the pain of two-thirds of the Jewish people being cut down and dying. The word for cut down (*karath*) in verse 8 is the same word for covenant, but here it is the idea of literally being cut in half. I know that what I just wrote is gruesome and given what I know about the Holocaust – it is beyond difficult for me to write. However, I must because missions towards the Jewish people and all people groups must not wait for any future time on a flimsy interpretation of Rom. 11:26.

Yes, we have the hope of the one-third being brought through the fire, being refined and calling upon Jehovah's name (true repentance) as the real and true remnant of Rom. 11:26. We have the relief for lack of a better word of Jehovah saying that he will answer them with the phrase – "They are my people (*Hu Ani Ammi*)." However, do you want to wait until two-thirds of a people group perish in a greater Shoah than the first? I cannot wait. Please do not wait for any person, Jewish or not, for any future time because James 4:14 is true for us all.

<u>Victory ... and the Feast of Shavuot (14:1-21)</u>
Being on the Mount of Olives with my mama in 2015 was a true joy. We could see the Eastern Gate. We could see Jerusalem in all of its glory. We began to discuss Zech. 14:4 and how Messiah Jesus would set his foot down and split the mountain in two from east to west to establish who truly was the King of Kings and Lord of Lords. We both got chills just thinking of that moment and then mama said to me, "I wish it could happen right now."

We both knew it could not happen because it was not yet time and since that day mama has joined Jesus and daddy in heaven. Now I consider 14:4 from a new perspective and imagine my impatient mama asking Jesus – "Is it time yet?" Yes ... I am being a bit fanciful but knowing my mama as I do – she is more than ready for the moment.

However, before the triumph of 14:4-21, there is the pain and questioning of what happens in the first three verses. Why is there yet one more time when Israel must face the threat of final destruction? Why must God wait until there is no hope to step in and save the day ... yet again? Eugene Merrill writes that the "purposes of God" prescribe that "triumph comes through tribulation."[188] I cannot disagree with him but I believe it is more basic than his idea – will we truly ever learn to be grateful unless God waits until we are most desperate for him? When we can no longer fight, because seriously when can we ever actually fight our battles, Jehovah steps into the fray and wins the war alone because we need him and not the other way around (v. 3).

Verses 5-15 can be categorized as a summarization of the events that lead up to the Feast of Sukkot (Booths as it is often translated in translations). Verses 5-8 recount the battle of verses 3-4 and the immediate aftermath when Jehovah rules over all the earth. There will no longer be any need for light because Jehovah is present (v. 6-8) and the geography of the Promised Land – especially Jerusalem for it will be lifted higher than it is already is at the present (v. 9-10).

The people will live in Jerusalem in freedom and in security and the word that is often translated as "utter destruction" can also be seen as the word "curse." For we can now see in verse 11 that the curse has been lifted from Jerusalem. However ... the survivors of those who sought the destruction of Israel in verses 1-2 will experience what I can only describe as the Indiana Jones disease.

Do you remember that scene in the first Indiana Jones movie when the Nazis opened the Ark of the Covenant and their faces began to melt and rot? Read verse 12 and tell me that this does not read exactly like what happened to those dastardly Nazis. Yes, panic will ensue (v. 13) because the plague spreads to all the animals that the armies of the anti-Christ as well (v. 15). However, and just like when the Israelites left Egypt in Exodus, the Jewish people will gather in the wealth of those who opposed God's plans (v. 14) and sought their destruction.

Bottom line – one does not seek to destroy God's covenant people, or they will be destroyed. In fact, there is an old Jewish joke that goes like this – "They tried to kill us. We survived. Let's eat." However, and finally, the remnant of God's Covenant People will finally get the saying correct when they say – "Satan tried to kill us again. Messiah Jesus saved us. Let's eat!" – for verses 16-21 will reveal the final and ultimate of all Jewish festivals.

---

[188] Merrill, *Haggai, Zechariah, Malachi*, 299.

As was briefly mentioned in chapter 11, Leviticus 23 provides an overview of the Jewish religious calendar. Passover, Unleavened Bread, and First Fruits are in the spring; Shavuot is in the Summer; and Feast of Trumpets (aka Rosh Hashanah), Yom Kippur, and Sukkot are in the fall.[189] Verses 16-21 deal with the feast of Sukkot and the ordinances are spelled out in great detail in Lev. 23:33-44. Sukkot, along with Passover and Shavuot, are also the three feasts, for it was commanded that all Jewish men are to appear before Jehovah with gifts for him (Dt. 16:16-17).[190]

Therefore, and I believe this is during the Millennial Kingdom, Jews and Gentiles from all over the world (v. 16-19). Those who choose not to attend Sukkot will be punished by drought for their disobedience. So, yes, the Millennium will not be perfect, but it will be holy – especially in Jerusalem (v. 20).

As we close this chapter, the last verse of Zechariah (14:21) contains a statement that might come across as unfeeling or odd—"there will no longer be a Canaanite in the house of Jehovah in that day." However, let us consider who the Canaanites were in Jewish history before we accuse Zechariah of being racist or bigoted.

The Canaanites represented evil and temptation to the people of God. The Canaanites introduced the people to Baal worship and sacrifice of their children. The Canaanites had repeatedly turned the hearts of the people away from God.[191] And, by the way, there are no more Canaanites alive, and so this term represents anyone who has a heart that is not holy and pure, for Jerusalem will forevermore be the City of God.

As we close this chapter, I am reminded of the song lyrics by Donnie McClurkin: "Holiness, holiness is what I long for, Holiness is what I need, Holiness, holiness is what You want from me." This is what Jehovah God will establish in the final feast of Sukkot for all those – Jews and Gentiles – who call on the name of Messiah. He will re-establish Jerusalem to be the city of holiness it was forever meant to be. And while this day is to come, we must seek ways to be even holier than we are now so that we can reach the remnant world for the Gospel before it is too late. Yes, holiness is what we need.

---

[189] I would never presume to set a date for Jesus' return and scripture tells me not to do so. I just want to note for curiosity's sake that Jesus fulfilled the spring feasts with his first coming, the Holy Spirit came during Shavuot (Pentecost), and the fall feasts are the only ones yet to be realized in any Christological way.

[190] This was why there were still so many people in Jerusalem on the Day of Pentecost (aka Shavuot) in Acts 2. They likely stayed in the region instead of going home and returning back for Shavuot. There were Jewish people from all corners of the world who heard Peter's message in Acts 2 and they then eventually took the message home.

[191] Merrill, *Haggai, Zechariah, Malachi*, 321.

Addendum Issue:
Importance of the Hiphil Verb

When I signed up to learn Hebrew at Southwestern Baptist Theological Seminary in 1999, I was actually excited to discover that Harry Hunt fit the optimal time slot for my schedule. Dr. Hunt was known to be the "hardest Hebrew professor" on campus, and he definitely deserved that title. Whereas many Hebrew professors only expected their students to memorize the Qal form of a verb in the direct and indirect (the most basic of all Hebrew forms), Dr. Hunt required of his students to memorize all forms of a verb – Qal, Niphal, Piel, Pual, Hiphal, Hophal, and Hithpael – and in the direct and indirect forms. In fact, one of the tests in Hebrew II was simply a blank chart with one Hebrew word as a starter, and the students had to fill in the rest of the chart. Yes, it was a very hard test!

Why am I sharing all these details with you? Well … I did make an "A" on the test, but that is not the reason. The reason is that when I see a Piel verb in Scripture, I automatically know that something intensive or intentional is happening. When I see a Hithpael verb, I automatically know that it is a reflexive action related to the Piel. I think you get an idea of where I am going. Dr. Hunt prepared his students not to just depend on a computer program but to really know Hebrew personally.

The Hiphil verb is something special, and the "minor prophets," if you ever find yourself reading in the original Hebrew, will discover that they really loved the Hiphil verb. The Hiphil verb, in the simplest definition, is the "causative" verb.[192] Hiphil verbs indicate that someone or something is causing the verb to react in a certain way. For example, in Zech 3:4b – "And to him He said, "See, I have removed (Hiphil Perf 1PS) your iniquity from you, and I will clothe (Hiphil Infinitive) you with rich robes" is how it is translated into English.

There is nothing wrong with the translation; however, I would argue in my opinion that there is richness or depth missing because the idea of the Hiphil verb is lacking. I wrote it out for my personal edification as I was studying these important prophets – "See, **I have caused your iniquity to be taken away** from you and **will cause you to be clothed**." Perhaps too many people believe there is not a great deal of difference, but the idea of God causing our iniquity to be taken away and God alone to clothe us impacts me on a very human level. This is the value and impact of the Hiphil verb in Scripture and, why it was been noted several times throughout the book.

---

[192] J. Weingreen, *A Practical Grammar for Classical Hebrew*, 2nd ed. (Oxford: Clarendon Press, 1959): 112. I used this source in honor of Dr. Hunt. An easier source for those who would like to study the Hiphil verb in great depth can be found at https://hebrew.billmounce.com/BasicsBiblicalHebrew-30.pdf.

Conclusion to *Missions in the Minor Key*

I pray that you have been blessed by this book and that the "minor prophets" will not seem so minor to you after finishing it. My love for these amazing men (even Jonah) has only grown as I have spent the better part of almost two years studying the Biblical text (both in English and Hebrew) and then writing the words that were before you. This is a personal journey that I will treasure forever.

I have also learned a great deal about myself—some good and some bad—as God has touched my heart and reminded me as I have read and reviewed certain texts. Let no one say that one can ever learn all that one needs to learn about God … we are always learning.

Writing this book also provided me a chance to recall some wonderful memories of mama and daddy, Roy and Val Blair, and many other people that I have mentioned. The people that God places in our lives for a moment or the people we call mama/daddy are there to teach us so much about God and ourselves. And this is something that these prophets have taught me as well from Hosea's painful marriage to Amos' willingness to leave the sheep to follow the Shepherd. I learned from each of these prophets something that will live with me forever, and I can only hope that the words that I pray God gave me will touch you as well.

I will not review each of the prophets in this conclusion. However, I cannot forget the message that Zephaniah taught me and the words of 3:2 – "She has not obeyed *His* voice. She has not received correction; She has not trusted in the LORD, She has not drawn near to her God." (NKJV). May we all be drawn nearer to God in the days and weeks to come and be willing to receive the correction and the love that God wishes to give us.

As I wrote in the introduction, I pray that after considering the message of these amazing men of God that you will consider more deeply the missional message they have for us as we live in the spiritual wilderness that surrounds us today. A message that we must learn as the twenty-first century church must make an impact on the world for Messiah Jesus that focuses on anything else but the spiritual to answer the hole which resides in their soul. For while I wrote often about my own heart to reach the Jewish people, the whole world is searching for the answer but they do not know where to look – and we are the only ones who can direct them in the right direction. They need the hope that is only possible through the God of the Hebrew Scriptures – the Scriptures of Messiah Jesus.

Made in the USA
Columbia, SC
03 October 2024

43029759R00124